"To capture the exhilarating, almost 150-year history of The Salvation Army in one short volume seems an impossible task, but Henry Gariepy has done it with verve, color, inspiration, and challenge. At the end, one is filled with a sense of wonder at what God has accomplished through this resilient, Spirit-filled movement. In this readable, alive history you meet mission-minded visionaries and compassionate innovators against in-justice, in the movement still motivated by the manifesto to be 'Christianity in Action.'"

General Eva Burrows, Rtd.

"In these lively pages Colonel Henry Gariepy, OF, Salvationist historian and biographer, invites us to join him on a globe-girdling, soul-stirring safari of Salvationist service, touching down in 118 countries across 140 years and more. This scintil-lating chronicle is replete with accounts of Army action and in-triguing cameos of heroes and heroines. Salvationists will read it with a swelling sense of gratitude for the privilege of being part of this story. Those new to the movement will find here a thrilling saga of Christianity in action."

General Paul A. Rader, Rtd.

"Colonel Henry Gariepy, The Salvation Army's foremost writer today, with his skillful weaving of narrative with fact and past with present, presents Christianity in Action as a superb telling of the fascinating story of The Salvation Army."

General John Larsson, Rtd.

"In this meticulously researched book, Henry Gariepy presents a fascinating heritage as he escorts the reader from the move-ment's birth in Victorian England to a present-day icon of mis-sion in far-flung places around the world. William Booth would be amazed to read this narrative about that for which he was di-vinely appointed to be its founder. And it reminds me why I'm proud to be a soldier in this magnificent mission!"

Commissioner Israel L. Gaither,
USA National Commander

**International Mission Statement
of The Salvation Army**

*The Salvation Army,
an international movement,
is an evangelical part
of the universal Christian Church.
Its message is based on the Bible.
Its ministry
is motivated by love for God.
Its mission
is to preach the gospel of Jesus Christ
And meet human needs
in his name without discrimination.*

ALSO BY HENRY GARIEPY

Daily Meditations on Golden Texts of the Bible
Man with a Mission
When Life Gets Tough
Light in a Dark Place
Treasures from the Psalms
Andy Miller: A Legend and a Legacy
A Salvationist Treasury
Songs in the Night
Mobilized for God: History of The Salvation Army, Vol. 8
A Century of Service in Alaska
A Pen of Flame (Editor)
100 Portraits of Christ
Healing in the Heartland
Guidebook for Writers and Editors
40 Days with the Savior
Challenge and Response
General of God's Army
Historic Highlights of The Salvation Army in Lancaster, PA
Wisdom to Live By
Christianity in Action
Portraits of Perseverance
Advent of Jesus Christ
Study Guide: Advent of Jesus Christ
Footsteps to Calvary
Study Guide: Footsteps to Calvary
Devotional Study of Names of Jesus
Salvation Army 101
Hallmarks of an Army (with Stephen Court)

Christianity in Action

The International History of
The Salvation Army

Henry Gariepy

Foreword by
General Shaw Clifton

WILLIAM B. EERDMANS PUBLISHING COMPANY

GRAND RAPIDS, MICHIGAN / CAMBRIDGE, U.K.

Published 2009 by
Wm. B. Eerdmans Publishing Co.
2140 Oak Industrial Drive N.E., Grand Rapids, Michigan 49505 /
P.O. Box 163, Cambridge CB3 9PU U.K.
www.eerdmans.com

Printed in the United States of America

15 14 13 12 11 10 09   7 6 5 4 3 2

Library of Congress Cataloging-in-Publication Data

Gariepy, Henry.
Christianity in action: the international history of The Salvation Army /
Henry Gariepy; foreword by General Shaw Clifton.
p.   cm.
Includes bibliographical references and index.
ISBN 978-0-8028-4841-3 (cloth: alk. paper)
1. Salvation Army — History.   I. Title.

BX9715.G37   2009
287.9'6 — dc22
2009023113

Dedicated to Marjorie,
my companion on life's journey,
"the wind beneath my wings,"
partner and editor par excellence
of this and all my writings

The Salvationist who captured my heart
and shared my journey (1948)

Contents

Contents

Foreword

Christian believers in every generation owe a profound debt of gratitude to those whose gifts enable them to write the history of the church. We cannot truly understand the present unless we have a reasonably clear grasp of the past. The path already trod lends light, not only to today, but also to the direction we are being called to follow for tomorrow.

This is why we are deeply indebted to Colonel Henry Gariepy for his one-volume history of The Salvation Army's origins and development right up to the present time. With considerable skill he has compiled a most readable record, crammed with human interest stories.

When we consider that the Army's own officially published history consists of eight lengthy volumes to date, the colonel's carefully crafted single-volume account is a remarkable achievement of selection, balance, insight, and concise clarity.

While this book is intended primarily for readers in the United States, it will serve most usefully far outside those shores and will appeal to readers both within and beyond the ranks of Salvationism.

Working and witnessing in 118 countries, the Army is a vast and complex part of the body of Christ. As the elected world leader of The Salvation Army, I feel honored to commend this telling account of our beginnings, our place in church history, our ongoing passion for souls and the less privileged, our role in the modern world, and, under God, our vision for the future.

GENERAL SHAW CLIFTON
The Salvation Army
International Headquarters, London

The Salvation Army is a multifaceted organization.
Art by Karen Yee Lim

Introduction

The Salvation Army has been acclaimed a phenomenon of religious movements, its name a byword around the world for its compassionate ministry. Its unity in 118 countries shines as a modern miracle in a divided world, and should make the United Nations blush with envy. Yet few know The Salvation Army — its history, global outreach, structure, vast array of services, ecclesiastical foundations, and mission.

Following a plethora of books about the Army over the years, why now a new book? Ironic as it may seem for such a high-profile organization, no contemporary book chronicles and defines the overall movement. The interminable tomes on the Army are now long out of date and out of print. Even the official eight volumes of its history have become for the most part a collector's item or resource for the devotee of Army history.

Furthermore, there is a need, both for those within its ranks and for those with interest outside it, for a definitive work on The Salvation Army. Literally millions of people each year are involved with or touched in some way by this movement. And for its members, each new generation must discover afresh and be reenergized by its roots. History can serve as the compass of the movement, helping chart its course amid strong winds and currents of change.

In the aftermath of the urban riots of the mid-1960s that turned some of our nation's inner cities into an inferno, The Salvation Army launched its Multi-Purpose Center in the riot-scarred ghetto of Hough, next to the heart of downtown Cleveland. The Center's galaxies of programs and services drew over a thousand persons a day through its doors. It became, in the words of the mayor, "a new hope and life for the community."

When Billy Graham came to Cleveland for his 1972 Crusade, he requested that we arrange for him to visit the Center. There he interacted with the youth and staff in the multiple programs serving the critical needs of that community, and even shot baskets with boys in the gym. Our tour ended in the chapel where I commented, "Billy, here is the core of this center. Here miracles have occurred as lives have been changed by the grace of our Lord."

I shall always remember his words. "Henry," he said, "this is truly Christianity in action!"

I responded, "Thank you, Billy, for the best definition I have ever heard of The Salvation Army."

The Salvation Army is Christianity in action, Christianity with its sleeves rolled up, out where the air is blowing, the issues are real, and people are hurting. Throughout its history it has served as the infantry of the militant Christian church. Though today more sophisticated, its mission remains unchanged — defined by one of its leaders, "to save souls, to grow saints, and to serve suffering humanity."

Now 143 years young, it remains an army without guns, an army of peace. In the words from Damon Runyon's *Guys and Dolls,* it is "a God-fearing Army."

The Salvation Army is seemingly everywhere, a signature movement on the landscape of many nations. Countless persons each year are the beneficiaries of its services. It is multifaceted and one of the most pluralistic of all organizations.

The *New York Times* in its November 17, 1999, edition featured a two-page article, "An Army Marching Smartly to Its Own Drummer." Writer Julie Connelly spotlighted the Army as the top charity in the United States the past year, with $1.2 billion raised. She attributed this fund-raising success "to the Army's clearly defined mission, being trustworthy in carrying out that mission, putting 84 percent of its funds back into direct services, and using superior marketing skills." The movement has come to have a claim not only on America's purse strings, but also on its affection.

A unique encomium came from the prestigious Booz Allen Hamilton global consulting firm, which cited the Army as among "the world's ten most enduring institutions" along with such venerable entities as Oxford University and the Olympic Games. It defined the Army as "iconic in its ability to motivate and inspire its workforce, exuding innovative capability, adaptive response, resilience and legitimacy."

In another article dated January 2006, Associated Press religion writer Richard N. Ostling gave his definition:

> Renowned for Christmastime bell-ringers with red kettles, and efficient canteens that served 4.8 million meals after Hurricane Katrina, The Salvation Army enjoys a kind of respect accorded few American charities. Yet the Army is not a charity. Rather, it's a rather small, distinctly conservative Protestant denomination that sponsors a massive and expanding philanthropic empire. Its doctrines are orthodox Christian. . . . Soldiers, the core group among members, take covenant vows that cover doctrine, loyalty, willingness to evangelize and help the needy, and clean living (no alcohol, drugs, gambling, pornography or profanity).

Rated by historians as the most successful religious movement of the nineteenth century, The Salvation Army has a colorful and captivating history. Born in the slums and saloons of East London, initially ridiculed and severely persecuted, it has become a worldwide movement with a practical brand of Christianity recognized by royalty and heads of nations. It has epitomized Kipling's model of one "who can walk with kings and yet keep the common touch."

But the history of the movement is not all progress and glory. William Booth acknowledged, "It is our troubles that give us our anecdotes." Valleys as well as mountain peaks make up the landscape of Army history, and both must be kept in our purview.

Historically The Salvation Army has remained a paradox. It emerged in the Victorian world of male domination, yet from its beginning it has accorded equality to women in its ministries and leadership. While adopting an apolitical stance, it worked for laws to protect the downtrodden and exploited. Internationally united under one general with headquarters in London, it nonetheless is managed autonomously and is multiculturally expressed in each of its member nations around the world. Small in size — under two million members — its influence far exceeds its numbers.

Salvationists have never subscribed to the artificial dichotomy between the sacred and the secular. The Army's founder, William Booth, summarized the approach to the down-and-out as offering "soap, soup and salvation." He reminded his followers that they must offer to the hungry bread for their bodies before offering the Bread of Life for their souls. The time-honored slogan defines its mission as "Heart to God, Hand to Man." Its spiritual and social work are as the two blades of scissors, each essential to the other to provide its cutting edge.

A history book, of necessity, has to be selective. This work omits historic details of interest only to Salvationists, details suitable only for the ongoing official history of the Army. Highlights, defining moments, and insights into the mission are presented here without the scaffolding that would compromise readability. Although written within an American context, this writing exudes an international scope that we trust will serve all readers interested in knowing more about the Army's origins and ongoing mission.

In presenting a definitive account of this unique and global organization, this historian acknowledges that he stands on the shoulders of pioneer writers whose recorded histories, biographies, periodicals, and chronicled data have receded into the archives of time. Yet they provide essential lamps on the paths of the movement's history.

History is always in the making with its inexorable and kaleidoscopic change. Events of today become history as the next day dawns. Cataclysmic events are reshaping our world as it whirls toward the dangerous uncertainties of the future. Besieged by global issues of ecology, poverty, the silent "tsunami of hunger," the HIV/AIDS pandemic, devastating natural disasters, war and terrorism, and potential nuclear holocaust, we stand at the threshold of both an unknown and a vastly different future. But The Salvation Army continues to serve amid the seismic changes of secular history, holding fast to the immutability of God's faithfulness.

May the reader find within these pages both information on and inspiration from this movement that God brought into existence and blessed.

ONE

In the Beginning

*Look to the rock from which you were cut
and to the quarry from which you were hewn.*

Isaiah 51:1

William Booth, born April 10, 1829, in Nottingham, England, was reared in poverty. As a lad he had a threefold longing — to rise above his adverse circumstances, to find God's purpose for his life, and to make his life count.

William was only fifteen when he heard an echo of the voice that turned Paul's life around on the road to Damascus. Spiritually precocious, he vowed, "God shall have all there is of William Booth." Years later it would be said that the secret of his life was that he gave his all to God, and he never took it back.

In 1846 there came to his hometown the noted American revivalist James Caughey of the Methodist Episcopal Church. He preached passionately for a verdict, inviting his hearers to kneel and pray at the communion rail to find forgiveness and freedom. He also emphasized the second work of grace, or "entire sanctification." His simple but compelling preaching, sharp mind, ready wit, and persuasive orthodoxy sparked the tinder in young William's heart, setting it aflame with a passion for evangelism. Caughey's ministry and preaching style helped shape Booth's preaching, and later his methods.

No hiatus occurred between Booth's conversion and the start of his lifelong ministry. He early organized street preaching, and at age seventeen walked long distances on Sundays to fill country preaching en-

1

William Booth

gagements. After taking a number of transient pastorates, in 1854 he found stability within the Methodist New Connection, one of the schismatic offshoots of early Methodism. Blessed with success in having converts, he was assigned in 1855 to the work of an evangelist. Ordained in 1858, he was appointed pastor to the church in Gateshead that for three years earned the name "the Converting Shop."

A Turning Point

The year 1861 was critical for William Booth. In that year it was decided whether he would be allowed to continue the revival work to which he was convinced he was called by God. The question came before the annual church conference held in May 1861. A long discussion ensued, with some denouncing the methods of revivalism.

Mrs. Booth had taken a seat in the gallery of the chapel. The result of the voting was announced, a compromise that would deny William

**The dramatic moment William Booth leaves Methodism, with Catherine
standing in the center of the gallery**

the opportunity for full-time evangelism. Questioned by a glance from
her husband whether he should accept such a compromise, Mrs.
Booth, rising from her gallery seat, in defiance of both rules and respectability, challenged their verdict with a clear, strong voice that resonated through the conference, exclaiming, "No, Never!"

This account, originally recorded in Frederick Booth-Tucker's history, repeated in Coates, *The Prophet of the Poor*, has been ascribed by
some to Salvationist folklore. However, early biographies, and a Mr.
Scowby who was an eyewitness, also reported hearing Catherine make her
famous cry, as did Dr. Townsend, a minister present on the occasion.[1]

Convention was flouted by this challenge of the verdict. Consterna-
tion overcame the dignified men below because a woman had dared to
utter a protest, or even to make her voice heard in the conference. Im-
pelled by that resolute exclamation, William courteously bowed to the
chair, and amid shouts of "Order, order" made his way to the foot of the
gallery stairs. There he and Catherine embraced, and went out to an un-
certain future. The issue between Booth and the convention proved intractable. In that moment the Rubicon was crossed: William Booth
took the first step toward his destiny.

Bramwell, William's son, writes of this turning point in his revealing book *Echoes and Memories:* "When he joined the Methodist New Connexion there was a distinct understanding with the authorities of that time that he was a minister for evangelistic work, in which he had already gained a great measure of success in various parts of the country. It was their subsequent refusal of that work which brought about the rupture."

Eight weeks after the conference, Booth resigned from the Methodist Church. He announced to the conference that he would do the work to which he felt God had called him, even if he went forth "without a friend and without a farthing." He had cut himself adrift from his church. After seven years of devoted service, he was now penniless, with a wife and four children to provide for. At thirty-two years of age, his prospects seemed hopeless. In desperation the family moved to London, where to meet their expenses Mrs. Booth took in two lodgers.

William Booth then became an independent, itinerant evangelist, conducting campaigns throughout Britain, supported by voluntary donations and the income his wife gained from preaching to her own well-to-do audiences. But he found himself out of favor within Methodism, for the church's respectability was offended by revivals for the working class.

A Methodist leader, Rev. John Telford, later expressed the view that became generally accepted: "General Booth, one of its zealous local preachers, was lost to Wesleyan Methodism, as at a later date he was lost to the New Connexion. There we trace the Providence that guides the Church's service. The worker needed a wider field, a freer hand than Methodism was then ready to offer him, and the result is one over which Christian men rejoice."[2]

Two

Booth Finds His Destiny

Once you were not a people, but now you are the people of God.

1 Peter 2:10

Evangelism and revivalism were thriving in mid-Victorian England. It was the age of Finney, Spurgeon, Moody, Sankey, Parker, and others whose meetings attracted thousands, with large numbers of conversions. Within that context William Booth served as an itinerant evangelist.

The great spiritual awakening in 1859 in England had brought into being the Home Mission Movement. One evening in June 1865, as William strode along the streets of East London, he came upon this group conducting a gospel meeting across from the Blind Beggar pub. He halted, listened with interest, and then was invited to "have a word." His commanding presence and forceful words captured the attention of passersby. Soon a crowd gathered. They heard sin denounced and the love of God proclaimed in a clear and powerful way.

The missioners began whispering to each other, "This is the leader we need at the Tent!" Seeking to reach the lost in East London and forbidden to hold meetings in parks, they had erected an old tent on a disused burial ground belonging to the Society of Friends. A few days later a deputation came to Booth to ask him to conduct their meetings in the tent. The evangelist who had been engaged had taken ill. Booth accepted the invitation to preach there in London's East End, beginning July 2, 1865.

William Booth preaching in the tent

The tent's less than hospitable backless benches could seat some 300 persons. Inside the closed canvas walls the air was heavy with a mixture of drunken vapors and noxious odors from the naphtha lamps hung on wires stretched between poles. Those who came were the unkempt and poorest in the spiritual wilderness known as London's Mile End, its name taken from a milepost.

The Army's first historian, Robert Sandall, reflects: "Could any setting have been more unpromising? Or could anything have seemed less likely to be the opening before him of the door of wider opportunity for evangelistic service?"[1] For William Booth, that weathered and worn tent became his tabernacle.

Booth would later recall that moment: "My field of labor was Mile End; my tabernacle, an old tent in a disused burial ground; my audience, a crowd of poor Whitechapellers; and the result — blessed be God! — was a few desolate souls at the mercy seat." Sandall further observes: "But for William Booth's seemingly chance encounter with the missioners at their open-air meeting, it is doubtful whether the Special Services Committee would have ventured to invite him to go to the Tent. Upon what fine points turns the providence of God!"

On that July night, toward midnight, as Catherine would later recall, a key grated in the lock, the door opened, and Booth, his eyes gleaming, strode into their living room. He then pronounced his historic words, "O Kate, I have found my destiny."

That moment of epiphany for William Booth echoed the sentiment of noted missionary C. T. Studd: *Some wish to live within the sound of church or chapel bell, I want to run a rescue shop within a yard of hell.*

In retrospect he reflected,

When I saw those masses of poor people, so many that they so readily and eagerly listened to me, following from open-air to tent, and accepting, in many instances, my invitation to kneel at the Savior's feet there and then, my whole heart went out to them. I walked home and said to my wife, "These are the people for whose salvation I have been longing all these years. As I passed by the door of the flaming gin-palaces tonight I seemed to hear a voice sounding in my ears, where can you go and find such heathen as these, and where is there so great a need for your labors? And there and then in my soul I offered up myself and you and the children to this great work. Those people shall be our people, and they shall have our God for their God." She smiled and took my hand, and we knelt together. That was the first meeting of The Salvation Army.

There, in the bleakest area of what was then the world's greatest city, William Booth found his destiny. In that inauspicious setting he was launched on his lifelong mission. The dilapidated tent became the Bethlehem of The Salvation Army, as unpromising as was the cattle shed for the Savior of the world.

Booth's Parish

Booth's mission was birthed in the middle years of the sixty-four-year reign of Queen Victoria when England was the world's dominant power. London was the hub of the British Empire during its apex of power. In East London, near the heart of the empire, poverty, hunger, unemployment, and crime stalked the streets. Prostitution for young girls became a way of life and for many their only means to earn a living. Lack of sanitation and clean water bred disease and the dreaded cholera and smallpox. One article described the scene: "the poor have been growing poorer, the wretched more miserable, and the immoral more corrupt."[2] Into this milieu of social pathology was born William Booth's Salvation Army.

William at first sought only to evangelize, channeling converts into the churches. But he had to abandon this aim because they would not go when sent; and those who did go were not wanted. Some Methodist churches introduced pew rents in their chapels, often as an intentional barrier to the poor. Booth also soon found that he needed the assistance of his converts to win others of their class.

He capitalized on the novel idea of taking religion to the people rather than waiting for them to go where they were not wanted, and he used the reformed sinners to bring their kind to the Savior. Both the religious cultural gap and the pragmatic approach led Booth to found his first mission — the East London Christian Revival Society.

As the work expanded, in 1867 the name was changed to the Christian Mission. In 1870 a constitution was written that placed William Booth, as general superintendent, solely in charge. In response to the harrowing plight of the poor, Booth and his early followers developed their mission as a synthesis of evangelism and social action, waging its war with the two-edged sword of the gospel and practical compassion.

Twenty-four-year-old George Scott Railton chanced on Booth's pamphlet *How to Reach the Masses with the Gospel*. "These," he exclaimed, "are the people for me." Ascetic in habits, Railton replied to the question why he traveled third class on the train: "Because there's no fourth class!" Scholarly in mind and passionate for evangelism, Railton rejected the rigid hierarchy and complicated liturgy of the established church, joining Booth as his private secretary in 1873. He became foremost among the noble oaks in the forest of early-day leaders and supporters of the fledgling movement.

The Army's triumvirate consisted of William as commander in chief, Catherine the chief adviser and a preacher in her own right, and son Bramwell the chief executive officer. Railton's loyalty and energetic support of the founder made him the closest confidant outside of Bramwell — the latter became the most valued assistant and leader of the early Army, serving devotedly for forty-eight years.

"The Salvation Army" Is Born

The name Salvation Army was adopted almost accidentally. An incident, now legendary within the movement, took place that changed the name of the Christian Mission. Early one morning in May 1878 Bramwell and Railton were summoned to meet with William Booth to review instructions for the day's work. William, in a dressing gown and slippers, walked up and down as he dictated instructions. Railton scanned the proofs of the eight-page annual report of the Mission and read aloud the words: "The Christian Mission is a Volunteer Army, recruited from among the multitudes who are without God and without hope in the world."

Young Bramwell exclaimed: "Volunteer! Here, I'm not a volunteer. I'm a regular or nothing!" William Booth paused, stepped forward toward the table on which the proof lay, pondered the text, then snatched up a pen and crossed out the word "Volunteer," substituting "Salvation."

The effect, recorded Bramwell Booth, of that one word upon him and Railton was extraordinary. "We both sprang from our chairs. I remember that I exclaimed, 'Thank God for that!' Railton was equally enthusiastic."

In that early morning dialogue, from the chrysalis of the Christian Mission there emerged The Salvation Army. From that moment its destiny was fixed. The change of name set the policy for warfare upon sin and human destitution. It was a call to arms.

Early in the formation of The Salvation Army William Booth gave the definitive statement: "The object and work of this Mission is to seek the conversion of the neglected crowds of people who are living without God and without hope, and to gather those so converted into Christian fellowship, in order that they may be instructed in Scriptural truth, trained in habits of holiness and usefulness, and watched over and cared for in their religious course."[3]

Of its beginning, Bramwell stated, "The movement was a new movement; we had no precedent to go upon, very little experience to guide us. We had to build the ship while we were at sea, and not only build the ship, but master the laws of navigation!"

Conceived of the Spirit of God, The Salvation Army was a child of the passion of William and Catherine Booth, both for their Lord and for the destitute people of their unconventional parish. For them religion

9

was not a refuge from the world, but a light to take into its dark corners. Booth and his Army were pragmatic rather than doctrinaire. They brought religion out of the clouds of ritual and into everyday life, and taught that a house or a factory or even a converted dance hall could be as holy a place as a church building. The bonds of convention were broken, and in the words of the late General Albert Orsborn, "The Salvation Army became the stormiest wind that ever blew through the halls of orthodoxy."

THREE

William and Catherine

*"Come, follow me," Jesus said, "and I will make you fish-
ers of men."*

Matthew 4:19

A movement is the lengthened shadow of its founder, and the shadow
of William Booth has today spread across the globe. Harold Begbie, in
the introduction to his two-volume biography of Booth, observed: "William Booth is likely to remain for many centuries one of the most signal
figures in human history . . . the greatest religious force of modern days,
and one of the most picturesque and heroic figures of the nineteenth
century."

Found among Booth's papers after his death were the resolutions
of a young man at age twenty, seeking to live a disciplined and dedicated life, dated December 6, 1849.

I do promise — my God helping — 1st That I will rise every morning
sufficiently early (say 20 minutes before seven o'clock) to wash, dress,
and have a few minutes, not less than 5, in private prayer. 2ndly That I
will as much as possible avoid all that babbling and idle talking in
which I have lately so sinfully indulged. 3rd That I will endeavour in
my conduct and deportment before the world and my fellow servants
especially to conduct myself as a humble, meek, and zealous follower
of the bleeding Lamb, and by serious conversation and warning
endeavour to lead them to think of their immortal souls. 4thly That I
will not read less than 4 chapters in God's word every day. 5thly That I

Catherine and William Booth

will strive to live closer to God, and to seek after holiness of heart, and leave providential events with God. 6thly That I will read this over every day or at least twice a week. God help me, enable me to cultivate a spirit of self denial and to yield myself a prisoner of love to the Redeemer of the world. Amen & Amen, William Booth.

Methodist Roots

Booth was christened an Anglican, but after his conversion he was nurtured within the Wesleyan Methodism tradition in Great Britain. Its teaching, including the doctrinal hymns of Charles Wesley, became the matrix of his theology, and later that of The Salvation Army. The dominant influence throughout his life was American revivalism, brought to Britain by Methodist revivalists James Caughey and Phoebe Palmer, and Presbyterian Charles Finney. *Lectures on Revivals of Religion* by Finney became the primary text for Booth, and was later required reading for his cadets in training. The revivals that swept Britain in the mid-1800s, with large meetings led by notable preachers, gave him his methodology and mission.

Booth devoured the story of John Wesley's life and his writings. He confided, "No human compositions seemed to me to be comparable to his writings, and to the hymns of his brother Charles." John Wesley's Arminian theology of "free salvation for all men and full salvation from all sin" early led the Booths to the conviction that conversion was not an end but a beginning.

Methodists admitted the gap that stood between them and the poor. Booth had encountered the abject poverty and vice on the streets of London that led him to his destiny of ministering to the least and the lost. He said, "We want the lowest of the low," and to reach the "lowest" he adopted methods entirely foreign to the religious establishment of his time. While these methods became popular among outcasts, they brought him into collision with the orthodox and the mob. His methods were a shock to the decorum of the religious world and the public.

Edward Rabbits, a wealthy boot manufacturer, impacted William Booth's life in two major ways. In 1851 Rabbits heard him preach, and, convinced that Booth could awaken the somnolent Methodists, he urged the young evangelist to preach full time. In response to his protest that he had no source of support, Rabbits agreed to support him for three months. This enabled William for the first time to go into full-time evangelistic ministry.

A Memorable Romance Is Born

The second major influence of Rabbits resulted from his inviting William to a dinner party at his home, along with a Catherine Mumford and her father. Both William and Catherine were committed to the Methodist reform movement, a revivalist branch of Wesleyanism. That evening William escorted Catherine home. The two immediately bonded, became engaged that year, and following a three-year courtship, were married in 1855. That first encounter evolved into one of the most remarkable and charming love stories in history, and William Booth's good fortune in meeting and marrying one of the most extraordinary women of her time.

Catherine was born on January 17 in 1829, the same year as William. Her education was superior to William's, but she recognized in him a man of extraordinary spiritual gifts and force of personality. Reared in the Wesleyan Methodist tradition, she read the Bible through eight times by the time she was twelve years old, according to her biographers.

Catherine's keen intellect and maturity were needful checks to William's mercurial spirit. Their frequent enforced separations from 1852 onward resulted in a voluminous treasure trove of letters, providing extensive insight into their struggles, concerns, faith, and everyday experiences. The affectionate and didactic letters from Catherine also reflected her life's work, that of guiding William. In Begbie's two-volume life of William Booth, over seventy-five pages are devoted to exchanged love letters. The long, reasoned letters from Catherine, often over two thousand words, were antidotes for William when he struggled with despair or self-pity. In a monumental work, David Bennett of Australia gathered all available letters and published them in a limited edition. The 180 letters from William and 167 from Catherine, written between 1852 and 1889, were largely extracted from the Booth papers in the British Museum.

During their early years in London, Catherine became better known, increasingly in demand as a preacher, and the principal breadwinner in the family. She proved to have surprising energy for one so frail and frequently indisposed. Congenitally ill, she still bore eight children in eleven years, and home-schooled them. Catherine was a major influence on the formulation of Army doctrines and its social service policies. Her writings and model of preaching would be a major means of liberating women from their subjugation in the field of Christian ministry. She alone among Army leaders never assumed formal rank as an officer.

In retrospect, that seemingly chance first encounter of Catherine and William at supper in the home of the boot manufacturer had the stamp of Providence upon it. In her declining years she became affectionately known within the ranks as "the Army Mother." She is also acknowledged as "cofounder" with William Booth, and often appears as such on the Army's letterheads and documents. William was the heart, Catherine was the brains. Catherine earned her own honored place in the pantheon not only of The Salvation Army but also of notable women of Christian history.

FOUR

An Army Is Formed

Put on the full armor of God so that you can take your
stand against the devil's schemes.

Ephesians 6:11

Soon synchronized with the 1878 change of name was the Army's quasi-military structure. The rhetoric of warfare, springing as it did from the pages of the New Testament, was common and translated readily to cultures of the day. The accoutrement of a uniform appeared in 1879, at first anything but uniform. But a standard uniform soon came into vogue. As "clothes made the man," so the uniform made the soldier. The women's straw bonnet, designed by Catherine, remained one of the Army's trademarks for almost a hundred years. Ultimately the design of uniform became standard and was modernized by minutes issued from time to time.

The uniform varied in accordance with national custom. Navy blue was adopted in the Western world, but in India native dress was adapted; conditions in tropical countries favored material light in texture and color. At Salvation Army international congresses the multicolored uniforms appeared as a rainbow of the Army's family of nations. As Salvationist Elizabeth Brengle testified from personal experience, the uniform served both as a witness to outsiders and as a benchmark of commitment for its members. It identified a Salvationist anywhere in the world, with many who traveled in uniform being stopped at airports and in public places by people with stories to tell or prayers to request. Symbolizing a person who cares and is available when needed, it

The earliest women's uniforms

has also served as proper attire in formal settings with heads of state and in official gatherings.

Accoutrements of an Army

An army needs a flag, and in September 1878 Catherine Booth presented Coventry Corps in England with the first Army tricolors, emblazoned with the motto Blood and Fire. It affirms in crimson the atoning work of Christ, in yellow the fiery baptism of the Holy Spirit, and in blue the purity of God. Once seen at countless nondescript street corners, today, as was said of the British ensign, the sun never sets on the flag of

The Salvation Army. It is a restless banner, proclaiming its own trinitarian message of the gospel in now over 100 countries. A miniature flag even traveled to the moon, aboard *Apollo 16,* carried by astronaut Captain John W. Young, commander of the lunar landing in April 1972. That flag is now exhibited at the Army's headquarters in Philadelphia.

Pseudomilitary terms soon emerged. Prayer times were "knee drills," giving of tithes in envelopes was "firing cartridges." Buildings were called "citadels," local congregations were "corps," members were "soldiers," and lay leaders were "sergeants," under a "sergeant-major."

Copious *Orders and Regulations* emerged after 1878, written by Railton and modeled on Sir Wolseley's *Soldier's Pocket Book,* ultimately one for soldiers and one for officers. A kind of "military etiquette," they stipulated conditions of membership, soldierly conduct, and advice on personal hygiene and health. Ranks soon followed, with full-time leaders designated officers with a hierarchy of ranks from lieutenant to commissioner. The militant songs born of the time suited well Booth's nascent army, such as the nineteenth-century English hymn "Onward, Christian Soldiers," written in 1871 as Booth's work was getting under way.

A new constitution was enacted in 1878 that confirmed the name change, included the doctrines, ascribed to Booth the title of general, and allowed him full autocratic control. His critics understandably seized on this. But he was in the company of his spiritual progenitor John Wesley, who has been described by his biographers as "an uncompromising autocrat."

Initially leaders recruited to the Army were sent out to do evangelistic meetings, with no further responsibility. But gradually there was the transition from itinerancy to fixed appointments at mission stations, at headquarters, or in delegated duties. By October 1878 the evolution from Christian Mission to Salvation Army was complete, led by Booth and championed by Bramwell, Railton, and Catherine. This fledgling army had but eighty-eight members and fifty-seven stations.

To meet the need of communication with its troops, and publicity for those outside its ranks, the *War Cry* was launched in December 1879, first as a monthly house organ and later as a weekly. From the start it was decreed that no reference could be made to partisan politics. Its early incarnation featured bold Victorian aesthetics, sensational stories of conversions, frontline reports of attacks and advances, and real-life spiritual adventures, and was considered worth its price of a penny. Salvationist historian R. G. Moyles describes the early editions as "Unabashedly jingoistic [in spiritual warfare], openly propagandistic, and thoroughly braggadocio." But he goes on to acknowledge that "the Army's religious tabloid was avidly read and universally loved by thousands of Salvationists and non-Salvationists alike."[1] No one then could have envisaged that this flagship publication of the movement would someday publish 136 editions in many languages and boast a robust circulation of over two million copies.

Supplies and Purchasing Departments sprung up to market its uniforms, flags, teaching materials, books, and Army memorabilia. These "trades," as they are known, carry a full line of both essential and novelty items bearing the Army's insignia. Structured on efficient business principles, they also often turn over a profit that is applied to the Army's mission.

The early properties acquired by the Army, totally unadorned, served pragmatically the Army's mission. A disused music hall, a converted dance hall, a spacious warehouse, a former skating rink — all were so plainly unecclesiastical as to free the irreligious from their inhibitions about entering a church. "Testimonies" — converts spontaneously witnessing to the miraculous change in their lives and the joy of their salvation — interspersed with choruses added interest and inspiration to the meetings of early days. Simple benches, called the "mercy seat," were a focal point for converts to pray as they sought and found salvation. A reporter from London's *Secular Review* was dispatched to describe an Army meeting, and in his lengthy report he described what he saw as "plain, vulgar, downright, most unfashionably earnest. This is simply an assembly of Christian enthusiasts who have no swelling organ, no white-robed choristers, no gaudily bedizened priests."

The Salvation Soldier

In carrying out the militant mission of the Army, converts were enrolled as soldiers. In 1882 the enrollment was formalized and all new soldiers were required to sign a document called the "Articles of War." This declaration, still in effect, now also known as "A Soldier's Covenant," affirms a profession of personal salvation, a pledge of separation from the world and of loyalty to Christ, support to the Army, and acceptance of the Army doctrines. (See appendix B.) A preparation course of up to ten weeks relates to the spiritual life, Army history, doctrines, and practice. In William Booth's army there would be no nominal members.

At the seventeenth anniversary celebration in July 1882, William Booth declared, "I want to say to every Salvation soldier, let us not trust in The Salvation Army, but in the mighty God who has made The Salvation Army. Our strength is not in our banners, nor our colors, nor our comrades, apart from the almighty power of God the Holy Ghost."

A unique and somewhat courageous inclusion in the articles as a condition of membership was a pledge of total abstinence from all intoxicating liquors and baneful drugs (tobacco was added in 1976). In no other Christian church at that time was any restriction placed, even upon its ministers, on the use of alcohol. The total abstinence requirement became binding on Army members throughout the world. The Salvation Army remains today one of the world's largest abstinence movements.

Many descriptions have been coined to soften the harshness of the word "death." But one of the most radical is the Army's descriptive phrase "promoted to Glory." In keeping with its quasi-military structure, it sounds a triumphant note that affirms belief in heaven and eternal life. It declares that death is not the end, but the beginning of a new and glorious life. The term, first used in the *War Cry* on December 14, 1882, found ready acceptance and has been used ever since. When a Salvationist dies, it is said that he or she has been "promoted to Glory."

A Meticulous Accounting

Bramwell Booth records: "Our movement was born in absolute penury. Buildings must be erected or hired. The poor and neglected must be cared for. Evangelists or leaders must be provided with their daily bread. The people lived from hand to mouth." He records that rich men often sent William Booth blank checks on condition that the amount he filled in should apply to his own personal use. Bramwell adds, "The checks were returned. William Booth largely supported himself by the slim profit from the sale of his books. For the Army he was ready to accept such gifts with both hands; for himself, not at all."

From the beginning William Booth practiced and required a meticulous accounting, calling in as needed experts in bookkeeping and auditing. He always had at least two persons involved with details on money matters, and required that balance sheets be prepared, audited, and published.

The Army went international in 1880, only fifteen years after its founding. Although still a Gideon's army, it was an army on the march. The successful financing of so sudden an expansion posed an arduous task. As the Army expanded globally, at work in twenty nations in 1886, it initiated what it termed its "Self-Denial Effort," whereby, for example, through sacrifice of dessert during Lent, the money saved was contributed to a special fund to help support its openings and work in other lands. This annual effort now raises many millions of dollars essential for the ongoing work in less economically developed countries.

Training of Leaders

Training for leadership soon became a priority, and the first training home was opened in 1879 in Manchester, England, where a few young men enrolled under the leadership of Ballington Booth, son of William. In May 1880 a training home for 30 women cadets was opened in London, quickly followed by a similar garrison for men.

In 1882 a large, former orphanage building at Clapton in northeast London was purchased. This building would become the Army's historic Congress Hall, an auditorium seating more than 3,000 persons, the scene of some of the Army's most notable gatherings. The property also provided accommodation for the housing and training of 400 cadets.

In 1904 the training period was extended from six to nine months; by then the number of cadets had swelled to 450. Thousands of cadets were trained there and commissioned to far-flung outposts of the Army world, until in 1929 the William Booth Memorial Training College at Denmark Hill, a suburb of London, was opened. The ever increasing acquisition of new training facilities and the expansion of existing ones around the Army world have culminated today in many state-of-the-art colleges and campuses that host the two-year resident course. An accredited academic component to the training now allows cadets to be awarded academic degrees as they are commissioned to their lifetime mission.

In 1978 a new word was inserted into the Army's lexicon, to be a part of every ceremony for the commissioning of cadets as officers. General Arnold Brown then acknowledged, "Some, I felt, did not understand that the granting of a commission not only admitted the recipient to officership, but also conveyed all that is commonly drawn from the term *ordination*."[2] Supported by Army leaders, he sent out in 1978 the directive that the revised wording of the commissioning statement should henceforth include the word "ordained." An April 2008 Minute from International Headquarters (IHQ) spelled out in further detail the procedure and ceremony, with three options for the officiating statement, including "Recognizing that God has called you, has equipped you and gifted you for sacred service, I now ordain you as a minister of the gospel of our Lord and Savior Jesus Christ, and commission you as an officer of The Salvation Army with the rank of lieutenant."[3] This sacred ceremony leaves no doubt of an officer's clergy credentials.

Around the Army world, cadets are commissioned officers and ordained annually, usually in spring, replenishing the ranks of leaders. Following the ordination, usually in a separate and public service, newly commissioned officers receive their first appointment, which grants them authority both to serve and to lead in whatever place and capacity they are given at that time.

General Albert Orsborn called this yearly reinforcement of leadership "the perennial springtime of the Army." The ultimate highlight event of the year is when the general comes to a country to conduct the ceremony. Since 1960 cadets have undergone a two-year residence course, then following their commissioning and ordination, they participate in five-year extended study institutes. Components of education include biblical studies, doctrinal studies, study in church history, practical field training (including social work, pastoral ministry, and public ministry), leadership, and administration. An immutable feature of all training colleges the world over is the daily "half-hour of power," dedicated to a corporate prayer period.

Salvation Army officership is not a career, it is a calling. Officers do not become officers by contract, but rather by covenant. They believe that where the world is at its worst there the church of Jesus Christ ought to be at its best. Theirs is a call to servanthood, not a short-term, but a lifelong, commitment.

In his message to 1,130 cadets worldwide in 2008, General Clifton stated,

> The one thing all cadets have in common is that all have been called by God to leave their secular walk in life to devote themselves full

time to the ministry of an officer of The Salvation Army. It is a privileged calling. Unless that divine calling has been experienced no person should offer to be trained as an officer. The life of an officer, whilst immensely rewarding, is also demanding and often stressful. At certain times of challenge and difficulty your abiding, settled sense of a sacred calling is all that will hold you secure and keep you pressing forward in your officer service.

In 1950 an International College for Officers (ICO) was instituted in London, described by General Orsborn as "an investment in the great intangibles." Twenty-six officers from different parts of the world come for the two-month training session and represent a microcosm of the international Army. The interaction and courses offered enhance knowledge and bonding of the Army's internationalism. Regional spin-offs of ICO, with their zonal acronyms — SACO, SPEAKO, AFCO — have been established in other parts of the Army world, with collaborative territorial leadership to promote advanced and specialized training.

Among other teaching programs, The Salvation Army Leaders' Training College of Africa (SALT), sponsored by IHQ and based in Harare, Zimbabwe, promotes education and training in fourteen African countries. Besides resident courses, training is provided through seminars and distance education, offering fifty-one subjects. It awards certificates or diplomas, and the associate in theology (Th.A.) degree through the Australian College of Theology.

Through gradual development Booth's warriors became a full-fledged army of God, with essential accoutrements and training for spiritual warfare in the front lines.

FIVE

The Sounds of Music

*Sing psalms, hymns and spiritual songs with gratitude in
your hearts to God.*

Colossians 3:16

The Salvation Army early took to heart the psalmist's dictum: "Make a
joyful noise unto the Lord." Brass band music, one of its most public
features, had its beginning in Salisbury, England, where Charles Fry
was leader of the Methodist choir and orchestra. Witnessing that the
Army was often attacked during their street meetings, he and his three
sons, in the late 1870s, offered to help protect these beleaguered meetings. When it was discovered that they were expert musicians, they were
invited to bring their instruments to accompany the songs. Soon they
became Salvationists, and in this unwitting fashion the first Salvation
Army band was born.

Their success led to the promotion of brass bands of varying sizes
and musical skills, which caught on rapidly, reflecting the British culture. By 1883 there were 400 Army bands within the British Isles. Soon
the singing was accompanied by tambourines, and ultimately timbrel
brigades of modern Miriams with their own flourish of creative chore-
ography.

Bramwell Booth was to say of the Army's music, which proclaimed
the gospel on the street corners to those who did not go to church,
"Ours is the marching chorus, the peripatetic organ."

The Fry family brass quartet on the rowdy street corner in Salisbury
in 1878 foreshadowed the day when brass bands would become a dis-

23

The Army has a diverse musical repertoire.

tinctive symbol of Salvation Army worship, when a Salvation Army band would be the first civilian band ever to play for royalty in the courtyard of Buckingham Palace, or when the band played at the Hollywood Bowl's Easter sunrise service, where the listening and viewing audience numbered 100 million. Such was the inauspicious step toward today's scene, with over 2,000 bands comprised of 45,000 members, all volunteers, dedicated to the ministry of music. Premier bands today, with the International Staff Band (London), inaugurated in 1891, considered the apogee, set the highest standards of musicianship capable of gracing any secular as well as sacred platform.

Bards and Bands

Booth and his Army took the unconventional step of adapting Army lyrics to the popular tunes of the day. Before the day of copyright restrictions, lyrics were adapted to ballads and love songs, and gave rebirth to such well-known tunes as "The Old Folks at Home." Booth shared Martin Luther's outlook: "Why should the devil have all the best tunes?" While Booth sanctioned indigenous hymnology, it became a supplement to the traditional hymns of the church. Subsequently many original works replaced the secular adaptations. "Music," he said, "is the wind to our sails." William appended his own byline to two memorable Army songs, "Send the Fire" and his signature song sung in other denominations as well, "O Boundless Salvation." (See appendix C.)

Richard Slater, a founding member of the Royal Albert Hall Orchestral Society in London, remembered as "the father of Army music," contributed hundreds of compositions. In 1883 Slater was put in charge of Booth's newly created Music Department, to coordinate and develop the Army's expanding music ministries, including band tune books and regulations. Such departments are today conventional in many territories and divisions of the Army. They are directed by Salvationists with professional credentials and have a wide impact on the development of the Army musical forces and program.

Apart from Scripture itself, the primary worship resource in The Salvation Army has been its official *Song Book,* published first in 1878 and updated for the fourth, and most recent, time in 1986. It occupies a distinctive place in the corporate worship and private devotion of Salvationists. In the British tradition of hymnals, it contains only the words, of over 1,000 hymns and 251 choruses; the music is published in a separate volume.

With an emphasis on gospel and devotional selections, it is replete with sections on each member of the Trinity, salvation, holiness, means of grace, and the Army's warfare. Its musical ecumenism is reflected in its range of songs, from Martin Luther's Reformation hymn "A Mighty Fortress" to Charles Wesley's 64 hymns to Fanny Crosby's 24 titles. Isaac Watts, John Newton, and other traditional lyricists contribute to the collection. A spate of contemporary collections and editions for accompaniment continue to enrich the Army's repertoire for worship music.

Salvationist lyrics and brass have given voice to their faith and mission. Herbert Booth and Evangeline Booth were two of the earliest of the Army bards, whose songs continue to be sung in Army meetings. Joining them in later years were well-known names to Salvationists such as Albert Orsborn, Catherine Baird, and Ruth Tracy. The following words from the pen of Ruth Tracy constitute but one of many songs born within their ranks that lead Salvationists the world over in a path of prayer and devotion in their worship:

> Lord, I pray that I may know thee, Risen One, enthroned on high;
> Empty hands I'm stretching to thee, Show thyself to me, I cry.
>   Show thyself to me, That I may reveal thy beauty;
>   Show thyself to me.

> All that once I thought most worthy, All of which I once did boast,
> In thy light seems poor and passing, 'Tis thyself I covet most.
>   Give thyself to me, That I may show forth thy power;
>   Give thyself to me.

> Only as I truly know thee, Can I make thee truly known;
> Only bring the power to others, Which in my own life is shown.
>   Show thy power in me, That I may be used for others;
>   Show thy power in me.

The fourth and final verse of one of Herbert Booth's songs leads the worshiper to a full consecration, following the first three verses that speak of bringing our heart, our life, and our sins to Jesus:

> I bring my all to Jesus; he hath seen
> How my soul desireth to be clean.
> Nothing from his altar I withhold
> When his cross of suffering I behold;
> And the fire descending brings to me liberty.

The Army's famous team of "the two Johns" (John Gowans [words] and John Larsson [music]) contributed twenty songs from their famous musicals to the Army's *Song Book*. These two officers became household names in Army circles as their full-length musicals, produced in virtually every Army territory and in every major language, powerfully presented the story of Army history and often left revivals in their wake.

Songster brigades are the "choirs" of the Army, and lend their inspiration in worship worldwide. The International Staff Songsters (ISS) in London, organized by Major Norman Bearcroft in 1980, became the standard-setting vocal group, their high-quality musical message resonating in international travels and recordings. At their inaugural presentation, General Arnold Brown announced, "I hope none of us will forget that the very first word sung by the ISS was 'Jesus.'"

The "Founding Fathers" of Army band music, Richard Slater, George Marshall, and Bramwell Coles, among others, laid the foundations that ultimately produced an abundance of Army musicians and music worldwide. Original compositions for the Army's brass bands proliferated in published band journals of meditations, selections, marches, hymn tune arrangements, and suites for concert performances. The repertoire was enhanced by compositions of highly regarded brass band composers Eric Ball and Erik Leidzen. The Army produced its own roster of notable musicians, including Ray Steadman-Allen, OF (Order of the Founder, defined in a later chapter), Sir Dean Goffin, Leslie Condon, and Norman Bearcroft. In recent years James Curnow, William Himes, OF, Robert Redhead, and Stephen Bulla have moved into the forefront of Army composers.

In 1920 The Salvation Army's brass band was invited to march in the annual Rose Parade in Pasadena, and has been represented ever since. It currently claims the longest tenure of any group in this granddaddy of all parades. In 1921 the Army held its first music camp, in New Jersey, later to be replicated around the world, hosting thousands of budding and advanced musicians in extended summer sessions. Soon the Army was publishing its own band and choral music with a varied repertoire of marches and meditations, and in 1928 published its own *Tune Book* of over five hundred tunes to accompany Army singing.

The Army's Lingua Franca

In addition to composing and publishing its brass and vocal music, the Army in 1889 established its own instrument-making factory in England. For many years its high-quality instruments were to be found in Army bands around the world, until the factory yielded to rising costs and increasing competition and closed in 1972.

Music festivals are popular events that feature the virtuosity and the virtues of Army compositions. The ultimate in Salvation Army musical expression takes place at its international gatherings, which are suffused with the quintessence of vocal and brass music from around the world.

Salvationist musicians have often excelled in the secular world as

Captain Margaret Davis performs in a London concert.

composers, arrangers, and performers. Among those holding principal chairs in brass sections of major orchestras are Philip Smith, for many years principal trumpet with the New York Philharmonic; Dudley Bright, the principal trombone of the London Symphony Orchestra; and Ronald Prussing, principal trombone of the Sydney Symphony Orchestra. Salvationist Stephen Bulla serves as arranger for the U.S. Marine Band. CDs bring the best of Army music into the homes of its members, complementing its burnished brass with vocal renditions from well-known artists, such as coloratura Captain Margaret Davis (Philadelphia).

Music, the universal language of mankind, is also the lingua franca of the Army world. It bonds its multinational members in an effective proclamation of the gospel message and nurtures the spiritual life of its followers.

Six

Early Persecution

Blessed are those who are persecuted because
of righteousness,
for theirs is the kingdom of heaven.

Matthew 5:10

The pattern of violence that stalked Booth's Army for thirty years was in the centuries-old tradition of opposition to anything deviating from the norm. Taking the gospel to the street corners and pubs, elevating women to equal status with men, and forming the organization in military ranks and structure were an assault on mid-Victorian culture and religious decorum. The unconventional tactics of Booth's Army incurred opposition from two ends of the social spectrum — from the mobs on one end and from churches on the other.

The Army's continuous campaigns against the evils of drink provoked support for violence from the brewers. Organized groups known as "Skeleton Armies" sprang up in various towns to attack the buildings and processions of the Army. Some shopkeepers kept eggs of vintage for sale at reduced prices for assailing Salvationists on the march.

The city of Eastbourne passed a law prohibiting street marches, with the intention of shutting down the Army's outdoor witness. Throughout 1891 the Army's marches were attacked in bloody encounters and riots by mobs bent on denying the Army its basic right. Many Salvationists suffered imprisonment and serious injury.

Sixty Army buildings were virtually wrecked by the mobs, all without redress or reparation. Editorialists, and even ministers, stoned Sal-

Citizens of Sheffield riot against the Army in 1882

vationists with words. In September 1882 one of Booth's first converts was struck by rocks and kicked severely, and died within a week. She became the Army's first martyr, but would not be the Army's last.

During one year, 1882, the number of Salvationists knocked down or otherwise assaulted in the United Kingdom was 669. More than one-third of them, 251, were women, and 23 were children. Eighty-six Salvationists, 15 of them women, were thrown into prison. All because they took part in religious meetings in their own buildings or in the open air.

Also in 1882 an afternoon procession in Sheffield was attacked with what newspapers called "savage ferocity." One lieutenant on horseback was so badly hurt that he remained unconscious for hours and never completely recovered from the injury; others were also severely injured. The *War Cry* recorded that "for over an hour musicians and officers were a target for thousands of brutal roughs to curse, spit upon and cover with mud, and wound with sharp stones." The general, marching with them, although derided, was uninjured. Amends were made by the city three months later when two large processions of Salvationists passed through the town guarded by police, and received scarcely a token of opposition.

William Booth himself was obliged to put on record the harassment of those early days: "If we opened the windows, mud and stones and occasional fireworks were thrown through. Consequently we had to sit and endure the stifling heat until it was impossible for delicate people to remain. Sometimes trails of gunpowder were laid, with the dress of one devoted sister actually set on fire during the service."[1]

Magistrates tended to protect the persecutors rather than the afflicted. Salvationists were often imprisoned, more than 600 in 1884. They refused to pay the fines imposed, in violation of their right to conduct street meetings. Bramwell Booth recorded:

> The children of this world were for once outdone in malevolence by the children of light! Always the chief opposition to the Army was from the churches. Every evil which could be imagined was told of us, and the tellers were from those whom we called our "fellow Christians"! Clergymen who had never been to a meeting of The Salvation Army, or spoken to a Salvationist in their lives, denounced us from their pulpits and wrote letters of ill will in the newspapers. The denunciation reached its height of absurdity when the Earl of Shaftesbury solemnly stated that, as the result of much study, he had come to the conclusion that The Salvation Army was clearly Anti-Christ. But fortunately, the tide of sympathy in the nation was too strong for them.
>
> We were fighting for freedom to proclaim the same Savior whom they honored. We were a menace to the "comfortable" worship of the day. Our people's zeal and joy put to shame the religion which consisted mostly in a listless rote. Ours was a practical faith. It appealed to the common mass. It offered a spiritual charter to the ecclesiastically disfranchised. It gave its message through the mouths of quite "vulgar" people — mechanics, domestic servants, factory girls, farm laborers.[2]

Booth's soldiers had to learn defensive tactics to survive. Elijah Cadman, one of the early leaders, would end a march loaded down by an armful of dead rats and cats. To drop them, he explained, would give the mob fresh ammunition.

On the brighter side, Charles H. Spurgeon, the most famous preacher of the day, on several occasions referred positively to William Booth. He came twice to lecture on behalf of the Mission, and gave his famous lecture "Candles" at an Army meeting.

A Turning Point

Opposition of the gangs as well as of the churches continued until the early 1890s. Finally on July 1, 1890, the Army was vindicated by Parliament rescinding the notorious law that violated human rights, winning the hard-fought battle to hold street meetings provided they were not causing an obstruction. Their marches, bands, and open-air meetings became a part of the religious landscape of England. The Salvation Army had fought and won the battle for the right of all public bodies to use the streets for lawful purposes, and to be protected when doing so.

William Booth was gaining both notability and notoriety. He lived and did his life work in italics. There was no one else like him. W. T. Stead, editor of London's eminent daily newspaper *Pall Mall Gazette,* wrote: "The Salvation Army is a phenomenon. It has done more to realize the ideals of almost every social reformer, secular or religious, than any other organization we can name. The enfranchisement of women, the greater simplicity of life, the obligation of altruistic service, the duty of temperance — all find in The Salvation Army more practical realization and more effective recognition than elsewhere. General Booth has done more to secure the attainment by this generation of the goal of human effort than all authorities put together."

"If William Booth had not been willing to make enemies," observes his biographer, Hattersley, "he would not have created the only remnant of the hundred-year Wesleyan schism that would survive into the twenty-first century. Unless he had been willing to offend there would have been no campaign for the undeserving poor."[3]

The Salvation Army became a living example of the words of Jesus to his followers: "Blessed are those who are persecuted because of righteousness."

SEVEN

Women in Ministry

There is neither . . . male nor female, for you are all one in Christ Jesus.

Galatians 3:28

The position held by women in The Salvation Army from the beginning has been unique. It was without historical precedent, and became one of the early defining distinctions of the new movement.

Catherine Booth

Although the British sovereign at that time was a woman, in mid-nineteenth-century England women played little part in government and leadership of the nation's affairs. In the church of mid-Victorian England, women were to be seen but not heard. At a time when education was the privilege of the male gender, women did not have the right to vote and held no positions of leadership in the church.

The Salvation Army acted on the conviction that a woman merited equal opportunities with a man in the work of evangelism. This principle was founded upon the sanctions of the Bible and the remarkable ability of women to be used of God. The first Christian Mission Constitution (1870) enunciated that women should have equal rights with men in the movement's work and government.

The Gauntlet Thrown Down

It all began when an American evangelist was assisted by his wife, Phoebe Palmer, a devout and eloquent woman whose teaching became popular. Anglican minister Arthur Rees was so incensed that he wrote a pamphlet denouncing a woman as a preacher of the gospel and attacking Mrs. Palmer. The idea of a woman preaching was viewed by many as scandalous. To Catherine, Rees' pamphlet was a gauntlet thrown down.

This attack outraged and galvanized Catherine into writing and publishing in 1859 a thirty-two-page rebuttal, a pamphlet titled *Female Ministry* that systematically defended the equality of women in ministry. Her polemic was supported by her astute knowledge of the Scriptures and the most careful biblical exegesis, demolishing arguments against women in ministry. She argued that 1 Corinthians 14:34-35, the solitary proof text used "to uphold the delusion and [enforce] it as a divine precept, binding on all female disciples through all time to seal woman's lips for centuries, was contrary to the example of Jesus. He could have summoned a legion of angels, yet accorded to woman the honor of being the first to announce the triumph of the resurrection." Her foundation text was Galatians 3:28: "There is neither . . . male nor female, for you are all one in Christ Jesus." Catherine's trenchant pamphlet not only proved useful for the radical position taken by the Christian Mission, but became a classic apologetic for women in ministry.

A Defining Moment

Catherine was convinced that the Holy Spirit endowed women with gifts and abilities to use in the service of God. While defending women's right to preach, Catherine herself had been struggling about the Lord leading her to preach, but had remained silent. One Sunday, at their Methodist church in Gateshead, Catherine surprised herself, her husband, and the congregation.

The scene was Bethesda Chapel, on Pentecost Sunday, 1860. A crowd of more than a thousand had gathered. Catherine sat in the minister's pew. Later on, telling of the incident, Catherine said, "It seemed as if a voice said to me, 'Now if you were to go and testify, you know I would bless it to your own soul as well as to the souls of the people.' I gasped and said in my soul, 'I cannot do it.' And then the devil said, 'Besides, you are not prepared to speak. You would look like a fool and have nothing to say.' He made a mistake! He overdid himself for once! It was that word that settled it. I said, 'Ah! This is just the point. I have never yet been willing to be a fool for Christ. Now I would be one!'"

As William Booth concluded his sermon that Sunday morning, Catherine, pale but determined, rose from her seat and walked to the front of the chapel. She later recounted the incident: "My dear husband thought something had happened, and so did the people. He stepped down to ask me, 'What is the matter, my dear.' I said, 'I want to say a word.'"

Booth himself was so astonished that he could only say, "My dear wife wishes to speak." Flora Larsson records, "The living volcano in Catherine's heart had burst its way out to liberty, with results such as even she at that moment could not foretell. William gallantly stood aside to let his wife mount the pulpit steps for the first time, but certainly not for the last."

Catherine openly confessed, referring to the Lord's leading her to preach, "I have been living in disobedience. I promised the Lord three or four months ago, and I dare not disobey. I have come to tell you this, and to promise the Lord that I will be obedient to the heavenly vision."

When she had finished speaking, the people were visibly moved. William was led to announce, "My wife will preach this evening." On that Pentecost Sunday in 1860, in response to the invitation of her husband, she preached her first sermon, "Be Filled with the Spirit," and opened a door for women yet unborn in The Salvation Army. It was a revolutionary step. From that time on Catherine shared in the preaching ministry with her husband.

Dr. Randall Davidson, chaplain to the archbishop of Canterbury, described Catherine Booth as one of the most remarkable women he ever met. After hearing her address a crowd for the first time, he said, "If ever I am charged with a crime, don't bother to engage any of the great lawyers to defend me; get that woman."

Some of Booth's "Best Men"

William Booth had early doubts about women preachers and Catherine's even more radical view of their having authority over men. He came slowly to the same conviction as Catherine with regard to woman's position, moving from doubt to tolerance and then to full support. She claimed that not only did redemption extend equally to woman, but she was intellectually, morally, and spiritually man's equal. Women won their place in the Army while still knocking at the doors of other churches and the professions.

Largely through the influence of Catherine Booth, women became increasingly prominent in the work of the early Christian Mission. As the work increased, and evolved into The Salvation Army, they came to take on leadership positions. Their success put the capstone on the contention that women's capacity to manage affairs at least equaled that of men.

The Army's employ of women as preachers and leaders courted strong opposition, especially from the established church. It was going against the tide of the culture and traditions of the day. But the resulting explosion of growth in the early years of the Army would have been impossible without its women officers. William Booth was constrained to say, "Some of my best men are women!" In later years he reflected: "She has filled with honor the most important positions of authority in our ranks, and directed with success many of our difficult enterprises. Indeed, she has justified every demand ever made by the Army upon her capacity, her courage and her love."

Long before suffragettes won the right to vote in England, Army lasses were playing a vital role in establishing the Army as a recognized religious revival movement in Victorian society. Diane Winston, in *Red-Hot and Righteous,* states that The Salvation Army was "the first Christian group in modern times to treat women as men's equals."[1]

In her book on The Salvation Army in Victorian Britain, Pamela J. Walker concludes: "The Salvation Army was among the first denominations to proclaim women's right to preach the gospel, and under its aegis thousands of working-class women assumed a spiritual authority that defied injunctions requiring female silence and submission. The Hallelujah Lasses were pioneers in establishing an authoritative, public, religious voice for women."[2]

Coming into Her Own

The Army was indeed a pioneer and pacesetter in providing equal opportunity of ministry for women, affirming and acting out the biblical principle of equality. Catherine Booth was obviously ahead of her time, but after her passing the Army did not keep pace with her vision and pronouncements. True, women did have broad and equal opportunities, but they were conspicuously missing from upper echelons of Army administration. In 2005, retired general Eva Burrows wrote in "The Dismantling of the Army's Glass Ceiling":

> Even today there have been few women divisional commanders, cabinet members, chief secretaries or territorial commanders. Women were often appointed to social and caring assignments such as with children, or the elderly, or homeless women and prostitutes; roles particularly deemed "women's work." Considering that women formed about two thirds of the membership of The Salvation Army, they were never given leadership in any way proportionate to their numbers. But things have changed and are continuing to change. The new awareness in Western culture of the significance and place of women in society has been a wake-up call to The Salvation Army. We are living in an age when woman is coming into her own.[3]

Recommendations of the 1991 International Commission on the Ministry of Women brought major change for married women officers. According to the new template coming from the Commission, married women officers no longer are given appointments as an accommodation to their husbands' but rather according to their gifts and abilities. The recommendations gave officer wives a rank in their own right, including that of commissioner, eventually opening the door for them as members of the High Council (the council that elects the general). Leaders were expected to assign women officers to positions that utilized to the fullest advantage their gifts. These and other changes help keep alive the dream of Catherine Booth.

Women take an active role in the pulpit.

Today women command corps, institutions, and divisions, and serve in national leadership. At the time of this writing a woman, Commissioner Robin Dunster, serves as The Salvation Army's chief of the staff, second in command of the international Salvation Army. And two of the movement's sixteen elected generals were women.

The contribution of women has been, and continues to be, incomputable in their roles of leadership in every facet of the Army administration and mission. All because, in an inauspicious setting and moment in time, one woman obeyed the Spirit's leading, stepped forward, and said, "I want to say a word."

EIGHT

Attacking a Monstrous Evil

Speak up for those who cannot speak for themselves,
for the rights of all who are destitute.

Proverbs 31:8

Beneath the veneer of respectability in Victorian England was a white-slave trade where girls were sold into prostitution, often by their own families, at the age of thirteen or even younger. Parliament had three times failed to pass legislation to raise the age of consent, set at thirteen in 1875. Bills had been passed by the House of Lords in 1883, 1884, and 1885, but failed before the Commons, thus encouraging perpetrators in what became known as the "white slave traffic." The flourishing trade tricked young girls into a life of debauchery, destroying their bodies and souls. This trade, which few in those days believed to exist, was a highly organized and lucrative business.

A Defining Moment

A defining moment came for the Army in 1885 when early one morning the caretaker at International Headquarters in London opened the front doors. There, clad in a scarlet dress, was a teenage girl, Annie Swan, who had slept through the night on the doorstep. She said to the surprised man, "I want to see General Booth." Annie's arrival at that doorstep would ignite one of the most explosive chapters in the Army's history.

The girl was ushered in to see Bramwell Booth, as the general was away. She told her horrifying story of how she had been lured from her home by an ad for domestic work and found herself trapped in a London brothel. When confronted by a "customer," she barricaded herself in a room. She heard the brothel keeper say, "Leave her there 'til morning and she'll come to her senses when she wants her breakfast." During the night Annie looked at a Salvation Army songbook she had carried with her that contained General Booth's address. At four o'clock in the morning she slipped out a back window of her locked room, walked the long distance to the Army's headquarters at 101 Queen Victoria Street, and slept outside until the doors opened.

Bramwell knew his wife Florence was involved in rescuing victims of the slave traffic. She had become appalled at the revelation that young girls were trapped by this vicious network and commenced a rescue work to house and secure employment for them. Annie's harrowing story galvanized Bramwell's resolve for the Army to investigate the vicious white-slave trade in England. Further revelations came to light when a number of girls were brought from the Army's rescue home by Florence and questioned. Bramwell recorded in his memoirs:

> From the earlier years there came to the Army's penitent-form unfortunate girls who looked to us for some means of enabling them to throw off the fetters of their deadly calling. Appalling revelation to find that young girls — children really, of 13 and 14 — were being entrapped by a vicious network and in their innocence condemned to a life of shame. Such anguish and degradation could not be matched by any trade in human beings known to history. That, no matter what the consequences might be, I would do all I could to stop these abominations, to rouse public opinion, to agitate for the improvement of the law, to bring to justice the adulterers and murderers of innocence, and to make a way of escape for the victims. The age at that time, wickedly and absurdly, was thirteen. We knew that the government was very tepid on the whole question.
>
> For many weeks I was like one living in a dream of hell. The cries of outraged children and the smothered sobs of those imprisoned in living tombs were continually in my ears. I could not sleep. I could not take my food. At times I could not pray.[1]

The War Is Launched

Bramwell set himself not only to rescue girls individually, but also to attack the very trade. This would be a moral war on the front lines, and he would need help. He enlisted as his ally William T. Stead, the crusading editor of the influential *Pall Mall Gazette.* Stead listened incredulously to the evidence presented to him of the abduction of girls by devious means into state-regulated brothels. The intelligence he then gathered through his own investigation was nightmarish — thousands of underprivileged, innocent girls, bought for a few pounds and shipped to state-regulated brothels in other countries. A worldwide trade was fueled by countless procurers and buyers.

Persuaded of the evil, Stead launched four explosive salvos, titled *The Maiden Tribute of Modern Babylon,* calculated to suggest that Victorian Britain was as venal as ancient Babylon in the gruesome evils of Britain's white-slave traffic. These horrifying disclosures, including testimonies of girls who had been abducted, turned a blazing spotlight on Britain's dark underworld and shocked the nation. The sensational exposé became a journalistic tour de force, "surpassing all that had been known in the history of journalism." The articles disclosed in graphic detail the entrapment and abduction of young underprivileged girls and their sale to London brothels.

The nation was roused to boiling indignation. One member of Parliament asserted, "The continental traffic in girls surpasses in villainy any other trade in human beings in any part of the world in ancient or modern times."

Catherine Booth appealed both to Queen Victoria and to Prime Minister Gladstone to forward the cause of a bill that was being introduced in the House of Commons. Her passion in attacking the evil was unsuppressed:

> I read some paragraphs from the report of a debate in the House of Commons which made me doubt my eyesight. I did not think we were so low as this — that one member should suggest the age of consent be reduced to ten, O my God! What is to become of the little girls of the poor, the working classes? I could not have believed that in this country such a discussion among so-called gentlemen could have taken place. I have been horrified by the moral obtuseness of the country's leaders that passed such a law which had lowered the age of

the protection of a female child to 12. The Legislature took care that such a child should not be empowered to dispose of her money or her property until she attained the age of 21, and yet they gave her power to dispose of her virtue when she was too young to know the value of it. Is there anything worse than that, think you, in hell?[2]

The Army, in what became known as the Purity Crusade, conducted seventeen nonstop days of protest meetings. A petition to the government was placed for signature in every Salvation Army building throughout the country, demanding legislation for the protection of children, and netting signatures of protest that broke through the apathy and stirred the conscience of the nation. It embodied four points: (1) the age of consent for girls was to be raised to eighteen; (2) the procurement of young for immoral purpose was to be made a criminal offense with a severe penalty; (3) police were granted the right to enter and search suspected brothels; and (4) the solicitation of women was made a criminal offense.

On July 30, 1885, a monster scroll of joined-together sheets, running over two miles long and bearing 393,000 signatures, was paraded, accompanied by a fifty-piece brass band. The rolled-up petition was borne on poles by eight cadets into the House of Commons. It petitioned for the age of consent to be raised to eighteen. At the same time, the general announced a scheme for the establishing of rescue homes.

Stead and Bramwell had spent long hours with the home secretary making proposals to strengthen the bill, including the right of police to raid suspected brothels and stamping out the intercontinental traffic in girls.

The government could do nothing but act. On August 14 the bill carried by 179 to 71 and became law, in conformity with the petition that included the suppression of brothels, except the age of consent was raised only to age sixteen. A thanksgiving rally was held for the passing of the act. Armed with new powers, the police entered and closed down many brothels.

In this David and Goliath combat, The Salvation Army's crusade had moved the world's most powerful government to a moral action that heretofore it intransigently refused to do. But the war was not over.

The Perils and the Prize

Stead, to solidify his facts, had conceived the idea of buying a young girl to prove that she could be bought cheaply from her parents — a nefarious possibility that many had refused to believe. Later he had her virginity medically certified to validate his integrity. But in his eagerness to prove his contention, Stead had broken the law. A scandal of megaton proportions captured the headlines. "This," one ill-wisher declared, with what seemed like reason, would "smash The Salvation Army" and bring about its demise.

An incredible turn of events occurred, as Stead, together with Bramwell and several others, was indicted for allegedly abducting Eliza Armstrong, age thirteen. The twelve days of hearings created a profound sensation throughout the country. Bramwell was acquitted, but Stead and his codefendants were judged guilty of abduction and served short prison sentences. The *Methodist Times* pertinently commented: "The sentence is founded upon the monstrous opinion that it was better for the crimes to go on than to be exposed."

The sensational trial further awakened the public conscience, and along with the Criminal Law Amendment Act, catapulted the Army into a position of unrivaled respect for its compassion and advocacy for those marginalized and without hope. The Army became known as the champion of the oppressed, a formidable opponent to evildoers, and a national bulwark against vice.

William Booth called upon his troops everywhere "To be a guardian friend of women. Let the men remember that God holds the strong responsible for the protection of the weak. Let the sisters hunt up the poor girls. Oh, that the time may come when not only the wicked but the weak will feel that whomsoever they see wearing a badge or uniform of a Salvation soldier is their friend and helper."

Each year on the anniversary of his conviction, W. T. Stead wore his prison uniform, which he regarded as a badge of honor. In April 1912 Stead paid a visit to William Booth. He knew that the aged and ailing warrior did not have much longer to live, and he wanted to say goodbye. He shared that he would be traveling to America on the new great liner. Booth asked the name of the ship. "The *Titanic*," he replied. Ten days later W. T. Stead went to meet his Maker, a victim of the most famous of all sea disasters.

The War Becomes Global

Other nations, as a result of the crusade, began to put their houses in order in raising the age of consent. In Japan licensed prostitution had been carried on with girls being openly sold to this trade. In 1900 The Salvation Army launched an attack on brothel keepers in Tokyo with a special edition of the Japanese *War Cry* that appealed to these enslaved girls to give up their lives of prostitution with an offer of help. The paper was distributed in the area of brothels, and as soon as the brothel keepers became aware of its contents, they hired men to attack the *War Cry* sellers. Army workers were violently attacked, but as a result the Japanese press came out on the Army's side, and many girls and parents sought the offered help. The government was forced to pass a law that no woman who wished to leave the brothels could be restrained for debt. In one year thousands of girls placed themselves for rescue in Army homes. By 1902, 14,000 prostitutes had escaped and renounced their activity.

In 1880 the Army had thrown down the gauntlet in England, and now neither country nor continent was immune from the Army's taking up arms where the evil existed to destroy innocent lives. Florence Soper, Bramwell's wife, had started the first home for rescued prostitutes, and carried on this work for thirty years. More such homes sprang up, providing a safe haven for girls. When Florence, who had pioneered these homes, died in 1957, The Salvation Army worldwide had 117 such rescue homes.

Human Trafficking War Continues

Now, more than a century after the Army's first victorious battle with human trafficking, it once again is at war against this evil and is rescuing girls from what has been termed "the mother of all women's issues." A July 22, 2006, issue of the Army's *All the World* magazine called sex trafficking of girls a $10 billion criminal industry that takes place through coercion, abduction, fraud, and deception.

Commissioner Helen Clifton, the Army's world president of Women's Ministries, has become a major and articulate spokesperson on this scourge that ravages the bodies, breaks the spirits, and steals the lives of countless girls and women. A gifted writer, she was a teacher

Attacking human trafficking worldwide

Top: **Antitrafficking training in China**
Center: **South Africa antitrafficking training group with Kathryn Burgmayer**
Bottom: **Antitrafficking training delegates in Mumbai, India**

before becoming an officer, and now draws on her training and gifts to address internationally the issue of human trafficking. She states, "Fighting the evil of sex-trade trafficking remains high on the agenda of the worldwide Salvation Army." In February 2008 she presented a global report on the Army's response to sex-trade trafficking, from which the following is taken.

In Malawi, Africa, the Army has a safe house for 16 girls and an education program that has reached some 5,000 girls. Congo and Angola have reached hundreds of vulnerable young people, sex slaves and parents through an effective educational program funded by Norway. In Ghana, thousands have been aided with an awareness program by leaflets and posters, along with accommodation for street girls in Accra to provide an alternative way of life. In Brazil a residence is underway for victims of trafficking and single mothers from the streets. Canada has established an extensive Anti-Trafficking Network and its advocacy has helped change laws and gain better protection for victims. The USA Western Territory has funded programs for residential services to survivors of trafficking in nine States. The UK produced 8,000 leaflets for soccer fans at the World Cup in 2006. "Stop the Traffick" is a global campaign based in London. In Asia where trafficking crime is spawned by poverty, oppression of women and sex tourism, the Army in Sri Lanka, Bangladesh and India intervenes with raising awareness and providing shelter and counsel for sex workers. A home for trafficked children has been opened in the Philippines, and two centers for women victims in Korea. In Sydney, Australia trafficking is high on the agenda of a newly-formed social justice group. The Army in Hong Kong reports work being done against human trafficking in China's Yunnan province where whole villages have lost their women and girls. In New Zealand the Army held a joint event with the Anglican Church in addressing the issue of trafficking.

Helen Clifton summarizes, "Today's sex slavery is a more hidden and subtle evil, even harder to tackle. But like Florence and Bramwell Booth in the early days of the Army, we refuse to close our eyes or accept it as inevitable."

The Salvation Army has mobilized its resources around the world to respond to the needs of sex-trafficking survivors, and to implement prevention strategies. Today its antitrafficking effort focuses on four core areas: (1) legislative and policy initiative, (2) awareness raising and training, (3) protection efforts, and (4) trafficking survivor services.

The Army endorsed the passage by the U.S. Congress in 2000 of the Trafficking Victims Protection Act. Lisa Thompson, U.S. national consultant for the Army's program, states, "We will continue to take positions on U.S. policy matters regarding sex trafficking, including emphasizing the link between sexual trafficking and HIV/AIDS, and we will oppose efforts to legalize prostitution." Her office has helped spearhead the Initiative against Sexual Trafficking (IAST), a partnership of faith-based children's and women's advocacy organizations united in seeking the abolition of sexual trafficking. It published an *Anti-trafficking Training Manual* to assist social service providers and others in recognizing and serving victims of human trafficking. The five-hour curriculum has been made available, and training sessions based on it have been sponsored in other countries. In November 2007 (as shown in the photo on page 45) delegates from six organizations came together in Pretoria, South Africa, for a training program hosted by Kathryn Burgmayer of Salvation Army World Services Organization (SAWSO) and Kristen Wiebe, director of World Hope International Anti-Trafficking and an attorney and recognized pioneer in this field, to develop action plans for programs to combat trafficking in their areas of work.

Kathryn and Kristen also conducted a similar training program in Mumbai, India, in collaboration with Project Rescue International, where Salvationists attended to strengthen effectiveness of their ministry in combating trafficking through outreach in red-light districts. They journeyed in March 2008 to war-torn Liberia. The following is adapted from Kathryn's report, which reveals that the Army's DNA to fight human trafficking is still found in the spiritual genes of the new generation.

The purpose of my trip to Liberia was to monitor a Salvation Army project designed to sensitize communities on trafficking issues and to protect survivors. The role of The Salvation Army in this project is to conduct awareness meetings and to develop Village Parent Groups (VPG) to serve as the eyes and ears for trafficking issues. Each VPG is connected to trained law enforcement and service providers to establish a referral mechanism of comprehensive care to victims of trafficking. The destruction, abuse, and evil that occurred during fourteen years of civil war is beyond comprehension. The infrastructure has been destroyed — schools, hospitals, government buildings. Many are living without water or electricity in dark corners of destroyed buildings. It has left a generation vulnerable to the ploys and lies of syndicates who seek to recruit and sell people for their exploitative purposes. The Army has remodeled apartments as an interim care center for victims of trafficking. My friend Kristen Wiebe and I interviewed many persons during the week about the current trends of human trafficking in Liberia, and we learned much by just sitting and listening to what they are witnessing. Some of it was so dark, stories that are so horrific they are hard to believe. My faith was challenged to know that God is able to help us make a difference in these extreme circumstances.

Salvation Army leaders in the Latin America North Territory, with headquarters in Costa Rica, have taken an active role in addressing the trafficking issue, including a "call to prayer and action for victims of sex-trade trafficking — a matter of grave concern." They sponsored programs for raising awareness, holding a protest march, and producing a workbook for parents and children at schools and day-care centers. In Guatemala, talks on sex-trade trafficking were given in the Army's schools and workshops were arranged for parents. In Cuba, every Army unit joined in the cry: "God, make it stop!" In the Dominican Republic, six corps held a day of fasting and praying for sex-trade victims, and offered counseling and workshops for women, mothers, and teenagers. Salvationists in El Salvador held a walk, carrying signs made by children expressing God's love and their protest against sexual trafficking. What is happening in these areas, and elsewhere, as reported in this chapter, symbolizes the Army's aggressive assault on this grotesque evil that is destroying millions of innocent lives around the world.

General Shaw Clifton in the summer of 2007 issued a further "call to arms" in the war against human trafficking:

I am calling the Army to prayer once again this year for those exploited and irreparably damaged as victims of this dreadfully evil trade. The matter is a core issue for the Army today just as much as it was in our early days. The holy instinct for addressing it can be said to be part of our DNA. Prayer, education, fund-raising and protection for the vulnerable, including children, are four powerful tools we are using. We can pray for the victims, for their families, for the relief agencies, for all working to reduce and to frustrate the evildoers, and for the forces of law and order.

Salvationists are helping lead the way in fighting on behalf of the least of the least, dismantling the brothels, breaking down the iron doors that keep captive children enslaved, bringing the evildoers to justice. In our time, William Booth's worldwide Army without guns is still at war, at the front lines to combat this monstrous evil. It serves in the spirit of its founder, who said of human suffering and injustice, "I'll fight! I'll fight to the very end."

NINE

In Darkest England

For I was hungry and you gave me something to eat, I was thirsty and you gave me something to drink, I was a stranger and you invited me in.

Matthew 25:35

Booth had become increasingly concerned about the social evils that ruined the lives of the people among whom he worked. In the 1870s he launched a chain of London soup kitchens that became known as Food for Millions, serving meals to the poor at token cost.

"As time wore on," he recounted in 1887, "the earthly miseries connected with the condition of the people began to force themselves more on my notice. I saw men walking about wan and worn with hunger. I saw others wallowing in drunkenness, vice and abominations which reduced them below the level of the beasts. I saw poor men and women and children compelled to live in hovels of the most wretched squalor and filth. I saw the people dying prematurely of disease for want of food and attention. Thousands of young women were being sacrificed to the gratification of the lusts of men who bought and sold them; and most agonizing of all I saw the indifference of those who had the means to help."[1]

Bitter Cry of Outcast London, a trenchant work by Andrew Mearns, had made a deep impression on him. In 1889 the East London dock strike by 75,000 workers highlighted the inequities of the working class and further aroused Booth's social concern. He was also influenced greatly toward social ministry by Major Frank Smith, who pioneered the

Army's social outreach in London, including hostels for the homeless, and by Salvationist women in the front lines, serving as "slum sisters."

The hostels for rescued prostitutes had been established, and Booth's sighting of men under London Bridge on a winter's night triggered his sympathies and set his mind working on a plan to launch more social services. What were the problems? How could they be solved? Gradually his ideas came together. By 1890 Booth would launch his most ambitious scheme — *In Darkest England,* arguably the most grandiose vision and monumental scheme for social reform ever devised up to that time.

Booth's Manifesto

Sir Henry Stanley, famed explorer, had recently returned from his epic journey through the remote equatorial jungles of Africa to find long-lost missionary David Livingstone. His book on his hazardous adventures, *In Darkest Africa,* became the best-selling book of 1890. It described the impenetrable jungle with its cannibals and pygmies and their impoverished lives of great limitation and disease. Using Stanley's book as his analogue, Booth seized upon the popular title, adapting it for his reform. In his preface he wrote:

> As there is a darkest Africa is there not also a darkest England? Civilization, which can breed its own barbarians, does it not also breed its own pygmies? May we not find a parallel at our own doors and discover within a stone's throw of our cathedrals and palaces similar horrors to those which Stanley has found existing in the great equatorial forest? How strange that so much interest should be excited by a narrative of human squalor and human heroism in a distant continent, while greater squalor and heroism not less magnificent may be observed at our very doors.[2]

W. T. Stead, after listening to Booth's expansive scheme and examining the manuscript, added his journalistic editing expertise to fashion the 140,000-word exposé and plan. In his preface Booth acknowledged Stead's "valuable literary help." But the newspaperman made it clear that the book was written by Booth, not himself. "I did the hack work" was the only credit Stead would ever take. He wrote to a friend,

"The sole responsibility and the dominating mind was his and his alone."

In 1890 Booth published his epoch-making book, *In Darkest England and the Way Out,* inscribing a loving dedication to Catherine's life partnership with him. Overnight it became a runaway best seller, the first edition of 10,000 copies selling out within a few days. Within a month 90,000 copies were in print; a year later the count had reached 200,000 copies, with further reprints in ensuing years. All profits from the sale were given to the scheme. By the end of 1890 it had been translated into Japanese, German, French, and Swedish. Initial response was sensational, and Booth's daring blueprint made him the most talked-about man in Britain, acclaimed as "the greatest publicist of his generation." Now the full text is on the Internet, and an excerpt from the book is in the *Norton Anthology of English Literature — Victorian Period.*

In Darkest England became Booth's manifesto for his salvation war, now on two fronts. Its publication became a major turning point, giving birth to the social wing of the Army. Theologically, he believed that a man's character, more than his environment, was the cause of his destitution. On one occasion he remarked, "It's not enough to take the man out of the slums, you need to take the slums out of the man."

"The Submerged Tenth"

Charles Booth, social researcher and contemporary of William Booth, from his extensive investigation of poverty in London, in 1889 authored the popular documentary *Life and Labour of the London Poor.* The two namesakes never met, and were poles apart in approach. Charles, the social scientist, saw the poor as those to be defined, counted, and classified. William, on the other hand, though he quoted statistics of Charles, said, "If a man is drowning, you throw him a rope. Argue how he came to be in such a precarious position and it will be too late to save him."

The figures in Charles's book led William to conclude that one-tenth of Britain's population lived in poverty, which William called "the submerged tenth." The *Darkest England* scheme targeted this group — those afflicted by poverty, vice, prostitution, homelessness, unemployment, and lack of safety.

William also borrowed a compelling metaphor put forth by the

**Some of the "submerged tenth"
addressed by William Booth's book**

poet Thomas Carlyle in his own lament for the poor. He wrote, "Mr. Carlyle long ago remarked that the four-footed worker [London cab-horse] has already got all that this two-handed one is clamoring for. There are not many horses in England, able and willing to work, which do not have due food and lodging and go about sleek coated, satisfied in heart."

Carlyle's standard for the London cab-horse became the standard Booth sought to establish for this "submerged tenth." He reminded his readers that every cab-horse in London has three things allotted to it by which it can earn its corn. When it is down it is helped up. While it lives it has food, shelter, and work to earn its keep. Thirdly, it was the law to help and care for the horse. Men who have fallen, he argued, should be treated with no less compassion. How many people in England, he asked, lived worse than the London cab-horse?

The Ambitious Scheme

Booth put forth his seven foundations that were essential to his *Darkest England* scheme: "First, it must change the man when his character and conduct are the reasons for his failure. Secondly, the remedy must change the circumstances when they are the cause of his condition, and lie beyond his control. Thirdly, any remedy must be commensurate with the evil with which it proposes to deal. Fourthly, the scheme must be permanent. Fifthly it must be practicable. Sixthly, it must not produce injury to the persons whom we seek to benefit. Seventh, it must not interfere with the interests of another."[3]

The first part of the book, "The Darkness," analyzed the problems. The second part, "Deliverance," proposed solutions in the form of a social triage divided among a city colony, a farm colony, and an overseas colony. The city colony would provide food and shelter for the poor, employment for the unemployed, a safety match factory, and other short-term social services.

The farm colony concept was the summit of Booth's dramatic social scheme. It would provide employment opportunity, and wholesome conditions for families outside the congested cities. People transferred from the city were to be established on farms to learn agricultural trades that would benefit them for the remainder of their lives. His idea was to teach agricultural skills on an estate of from 500 to 1,000 acres that was suitable for market gardening, and have the residents and program self-supporting.

Francis Thompson, author of *The Hound of Heaven*, who himself had sounded a strong lament on the misery of the poor, wrote, "I read with painful sympathy the book *In Darkest England* and rise from the reading of it with a strong impression that here is at last a man who has formulated a comprehensive scheme, and has dared to take upon himself its execution . . . in God's name, give him the contract. And, except in God's name, it were indeed wanton to try it."

An appeal for 100,000 English pounds to finance the scheme was oversubscribed by a public whose conscience had been stirred. Food depots, shelters, rescue homes, and labor bureaus were set up, and farms were purchased, all under the new social wing of the Army. The support given the *Darkest England* scheme and the programs established turned Booth's Army into a major social service movement. By 1890 The Salvation Army alone, with 10,000 officers and over 4,000 stations, had the resources to launch and oversee such a scheme.

The Mixed Results

A farm colony with 3,000 acres was established at Hadleigh, England, with 215 men. At its peak it bred pedigree horses; grew grain and root crops; maintained several herds of cattle, some 300 pigs, and 800 sheep; and dedicated 200 acres to gardening and fruit orchards. The

Hadleigh farm still serves today, albeit in a different fashion. At the time of this writing, the farm is scheduled to host the mountain biking events for the 2012 Olympics in London, and is described by the Olympic Committee chairman as "a world-class venue for the Games." Three farm colonies were also established in the United States, but all three failed within ten years due to insufficient funding, poor land, and lack of knowledgeable workers.

The overseas colony enabled the poor of the cities to find work overseas, primarily in Canada, Australia, and New Zealand, through the Army's emigration bureau.

Booth wasted no time in implementing his ambitious scheme, commencing in 1891, within a year of the book's release. Major Frank Smith, a major contributor to the outline of the plan, was his choice to take charge of what became the new social wing of The Salvation Army.

Though the farm colonies did not succeed, and the overseas colonies were short-lived, a number of the most needed and viable programs became upgraded as permanent expressions of the Army's social work, transforming the Army into a major social as well as evangelical movement.

In his scheme Booth disclosed, "Perhaps nothing more vividly suggests the varied forms of broken-hearted misery in the great City than the statement that 18,000 people are lost in it every year, of whom 9,000 people are never heard of any more in this world." In response, a Missing Persons Bureau was initiated to help find those who dropped from sight. His army of soldiers and officers would serve as sleuths, and with this program expanding worldwide, would ultimately find over a quarter-million missing persons, with many heartwarming results and stories.

"We have commodities," said Booth, "which provide a means of immediately employing a large number of men. I propose to establish in every large town what I call 'A Household Salvage Brigade,' a force of collectors, who will patrol the whole town as regularly as the policemen, with the task of collecting the discards of the houses. Our uniformed collectors would call twice a week with the hand barrow or pony cart to collect for utilization the waste of London. In return the men would receive food and shelter and advancement in employment. Goods collected would be repaired as needed and sold to those unable to buy them new."

In 1897 the salvage idea — the harvesting of discarded household goods — took root in the United States, a natural resource with its prosperous and large population. It began with a simple peddler's pushcart that sought salable discards to help support a shelter in New York. Success in donated items resulted in an increasing number of carts going out, and returning with clothing, furniture, and salable items. This modest beginning of pushcarts and horse-drawn wagons became the precursor of today's fleets of trucks, picking up valuable discards and providing employment and recovery for men and women. Known today as Adult Rehabilitation Centers, with thrift store outlets, it is one of the Army's most successful programs.

Booth incorporated a strong work ethic in his social programs. "Mere charity demoralizes the recipient," Booth said. His principle was to never give something for nothing. To do so was to rob man of his dignity. He knew that giving can pauperize and not truly remove poverty. Men in his programs were put to work to earn their keep and progress toward becoming self-sustaining. The programs put into practice the old adage "Give a man a fish and you feed him for a day. Teach a man to fish and you feed him for a lifetime."

Another offspring of the *Darkest England* scheme was the opening in 1891 of an Emigration Bureau in London. Men from the Hadleigh Farm Colony, after training, emigrated to Canada in 1901. In the wake of its success, the Army encouraged general emigration on a large scale. The general laid down three principles for the program: it was to be (1) helpful to the individual, (2) acceptable to the old land, and (3) advantageous to the new country. In 1905 the Army's own emigrant ship, which it had secured, sailed from Liverpool with 1,000 new citizens for Canada, with frequent sailings thereafter. By 1938 a total of 250,000 men, women, and children had settled overseas, in Canada, Australia, New Zealand, and the United States. Canada alone welcomed over 200,000 who were chosen and assisted by the Army's Immigration Bureau at a time when that country was actively seeking immigrants. The bureau also provided further assistance for those who sought to make a new life in their adopted countries.

"The Salvation of the Unfit"

The scheme was not without its detractors, led by Professor Huxley, an avowed agnostic. In a protracted correspondence to the *Times,* he condemned Booth and his scheme. When it was suggested that Booth should reply to Huxley, his response was: "Don't answer criticisms. Let's get on with the work." To another source of criticism he did reply: "They believe in the survival of the fit. The Salvation Army believes in the salvation of the unfit."

But Booth did answer his critics on fiscal accountability with a unique initiative. In order "to satisfy all sincere persons, and in the hope of removing those doubts and of correcting misrepresentations, General Booth has invited an examination by a Committee of Inquiry." The independent panel reviewed the Army's accounts, and after careful and prolonged investigation pronounced them sound, even praising Booth's financial acumen and fiscal integrity.

The unique dynamic that distinguished the Army from other philanthropies was the linking of the social and spiritual thrusts. The holistic approach for addressing social problems became a forerunner to today's faith-based initiatives in partnership with government aid programs. Charles Haddon Spurgeon, famed Baptist preacher, had discerned the irreplaceable value of the Army in its war on poverty and social issues: "If The Salvation Army were wiped out of London, five thousand extra policemen could not fill its place in the repression of crime and disorder."[4]

The Match Factory

A subsidiary enterprise of the *Darkest England* scheme reflected Booth's innovative and unconventional approach to solving social ills. He ordered the investigation of a large match factory, which produced evidence not only of the appalling working conditions and low pay, but also of dozens of cases of phosphorus necrosis, or "phossy jaw," a painful and often fatal disease attacking the teeth and jawbone, causing the jaw to rot with horrible disfigurement and suffering. The big match firms were aware of these evils but callously refused to take steps to remedy them.

On May 11, 1891, General Booth opened a factory to produce matches where the dangerous yellow phosphorus was not used. It employed one hundred girls and used only the safe phosphorus, and paid an adequate living wage. The *Darkest England* matchboxes soon were a welcome and familiar sight throughout England and today are museum pieces. England's biggest match manufacturer, Bryant and May, was moved to adopt the safety match and introduce factory reforms. By 1900 the large factories had been influenced to change their methods and the *Darkest England* factory was closed down. Parliament passed a law in 1908 restricting the unsafe phosphorus formerly used.

The Army's matchbox

Booth had described his *Darkest England* scheme as "better to build a fence at the top of the precipice" than to attempt to rescue a man once he had fallen off. As time went on, his scheme and its many offshoots pushed the "fence" of his parable farther and farther back from the edge of the precipice.

TEN

The Army's Theology and Ecclesiology

I know whom I have believed, and am convinced that he is
able to guard what I have entrusted to him for that day.

2 Timothy 1:12

The Salvation Army was born in the tidal wave of evangelical revivals and awakenings that swept across England and America in the mid–nineteenth century. J. Edwin Orr, who chronicled these awakenings, observed that The Salvation Army was the most enduring result of the midcentury awakening in England.

In earlier years the movement had an aversion to referring to itself as a church. It emphasized its identity as a Christian mission, free from what it viewed as ecclesiastical trappings. Its mode was pragmatic rather than doctrinaire. Only in the most recent edition (1998) of its official *Handbook of Doctrine* has the word "church" found its way into the Army's lexicon. Through writings and international symposiums the Army has come to a new and clearer understanding of its ecclesiastical history and identity. Every officer is ordained and its soldiers are ecclesiastical members engaged in regular worship and evangelism. Its mission statement declares the Army as an "evangelical part of the universal Christian Church."

The foundation for the Army doctrines was that articulated by the Methodist New Connection and the Evangelical Alliance. Booth's earliest East London Christian Revival Society had appropriated seven doctrines by 1866, but by 1870 the doctrines had expanded to ten. Later, influenced by John Wesley's teaching, the doctrine of sanctification was added. William Booth wrote to his son Bramwell, "Under God, Wesley made Methodism not [only] by converting sinners, but by making well instructed saints. We must follow in his track, or we are a rope of sand." The Deed Poll of 1875 gave legal status to the Army, and the Deed Poll of 1878 affirmed those eleven doctrines as intrinsic to The Salvation Army. (See appendix A.)

These articles of faith were interpreted in its official book of theology, the *Handbook of Doctrine,* which appeared in 1923 and was updated in 1969. An appointed Doctrine Council is entrusted to be a "faithful custodian of Army doctrine, help Army beliefs to be taught effectively, undertake interchurch dialogue, and to keep in touch with theological trends internationally." In 1992 the new International Doctrine Council responded to its mandate to produce "a fresh approach" with the 1998 edition, titled *Salvation Story,* which states that "its purpose is to provide a testament to the faith that is shared by Salvationists all over the world."

The Army's doctrines define its being and chart its purpose. Commissioner William Francis, chairman of the Doctrine Council, in 2008 stated, "The Salvation Army doctrines are its theological underpinnings that provide the firm foundation for the drama of its mission. What we believe to be true about the Scriptures, the Triune God, sin, salvation and sanctification supports and empowers that mission."

William Booth could not accept the Calvinist doctrine of "election" that predestines those to be saved. Catherine was unambiguously explicit regarding the position they adopted: "The idea of anything like the selection of one individual to enjoy the blessedness of divine favor forever, and the reprobation of another to suffer all the pains and penalties of damnation, irrespective of choice, conduct or character on their part seemed to be an outrage."[1] Booth and his followers did not enter into contention with Calvinism, but rather went on with their proclamation of the gospel to the "whosoever."

Salvation Army Ceremonies is the handbook used by officers for marriage ceremonies, enrollment of soldiers, dedication of children, and funerals. General Burrows commissioned Colonel John Larsson to soften and modernize its wording while maintaining the spiritual standards and application of the sacred covenants. Larsson said this last edition, published in 1989 and used throughout the world, included "far-reaching changes."

The Church's Exclusion

On one occasion Army leaders approached the dean of St. Paul's to inquire if the Army's recruits could attend a service in the Cathedral, which was but a stone's throw from its headquarters. They did not propose that any Army leader take part in the service, but that the poor working-class people the Army had recruited might be part of the congregation to worship under the leadership of the church, and perhaps to sit under the preachment of Dr. Liddon, the notable pulpit figure of St. Paul's.

Bramwell reports: "The Dean asked, after a few kindly words, whether most of our people, being working people, did not wear hobnailed boots. I agreed that this might be so, and he said that St. Paul's had not long ago been repaved at great expense, and that he feared the marble might be scratched. Surely, I said, you would not consider that a sufficient ground for keeping them out of a place set apart for the national recognition of religion. But he had made up his mind."

In another setting, when Booth sought to bring his recruits to a church, they were told they must come in by a rear door and sit in an inconspicuous section of the church. The growing number of recruits in Booth's Army were excluded or ostracized from the church of that day.

Not all church leaders saw the Army as vulgar and heretical. Cardinal Manning, head of the Catholic Church in England, paid his tribute to Booth's Army: "The work of The Salvation Army is too real to be disregarded," and he noted two characteristics: "self-sacrifice, and the love of souls."

The Church Seeks an Alliance

Two factors eventually resulted in an extraordinary development between The Salvation Army and the established church. First, it was noted that the Army was unusually effective in its mission to the working classes and in addressing the critical social needs of the day. Secondly, the Anglican Church was not reaching the urbanized masses participating in the Industrial Revolution, and was suffering serious attrition in its clergy and membership.

In 1882 the Anglican Church appointed a committee to explore the possibility of an alliance with The Salvation Army, to bring the Army under the wing of the church. This was a bold initiative by the Church of England toward the upstart Army. The church committee had impressive members, including Dr. J. B. Lightfoot, the bishop of Durham, and Dr. Archibald Tait, who later became archbishop of Canterbury.

The archbishop of York (Dr. Thomson) wrote to the founder: "Some of us think that you are able to reach cases, and to do so effectually, which we have great difficulty in touching. They believe that you are moved by zeal for God, and not by a spirit of rivalry with the church." Bishop Dr. Lightfoot echoed the sentiment: "The Salvation Army has taught us a higher lesson, 'Go ye into the highways and hedges, and compel them to come in.' Whatever may be its faults, it has at least recalled to us the lost ideal of the work of the church, the universal compulsion of the souls of men." Negotiations lasted for several months.

Although the Army was spreading successfully throughout the world, its finances were precarious. The resources of the Anglican Church and its backing would provide fiscal stability and respect, both in short supply.

However, the difficulties of such a union were great, from the Army's point of view. Negotiations eventually centered on what place would be given William Booth and his officers in the Anglican Church, especially the female officers, and the sensitive issue of the Army's position on the sacraments (to be covered later in this book). The Anglicans could not accept the ordination of women or the Army's unorthodox view of the sacraments. After a number of joint sessions, the effort was abandoned.

St. John Ervine, Booth's biographer, described the final decision: "The absurd evangelist who once banged a Bible and waved an umbrella to attract attention on Mile End Waste, was now being entreated to help the established church to relate itself to the poor! Booth had not raised his Army to be spoil for the Church of England; he had raised it to make war on hell. And he, better than any of these bishops and canons and deans, knew how to lead it into battle."

Bramwell Booth clearly enunciated the Army's position: "We believe that our Lord Jesus Christ has called us into His Church of the Redeemed, by the Holy Spirit of God; that our salvation is from Him, not by ceremonies or sacraments or ordinances, but by the pardoning life-giving work of our divine Savior."[2] Dr. Lightfoot himself at the time seemed to agree with Bramwell's view: "The Kingdom of Christ is in the fullest sense free, comprehensive, universal. It has no sacerdotal system. Each individual member holds personal communion with the Divine Head."

The Anglican Church and the Army went their separate ways. Having failed to secure The Salvation Army as an auxiliary, the Anglican Church later that year established the "Church Army." It copied the Army's use of uniforms, songs, terminology, and open-air meetings, and continues to operate today as an arm of the church in Britain, Australia, Canada, the United States, and other parts of the world.

Ecumenical Alliances

The Army, a founding member of the World Council of Churches (WCC) in 1948, became increasingly uncomfortable in the late 1970s with an official statement calling for "eucharistic unity." A turning point came when the World Council granted funds to a guerrilla organization in Rhodesia-Zimbabwe that was implicated in the murder of two Salvation Army missionary teachers. Some viewed this as an espousal of the violence of liberation theology. Following two years of dialogue, in 1981 the Army advised the WCC that its nonobservance of the sacraments, its position of equal ministry for women, its nonpartisan political stance, along with its cited priorities of evangelism and concern for the poor, made it reach the decision to withdraw from full membership. The Army petitioned for "fraternal status," which was granted, allowing participation in WCC events and service as the Army may consider appropriate.

The Salvation Army has been an active member of major ecumenical organizations. In 1960 it became a denominational member of the International Holiness Association, founded in 1893 to propagate and preserve Wesley's holiness teaching, in 1997 renamed Christian Holiness Partnership. In 2006 Commissioner Chun Kwang-pyo, territorial commander, was elected president of the National Council of Churches in Korea, and in 2007 Commissioner Betty Matear was elected moderator of the Free Churches in England, and by virtue of that office became one of several copresidents of Churches Together in England. In the USA The Salvation Army has long been an active member of the National Association of Evangelicals. This group boasts an aggregate church membership numbering in the tens of millions among its sixty denominations, and is dedicated to coordinating cooperative ministry for evangelical denominations in the United States. In January 2007 Commissioner Todd Bassett, retired Salvation Army national commander, became executive director of the association. Salvationist leaders are making their mark in ecumenical church leadership around the world.

Officers of The Salvation Army serve as chaplains in the military. Captain Kenneth Hodder, who had earned a Phi Beta Kappa key, served in the U.S. Navy, and later became U.S. national commander. Colonel Giles C. Barrett was awarded over twelve medals for his service in World War II, including the Purple Heart. Others in the USA, Britain, Australia, and around the world have given distinguished service in the armed forces of their countries.

Holiness Emphasis

A theological hallmark of The Salvation Army has been its emphasis on holiness. Holiness became staple theology in the early days of the Army, enshrined in its tenth doctrine, which declares, "It is the privilege of all believers to be wholly sanctified, and that their whole spirit and soul and body may be preserved blameless unto the coming of our Lord Jesus Christ." Of its eleven doctrines, this is the only one couched in the language of Scripture — 1 Thessalonians 5:23, affirming the Army's belief in holiness of heart.

Salvationists do not perceive holiness as moral exclusivism, but as "the privilege of *all* believers" for the purifying and empowering work of the Holy Spirit in the Christian life. They believe holiness relates to the totality of life, "their whole spirit and soul and body." Such holiness is a lifelong process by which hearts and minds are conformed to Christ, and places the believer at God's disposal in a courageous and compassionate service to others.

In summary, Salvationists believe that God the Father purposes our salvation, God the Son provides our salvation, and God the Holy Spirit perfects our salvation.

The Army *Song Book* is replete with songs on holiness. Sunday morning worship had long been designated a "holiness meeting," with emphasis on the deeper life, whereas the Sunday evening meetings of the past were designated "salvation meetings," with emphasis on evangelism.

In the late 1800s a new star made his appearance in the international firmament of the Army. Rev. Samuel Logan Brengle, after earning his academic and biblical study degrees, arrived in London from three thousand miles across the Atlantic. He had turned down the call

Samuel Logan Brengle

to the pulpit of a large Methodist church in America built by millionaire Studebaker, to embrace the debt-ridden itinerant evangelism of Booth's Army.

Booth at first accepted his services grudgingly, thinking Brengle would not stay, and set him to work cleaning other trainees' boots at the training garrison. "Have I followed my own fancy this distance to black boots?" Brengle asked himself despairingly as he went about his task in a gloomy cellar. Were all his educational advantages and talents being thrown away? Then the Holy Spirit brought to his remembrance his Exemplar, Jesus, bending over the feet of rough unlettered fishermen. "Lord," he whispered, his pride abated, "Thou didst wash their feet; I will black their boots."

The Lord would use Samuel Brengle for almost half a century as the Army's "Apostle of Holiness." He wrote more than a dozen books on the deeper life, which received worldwide acclaim among holiness churches. Brengle became the Army's first American-born commissioner, and through his teaching and writing continues to be one of the most influential leaders in the history of the movement.

As an ongoing memorial to Brengle, the Army instituted in 1947 its first Brengle Memorial Institute, a weeklong institute on holiness held annually in Chicago. Its purpose was to perpetuate the teaching of holiness as taught in the Bible and exemplified in the life and legacy of Brengle's writings. Conducted during the summer recess at the Chicago School for Officer Training campus, it hosted some fifty officer delegates. Subsequently the concept and program were replicated around the Army world, and included soldiers as well as officers, reinforcing the Army's hallmark of holiness teaching in its ecclesiastical structure and practice.

Also nurturing the spiritual life of the Army in the USA since 1970 has been the gathering of Salvationists in Colorado to an annual Soldiers National Seminar on Evangelism. Over five thousand Salvationists have benefited from this program.

Prayer Power

A movement called "24-7 prayer" started in September 1999 when young people in England conceived the novel idea of praying nonstop for a month. It was reported, "God turned up and they couldn't stop until Christmas!" This birthing of the modern-day 24-7 prayer movement was replicated in the USA and elsewhere, as it spread globally among denominations and age groups.

The Salvation Army quickly caught the prayer fever, beginning in 2001 in the United Kingdom and followed by hundreds of nonstop prayer chains around the Army world. Prayer rooms were established in corps, at training colleges, at summer camps, and at headquarters, with groups pledged to pray for twenty-four hours a day for a week or more.

In the USA East, Major Janet Munn, Territorial Ambassador for Prayer, on a DVD explains the 24-7 prayer process. In that territory prayer nonstop went from June 9, 2006, through June 8, 2007, with over two hundred prayer rooms established through the year, many of which remain as dedicated places for prayer.

In Vancouver, what started as a one-week commitment has continued, as of this writing, for nearly three years. New Zealand has witnessed twenty months of unbroken 24-7 prayer to date, and reports that "24-7 prayer has become part of the regular rhythm of corps life in many places." Other Army territories followed suit with a full year of nonstop prayer.

Youth continue to be a major part of the Army's commitment. Fasting often accompanies the prayer covenant. The movement receives further impetus by 24-7 state-of-the-art Web sites defining and promoting the prayer networks.

If it be true that God's Army moves forward best when on its knees, these youth and prayer warriors give great hope for the movement's future.

Continued Renewal

An outgrowth of the Army's 1994 International Conference of Leaders in Hong Kong was General Paul A. Rader's decision to clarify and reemphasize those aspects and practices integral to the unity, progress, and health of The Salvation Army. The International Spiritual Life Commission was convened to review ways in which the movement cultivates and sustains the spiritual life of its people. Commencing in 1996, its eighteen members from a broad context of the worldwide Army met over the next two years to identify and address the range of issues dealing with the spiritual life of the Army. The commission sought to provide guidelines and strategies that would be relevant to all countries and cultures in which the Army operates. Extended discussions resulted in promulgation of "The Twelve Calls to the Army World," relating to such dynamics as worship, Bible study, prayer, spiritual disciplines, evangelism, servanthood, discipling, holiness, the Bible, and family values.

The final report, disseminated worldwide in 1998, included these seminal concepts, with task forces organized in Army territories to implement recommendations:

> The Salvation Army has a God-given freedom in Christ . . . to be warmly embraced and positively engaged to the glory of God and for the extension of his Kingdom. It is firmly rooted in the Army's tradition . . . and points the way ahead for what God has planned for his people. Integral to the Army's life are its ministry to the unchurched, the priesthood of all believers, personal salvation, holiness of life, the use of the mercy seat, and social ministry. . . . The springs of our spiritual life are to be found in our turning to God in worship, in the disciplines of life in the Spirit, and in the study of God's word.

In April 2004, 126 international, territorial, and command leaders of the Army were convened by General John Larsson for an eight-day triennial conference, this time meeting in New Jersey, USA. Prior such conferences were held in Melbourne (1988), Hong Kong (1995), and Atlanta (2000). The stated purpose was to "discover those new things that

God wants us to do," based on the theme from Isaiah 43:18-19, "Renewal — See I Am Doing a New Thing." Issues examined included "How to keep The Salvation Army focused on its mission, the challenge of world evangelization, reaching and holding children and youth for Christ, new trends in reaching out with the gospel to women, combating social evils — with focus on human trafficking." The conference explored lifting the age limit for training of officers along with individually tailored training programs. It addressed the challenge of finding financial resources for the Army to sustain its mission in needy parts of the world. How to encourage more prayer in the corporate life of the Army was also on the agenda for discussion.

A "Declaration of Renewal" was drafted, signed by all 126 Army leaders, and disseminated to the Army world. Among other statements, it declared, "We embrace the future, desiring to know our potential as God sees it. We affirm that the essence of Salvationism is the love of Jesus Christ that knows no boundaries, calling us especially to the lost, the marginalized, the exploited and the neglected."

The foundations of The Salvation Army's spiritual heritage and mission have not been immune to assault from the winds of change blowing across the religious landscape of the world. There is constant tension of not allowing its social work to diminish the primacy of the spiritual, and this has not always been resisted with total success. But there are encouraging barometers of spiritual life. A major dynamic comes from its youth, who engage in summer missions to needy places in the world, who attend weekend fasting and prayer retreats, and who witness to the work of the Holy Spirit in their lives. Leadership conferences and initiatives also help to keep the Army's spiritual compass pointing in the right direction.

Shaw Clifton, in an April 2006 interview with Sue Warner in the Army's *New Frontier* periodical, enunciated the dual beliefs and praxis of the Army as "a Church and more. We are a church in every possible sense of that word — legally, socially, theologically. We can talk about ourselves as a religious body; we can talk about ourselves as a charitable organization, a movement, a collection of like-minded persons — but with ultimate loyalty to the Lord Jesus Christ. And of course, we're a human service agency at the same time. Throughout our history we've moved from being an evangelical mission to becoming a fully-fledged Christian denomination. We're not a parachurch. I see the General as a worldwide head of a Christian denomination as well as leader of all of those other manifestations of our life." Such is the ultimate and official statement on the ecclesiastical status of The Salvation Army.

In 2008 a landmark booklet was produced, *The Salvation Army in the Body of Christ, an Ecclesiological Statement.* Its thirty-five pages present the most definitive statement of "where the Army stands within the body of Christ." It came out under the aegis of the general, the International Doctrine Council, and the International Management Council. The two high-level multiethnic commissions represent the Army's global membership, symbolized by issuing the text in English, French, and Spanish. The following defining statements are extracted from its contents.

> Believers stand in a spiritual relationship to one another, which is not dependent upon any particular church structure. The Salvation Army, under the one Triune God, belongs to and is an expression of the body of Christ on earth, the Church universal, and is a Christian denomination in permanent mission to the unconverted, called into and sustained in being by God. Denominational diversity is not self-evidently contrary to God's will for his people. Inter-denominational harmony and cooperation are to be actively pursued for they are valuable for the enriching of the life and witness of the Body of Christ in the world and therefore of each denomination. The Church universal includes all who believe in the Lord Jesus Christ, confessing him as Savior and Lord.

> We do not believe that the Church universal depends for its existence or validity upon any particular ecclesiastical structure, any particular form of worship, or any particular observance of ritual. The Army has been led of God to adopt [among others listed] the following characteristics: its teaching concerning sanctification and holy living; its teaching that the receiving of inward spiritual grace is not dependent upon any particular outward observance; its preference for non-liturgical and flexible forms of worship, seeking to encourage spontaneity, for example in prayer and in spoken personal testimony; its tradition of inviting public response to the presentation of the gospel message, and its use of the mercy seat for this and other spiritual purposes. We do not believe it is our task to comment negatively upon, or to undermine, the traditions of other denominations.

This document was designed to define and to put to rest any ambivalence by its members or others on the ecclesiology of The Salvation Army.

ELEVEN

The Sacramental Salvationist

These are a shadow of the things that were to come; the reality, however, is found in Christ.

Colossians 2:17

One difficulty for the Army in the early days related to its position on the sacraments of baptism and communion, two time-honored rituals and traditions of the church. Early in its history, in 1874, the Lord's Supper was administered monthly to all members of the group; the Army was the first to allow women to administer the sacraments. The sprinkling of water in baptism was viewed as a symbol and left optional for followers.

A sense of misgiving arose and became more evident within the growing work. William Booth and early leaders were heavily influenced by Catherine, who had an aversion to anything that might tend to substitute some outward act or compliance for the fruits of practical holiness, or become a substitute for inward grace. Also, a chief danger was seen in the disunity among churches in their spirited debate and divisiveness on the theological meaning and proper administration of the sacraments.

Furthermore, it was unthinkable for the Army to use, as did some churches, fermented wine because many of its men and women were rescued drunkards, and nonalcoholic grape juice was unavailable in Britain at that time. Then there was the issue of women administering sacraments, which was scandalous to many good people. Also in dispute was who should be allowed to partake of the sacrament.

Dr. David Rightmire, in his seminal book on the Army and the sacraments, has written:

> The decision to abandon sacramental practice was, in part, motivated by an avoidance of external religion, a desire to advance as a pragmatic theology. . . . Utilitarianism was one standard used to abandon sacramental practices. Anything that got in the way of Booth's central soteriological [salvation] task was considered expendable. . . . The Salvation Army, as part of the 19th-century holiness revival, subordinated its sacramental theology to pneumatological [concerning the Holy Spirit] priorities. Consequently, the real presence of Christ is mediated to the believer through the sanctifying work of the Holy Spirit apart from outward forms, subordinating ecclesiological and sacramental concerns to the experience of "closer communion" with Christ through the baptism with the Spirit.[1]

The Army had before it, and was influenced by, the example of the Quakers, who, while manifesting holiness, abstained from the sacraments. Their witness to the inner experience of grace was real without the external rituals. Gradually William Booth was led to the same conclusions as George Fox and his Quakers, that the sacraments were but symbols of spiritual truth pointing his followers to seek the substance rather than the shadow. The Quaker position provided a theological precedent for justifying the Army's stance. Booth also was motivated to "avoid the grave dissensions" often associated with the observance.

Salvationists find concurrence with theologian Emil Brunner, who wrote: "The decisive test of belonging to Christ is not reception of baptism nor partaking of the Lord's Supper, but solely and exclusively a union with Christ through faith which shows itself active in love."

The Army also early ceased performing baptism. Army leaders perceived a lack of scriptural basis for a claim that it is essential to salvation, and they saw the overwhelming evidence to the contrary of multitudes who became "new creations in Christ" without outward baptism. Again, the conflicting views still blatantly held, as to the method of its practice, discouraged its adoption.

For George Scott Railton there was only one baptism — the baptism of the Holy Spirit — and only one communion with Christ — the communion of a cleansed heart devoted to his service. Booth came to suspect symbolism, believing that men are only too ready to adopt excuses and lean upon a formalism rather than upon God. Dr. Benson, soon to be archbishop of Canterbury, was among a number of church leaders who applauded Booth's decision not to celebrate the sacraments.

The following is excerpted from a published interview with Booth:

> In the first place, we do not consider that the Sacraments are essential to salvation, and in this matter, as I know quite well, I have with me some of the most eminent members of the English Episcopal bench, who have admitted to me, in conversation, what they would never dare say. Men and women are constantly in danger of putting their trust in ordinances, and thinking that baptized communicants must be in a secure position, no matter how inconsistently they are living. We attach great importance to that wonderful statement of John the Baptist, "I indeed baptize you with water, but He shall baptize you with the Holy Ghost and with fire." Further, we never disclaim against the Sacraments; we never even state our own position. We are anxious not to destroy the confidence of Christian people in institutions which are helpful to them.[2]

Commissioner Harry Williams led The Salvation Army delegation to the fifth assembly of the World Council of Churches in Amsterdam in 1975. He had earlier reported reported: "We remain a tiny minority in this now vast company, a decimal point of dissent within this Eucharistic church, yet once again our distinctive ministry made delegates ponder the fundamentals of the Christian faith."[3]

In reality, The Salvation Army substituted its own rituals. Infants were no longer baptized; they were dedicated, with parents vowing to raise them according to Christian practice. The public enrollment of senior soldiers (lay members) and the signing of the "Articles of War" became a ritual within the Army. In the end, the Army came to lean upon its own external symbols and rituals, including its uniform, flag, songbook, and mode of worship. These were looked upon as aids, not to be espoused as a medium or requisite of salvation, or of the spiritual life.

The Army's position on the sacraments remains to many its single most difficult issue to explain and understand. Discussion on the sacraments continues among its members, in particular those who come to the Army from other churches. Two of the early issues no longer pertain — women in ministry and the unavailability of nonalcoholic grape juice.

High on the agenda of the International Spiritual Life Commission appointed in 1998 was discussion, among other issues, on the sacraments. After over a hundred years of holding to a nonobservance of the sacraments, it reemphasized the Army's long-held belief that no particular outward observance is necessary for inward grace and that God's grace is freely accessible to all people at all times and in all places.

Commissioner Philip Needham has enunciated a perspective on the issue:

> In order for there to be true unity in the (universal) gospel, there must be freedom in the diversity of culturally conditioned forms, rituals, ceremonies and governments in the Church as a whole. In order to protect this universality, the church must allow for considerable diversity in the expression and nurture of faith, so that acceptance of the gospel does not depend upon simultaneous acceptance of a particular culture or ecclesiastical tradition and thereby nullify the universality. It is a disservice to the gospel to insist that grace must be received through the mediation of a particular ritual or procedure, and there is no evidence in the New Testament from which a case can be argued for such a view. Grace is immediate and accessible.[4]

General Shaw Clifton in 2006 shared at an Army International Theology Symposium in South Africa a paper entitled "Our God-Given Position on Sacraments — a Candid Reflection." An excerpt reads:

> Even a cursory perusal of the literature (which is truly vast) reveals that this is a turbulent and theologically complex area of Christian thought. The history of sacraments in the churches has been marked by strife at every turn. The divine and consistent leadings of God among us for many generations have blessedly freed us from all of that. . . . Let us suppose for a moment that the vast majority of Salvationists were to become persuaded that God, who raised us up and led us faithfully for generation after generation along the oft-lonely path of nonobservance, has in fickle capricious or arbitrary fashion suddenly changed his mind, contrary to all we know of his divine nature. Even then, even if God were somehow willing upon us an out-of-character doctrinal U-turn, the implications of tangential change are incredibly complicated. . . . Ecumenical friends can readily grasp that we respect their observances deeply, but that we have a different calling.

**General Orsborn (ret.) tells Major Gariepy of
the "Army's sacramental song" (1966).**

Salvationists are not nonsacramentarian. They identify with Frederick Buechner's definition: "A sacrament is when something holy happens. Needless to say, church isn't the only place where the holy happens. Sacramental moments can occur at any moment, any place, and
to anybody." For the Salvationist, the truly sacramental interpenetrates
all of life. It can occur in an encounter with God's majesty in nature, a
moment in worship, a passage in a book, a stirring melody, an anointed
preachment, an epiphany in the Word or in prayer. Salvationists take to
heart Jean-Pierre de Caussade's words in his classic writing *The Sacrament of the Present Moment:* "God speaks to every individual through
what happens to him moment by moment."

Among the Salvationist treasury of devotional songs is one written
by General Albert Orsborn (1946-1954). In a 1966 visit with the author,
he described it as the "Army's sacramental song." The words speak not
of a ritual, but of the sacramental life:

The Sacramental Salvationist

My life must be Christ's broken bread,
My love his outpoured wine.
A cup o'erfilled, a table spread,
Beneath his name and sign,
That other souls, refreshed and fed,
May share his life through mine.

My all is in the Master's hands
For him to bless and break;
Beyond the brook his winepress stands
And thence my way I take,
Resolved the whole of love's demands
To give for his dear sake.

TWELVE

William Booth's Legend and Legacy

The steps of a good man are ordered by the LORD.

Psalm 37:23 KJV

William Booth in his lifetime went from being the most criticized to the most acclaimed man of his day. He became a legend in his lifetime. But he was not altogether as successful on the home front with his children as he was on the front lines of his Army's mission.

The Booth Family

The eight Booth children shared their parents' passion for mission, except for Marian, because of her physical limitations. In the formative years The Salvation Army was largely a Booth affair. William's children received preferential treatment for appointments and were often put in charge of the work in a major country. His married daughters took on their husbands' names but retained the family name, and the husbands took on the Booth name as well; Emma's husband became Frederick Booth-Tucker; likewise the other husbands. Eminent titles assumed by the Booth household included "chief of the staff," "the *Maréchale*," "commander." This nepotism, seized upon by his critics, proved to be a chink in the founder's armor.

The faith and foibles of the colorful family have been recounted many times, detailing how William's devotion to his Army, as "General first and father afterwards," led to irreconcilable breaches with most of his children.

Bramwell, the elder son, and his father's lifetime partner in the salvation war, served as his chief of the staff, second in command, for more than thirty years. A master organizer, Bramwell developed the Army's infrastructure and ran the organization in the early years when the general was away conducting campaigns. Evangeline led the Army in the States for thirty years and went on to become the fourth general. Emma was killed in a train wreck in Missouri in 1903, a traumatic loss to both William and her husband Frederick Booth-Tucker, who had led the work in America with her.

Lucy stayed within the Army — Commissioner Mrs. Lucy Booth-Hellberg — continuing as a territorial commander in her own right after her husband's death. Marian was fragile but still was a captain; she was in the background when she died in 1937. Emma, Marian, Bramwell, and Eva remained close to their father and faithful to the cause. The other three, having served in major appointments, resigned after a falling out with their father and Bramwell's autocratic practice. Booth children who left the Army remained workers in the cause of religion. The training and influence of the parents had left its indelible imprint, including the parents' charisma.

The first to leave were Ballington and his wife Maud. In charge of the work in America, their leadership was crowned with success. They resigned in 1896 because of the autocratic rule of William and Bramwell. In addition to forming a loyal following, they founded the Volunteers of America, patterning it after the Army's structure. The gifted Herbert and charismatic Catherine ultimately departed from the one who was "their General first and father second."

Booth's Most Painful Loss

Miss Jane Short, who lived with the Booths as a "paying guest," had intimately observed their home life and family relationships. She later recalled of William, "His love for his wife was the most beautiful thing I have ever known. It really was an exquisite thing. I may forget other things about them, but I shall never forget the General's love for his wife." William's love for Catherine was especially notable during her last days.

Catherine suffered excruciatingly from cancer during her final two years. "Do you know what was my first thought?" she gently asked William. "That I should not be there to nurse you at your last hour." William wrote in his diary: "She took hold of my hand, took the ring off her finger, and slipping it on to mine, said, 'By this token we were united for time, and by it now we are united for eternity.' I kissed her, and promised that I would be faithful to the vow and be hers and hers alone forever and ever."

The eve of William Booth's grandest vision coming to fruition was overshadowed by his most severe personal loss. The Christmas 1889 issue of the *War Cry,* printed amid Catherine's prolonged and painful ordeal with cancer, conveyed a message from her to Salvationists around the world: "The waters are rising, but so am I. I am not going under, but over. Don't be concerned about your dying; only go on living well, and the dying will be all right." On October 4, 1890, the Army Mother was "promoted to Glory." Her passing ended one of the great love stories of the Victorian world.

Rev. Hugh Hughes eulogized in his memorial sermon: "The achievement which will immortalize her memory is the fact that she more than any other of her sex has vindicated the right and duty of women to preach. Her book upon the subject is the most masterly and successful argument I have ever read. Catherine Booth came to crown the social evolution of our time by accomplishing the religious emancipation of woman."

Harold Begbie, William Booth's biographer, recorded: "So passed away one of the most remarkable women of the nineteenth century, whose beautiful spirit impressed itself alike upon the most exacting of her intellectual contemporaries and upon vast masses of the poor. The growth of her spiritual power seems to me like one of the miracles of religious history."

Some eight years after her passing, William Booth added his touching postscript: "Had the ordering of things been left with me, I would have kept her by my side so long as my place was on the battlefield. I would have ordained that we should have laid down the sword together, and passed together through the Gates of Gold into the presence of our Lord. It was ordered otherwise. The sense of the loss I suffered eight years ago grows keener and keener as the days and the months go by; but all the time there is the unspeakable consolation arising from the feeling that, although not with me, she is only gone on before."

William Booth's Recognitions

Cecil Rhodes, premier of Britain's Cape Colony in South Africa, accompanied William Booth in 1898 to see the Army's farm colony at Hadleigh in England. The political situation in South Africa was dangerous at the time, with an expectation of war. Rhodes showed keen interest in the Army's agricultural scheme, and how it tied into its social work, and ultimately presented the Army with a 3,000-acre farm in Rhodesia. What touched Rhodes most deeply was that on their return journey by train to London, Booth put his hand upon him and said, "You are a man with much depending on you just now. Tell me, how is it with your soul?" The world-famous magnate replied, "Well, General, it's not quite so well with my soul as I could wish." Booth received Rhodes's permission to pray for him, and they knelt there and then in the railway carriage as Booth prayed for the famed pioneer. In parting, Rhodes confided, "I am trying to make new countries; you are making new men." Just before Rhodes died in 1902 at the early age of forty-nine, he confided that William Booth to him was still "the only one who believes I have a soul."

Following his early rejection by the churches and castigation by the media, as Booth's Army achieved recognition for its international success in evangelism and human services, he was accorded the highest honors. Visits to the United States were reported as having "hurricane welcomes." He was warmly received by President William McKinley on February 10, 1898, and invited to open the Senate in prayer. In both 1903 and 1907 he was received by President Theodore Roosevelt, and in 1903 he was invited by the president to again open the Senate in prayer. The colorful president described his visitor: "General Booth is a steam engine in trousers. At 78 years of age he is a bundle of energy, a keg of dynamite, an example of perpetual motion."

A highlight of Booth's life occurred in 1904, at age seventy-five, when he was granted an audience with King Edward VII. Booth prepared himself symbolically by washing his hands in a workman's bucket. "You are doing a good work, General Booth," lauded the king. "Tell me, General," asked the sovereign, "how do you get on now with the churches? What is their attitude towards you?" The old man's eyes twinkled, and he answered, "Sir, they imitate me." At which the king laughed with a good understanding.

The king, enjoying the dialogue, asked him to write in his autograph album. The aged warrior bent forward to sum up his life's work: "Your Majesty, some men's ambition is art. Some men's ambition is fame. Some men's ambition is gold. My ambition is the souls of men."

On April 6, 1904, he paid his second visit to Buckingham Palace, this time for an audience with Queen Alexandra. The visit, which included the presence of Princess Victoria, was reported as exceedingly friendly.

On one occasion Booth, seeing the need for improving the Army's work in prisons, decided to "go to the top" and made an appointment with Winston Churchill, then home secretary. He explained the Army's prison work and the need to improve access to the prisoners. After a lengthy discourse, Churchill asked, "Tell me, General, am I converted?" The general hesitated, but though Churchill was an important politician, he could not compromise. "No, Mr. Churchill," he answered, "you are not converted, but I think you are convicted." Churchill smiled. "You can see what is in me." Following further discussion between Bramwell and officials from the home office, broad agreement to the plan was announced.

Booth received the Freedom of the City award from four different cities. Freedom of the City of London was bestowed on October 26, 1905, as 1,000 of his officers escorted him from the Army's IHQ to the famed Guildhall. To London's elite who were present for the occasion, in one of his most notable speeches, he shared,

> The Salvation Army is coming to be known as, and to be seen to be what it professes to be, the friend of the hopeless. Forty years ago, when it commenced in the old burial ground, to which reference has been made, it was then that I consecrated myself, and my wife and children, and all I possessed to labor for the benefit of the poor and outcast. The Salvation Army has followed the injunctions of our Lord, who said when we made our feast we were not to invite those who could invite us back again. But the Army has invited the drunkard, the harlot, the criminal, the pauper, the friendless, the frivolous throngs to come and seek God. It has gone to those classes who are not found in the churches, who are without hope and help, who are friendless.

The ceremony was followed by a luncheon at the Mansion House, and then a tour of several of the Army's shelters and centers in the city.

William Booth in Oxford doctoral robe

Nottingham, birthplace of Booth, where he had known only poverty and destitution, was not to be outdone by London. On November 6, 1905, it presented its illustrious son with the Freedom of the City, as "the greatest man that Nottingham has ever bred or seen."

A letter inviting him to receive an Honorary Doctor of Civil Law degree from Oxford University in part read, "I should like this famous and ancient University, of which I am now the Head, and which has played so notable a part in the history of our country — to have the privilege of setting its seal upon the noble work that you have done for so many years, and are continuing to do, for the people of all countries — a work excelled in range and beneficence by that of no living man." On

June 26, 1907, he received the prestigious degree along with venerable cohonorees — the American ambassador, the prime minister, the speaker of the House of Commons, Auguste Rodin, Rudyard Kipling, and Samuel Langhorne Clemens (Mark Twain). The citation in Latin translates: "O Man, Most Venerable, Compassionate Patron of the lowest of the people, and Commander of the Army for the winning of souls, I admit you as a Doctor of Civil Law to this ancient University." The Oxford award symbolized that Booth's Army had gained acceptance with polite society.

Kipling, who had met Booth earlier, recounted, "I conceived great respect and admiration for this man with the head of Isaiah and the fire of the Prophet. At Oxford when degrees were being conferred, he strode across to me in his Doctor's robes, which magnificently became him, and 'Young feller,' said he, 'how's your soul'?"

One report observed: "It was the singular merit of this man that he had achieved renown, alike in this country and in foreign lands, not by any great actions performed either in war or statesmanship or in the art of science. By a new and different path he made his way. His work had been to create an institution for enabling the lowest of his fellow creatures to raise themselves to a better mode of life."

International honors paralleled what was happening in England. In 1907 he had audiences with the king and queen of Denmark, the king of Norway, the queen of Sweden, and the emperor of Japan. Salvationists viewed with pride these eminent recognitions of their commander in chief who had risen from Mile End Waste, now in his vintage years to be received in royal palaces and parliaments of the world. William Booth had become one of the most picturesque of patriarchs. His iconic figure was known in nearly all nations, his work recognized in nearly every land. He had been welcomed in the capitals of the world by heads of states and churches, as well as by the multitude.

Final Words

At eighty years of age, when it was evident that Booth's sight was irrevocably gone, Bramwell broke the melancholy news to the aged warrior. After a pause the father said, "I shall never see your face again?" "No, probably not in this world," replied Bramwell. The father then took hold of his son's hand and replied calmly, "God must know best." And

William Booth gives his final address at Royal Albert Hall.

after another pause: "Bramwell, I have done what I could for God and for the people with my eyes. Now I shall do what I can for God and for the people without my eyes."

On May 9, 1912, seven thousand Salvationists crowded into London's Royal Albert Hall for what would be William Booth's last public address. They heard their general take leave of them in his valedictory statement, "I am going into dry dock for repairs."

Incredibly, even now, without the aid of amplifiers he made his last and his most memorable speech. His parting words became indelibly inscribed on the hearts of those who heard them and upon succeeding generations of Salvationists. The flame of his spirit flared highest as the candle burned near to its end.

While women weep as they do now, I'll fight;

While little children go hungry as they do now, I'll fight;

While men go to prison, in and out, in and out, as they do now, I'll fight;

While there is a drunkard left,

While there is a poor lost girl upon the streets,

While there yet remains one dark soul without the light of God,

I'll fight — I'll fight to the very end.

At the conclusion his hearers remained silent. They knew that William Booth had spoken to them for the last time.

Near the time of his passing, Booth's final pronouncement would resonate with Salvationists in years to come: "The promises of God are sure if you only believe."

THIRTEEN

"The General Lays Down His Sword"

Be faithful, even to the point of death, and I will give you the crown of life.

Revelation 2:10

A little over three months after his valedictory, on August 20, 1912, William Booth joined the company of immortals in the history of the Christian church. The next day it was announced, "The General has laid down his sword." The struggling evangelist who had preached in a tent on a disused burial ground, had raised the Army flag in fifty-eight countries, and had overseen more than 15,000 preaching the gospel in thirty-four languages left a legacy of social services bringing comfort and hope to the countless destitute of the world.

For three days at the Army's Clapton Congress Hall, 65,000 people filed by the old warrior's casket to catch a final glimpse of God's soldier. On August 27, with 5,000 Salvationists marching six abreast behind the cortege, Booth was borne to the vast Olympia exhibition hall in West London where 35,000 people flocked to the memorial service.

An Eloquent Epitaph

It was later reported that unknown to most, royalty was there too. Far to the rear of the hall, almost unrecognized, sat Britain's Queen Mary, a staunch admirer of Booth, along with her lord chamberlain, Lord Shaftesbury. At the last moment the queen had elected to come without notice, and there was no other seat to be had. Beside her, in an aisle seat, was a plainly dressed woman. Shyly she confided her secret to the queen. Once she had been a prostitute and Salvationists had rescued her from that life. Years later, at a meeting, General Booth heard her story and told her gently: "My girl, when you get to Heaven, you'll have a place of honor, because Mary Magdalene will give you one of the best places."

The queen was curious. Was it this that had brought that woman here? That, the woman confessed, and the flowers — three faded red carnations that all through the service were the only flowers that lay on Booth's casket. She had come early to claim an aisle seat, guessing that the casket would pass within feet of her — and as it did she unobtrusively placed the flowers on the glass lid. Deeply moved, a queen heard that day a prostitute pronounce perhaps William Booth's most eloquent epitaph: "He cared for the likes of us."[1]

The Last Journey

Next day forty Army bands with 10,000 uniformed Salvationists fell into step behind the horse-drawn bier bearing William Booth to his final resting place. The cortege proceeded slowly from the Army's International Headquarters to Abney Park Cemetery where he would be laid to rest beside his beloved Catherine. The acting Lord Mayor of London stood in silent salute as Booth passed by on his last journey. City offices were shuttered; the flags of nations had slipped gently down to salute him.

London's *Daily Telegraph* reported: "He belonged to the company of saints." "No man of his time did more for the benefit of his people," claimed the *New York Times*. Around his grave lay a carpet of flowers, including wreaths from reigning King George V and Queen Mary, from Queen Alexandra, the German emperor, and the American ambassador.

The people of London gave their own tribute as tens of thousands made the city streets impassable as they strained to see this most unusual funeral procession of the champion of the common man. Harold Begbie, who knew Booth well and whose monumental two-volume *Life of William Booth* stands as the Everest of books about him, described him as "This Moses of Modern Times" and wrote the following in Lon-

William Booth's funeral cortege in downtown London

don's *Daily Chronicle* two days after his death: "Scarcely could you find a country in the whole world where men and women are not now grieving for the death of General Booth. Among people of whom we have never heard — perhaps the most universal grief ever known in the history of mankind. Never before has a man in his own lifetime won so wide a measure of deep and passionate human affection."

A photograph of the funeral procession passing through the cemetery gates shows a nonuniformed male figure among the mourners in the forefront of the march. It is Herbert Booth, the gifted third and estranged son of William and Catherine, who had left the ranks when in command of the Army in Australia ten years before. He crossed the Atlantic to attend his father's funeral, saluting as the coffin was lowered into the grave. One wonders what his thoughts were that day as band after band on the long journey through the stilled city streets played the Army's funeral march, "Promoted to Glory," composed by Herbert at the time of his mother's passing in 1890.

An Enduring Legacy

John Wesley is said to have preached 40,000 sermons and to have traveled 250,000 miles. The number of sermons William Booth preached during his sixty years of evangelistic campaigning was, on a low estimate, between 50,000 and 60,000; and for every mile that Wesley traveled, Booth traveled many times over. Wesley, of course, had to go on horseback or by coach. But harnessing the forces of locomotion, Booth was the Methodist circuit rider brought up to date, a pioneer motorcar evangelist. His journeys were all in pursuit of his supreme mission — to bring others to Christ. With the exception of 1905, in his later life he traveled every year, visiting the Army's global expansion.

W. T. Stead wrote: "Thanks to the facilities of modern travel William Booth has been seen by the greatest number of human eyes, his voice heard by the greatest number of human ears, has appealed to a greater number of human hearts, in a greater number of countries and continents, than any man who has ever lived upon this planet."[2] Nor could any preacher have made a pulpit of so many strange platforms. The theater stage, the grandstand of the racecourse, the footboard of the railway carriage, the captain's bridge, the stall in the marketplace, the drinking trough on the village green, the magistrate's bench, the convict prison, the sheltered inlet by the sea, the dais of the American Senate, the rostrum of the London Guildhall, the Indian pandal, the university quadrangle — they all served his purpose. Upon his death he was hailed as "one of the most remarkable figures in the religious history of the world."

William's congregation was the poor of London, with much of polite society regarding him and his army as fanatical and vulgar. He left no largesse to his family, only a pittance, having lived impecuniously throughout his life. This prophet of the poor left a legacy of incomputable worth to humankind around the world.

Jeremiad Voices Quelled

But there were jeremiad voices that characterized the Army's phenomenal progress as a mushroom growth. The editor of *John Bull* prophesied that "the old General's death spells the death of The Salvation Army." Some pundits had predicted that The Salvation Army would not outlast William Booth.

Booth's death left a painful void. For forty-seven years he had led his forces; they grew from a nondescript street mission to a global movement. Salvationists had not known another general. However, the Army continued to move forward, building strong infrastructures on the foundation that had been laid. The great expansion of the Army would testify to the truism that "God buries his workmen but carries on his work."

Vachel Lindsay, an itinerant poet who had once been sheltered by the Army, wrote what became his best-known poem as a tribute: "General William Booth Enters into Heaven." It opens with "Booth led boldly with his big bass drum"; interspersed in the verses are the words "Are you washed in the blood of the Lamb?" Lindsay describes a motley group Booth brings to heaven, "from the ditches and alleyways," for "Every slum had sent its half-a-score / The round world over. (Booth had groaned for more.)" The ballad ends with Booth seeing Jesus, who comes "gently with a robe and crown for Booth the soldier." Lindsay himself had experienced the Army's helping hand, and wrote his poem in gratitude. He said, "The poem is my monument, and I hope that my entrance in Heaven will be as certain as his."

Within days of his father's passing Bramwell proposed as a national tribute to William Booth a memorial training college. This was erected in 1930 at Denmark Hill in London. Among contributors was the Right Honorable Winston Churchill. This college, still active, has trained thousands of cadets and sent them on their lifetime mission around the world, a fitting and living memorial for the Army founder.

FOURTEEN

The Army's High Council

We have different gifts, according to the grace given us . . .
if it is leadership, let him govern diligently.

Romans 12:6, 8

Whenever the Army's High Council meets, it is election time in The Salvation Army. The council constitutes the highest level of Salvation Army leadership, the constitutional body that elects the general at the retirement of the existing officeholder; it also may remove generals who can no longer fulfill their duties. It is not a governing body of The Salvation Army, and has no continuity between meetings. The High Council is somewhat the Army's equivalent of the College of Cardinals of the Roman Catholic Church.

But there was not always a High Council. Beginning in 1870 the Christian Mission was governed by its annual conference, modeled on the Methodist Church pattern. Booth found this cumbersome. In 1877 a gigantic change took place as the annual conference voted to move from a democratic system to an autocracy, giving Booth sole authority for the movement.

The Foundation Deed of 1878 established the legal basis that completed the evolution from the Christian Mission to Booth's Salvation Army. This deed provided for the general to nominate his successor by placing the name in a sealed envelope and depositing it with his attorneys. Upon death or resignation of the general, the envelope was to be opened to reveal his successor.

A Historic Fireside Chat

William Gladstone, Britain's famous four-time prime minister, on December 21, 1896, invited William Booth for a visit in his home. Chatting by the fireside, they entered into a conversation that was to change the course of Army history. Booth mentioned the Deed Poll of 1878 that established the mission as The Salvation Army and gave each general sole right to appoint his successor.

Even the pope, Gladstone pointed out, enjoyed no such authority; his successor was elected by the College of Cardinals. The prime minister paused, and then inquired, "But suppose some General becomes unfit or unworthy? What provision was there to remove such a General?" Gladstone further commented that the method of nomination left no provision for "calamity, incapacity or heresy."

Booth had to admit there was none. Gladstone in that fireside chat had given Booth something to ponder, and can be credited with prompting one of the most important developments in the infrastructure of The Salvation Army, and one that would enable it to survive a coming crisis.

This point was further emphasized when an explosion occurred near William and his eldest son and heir apparent when they were in a taxi. "What a mess the Army would have been in," said William, "had we both gone to Heaven at the same time."

Seven years after Booth's conversation with Gladstone, this weakness was rectified. The 1904 supplemental deed empowered a High Council, made up of commissioners and territorial commanders, to remove from office any incumbent general who had become, for whatever reason, unfit to continue to exercise oversight of the Army. It could be convened by the chief of the staff and four commissioners, or by any seven commissioners. Thus it was originally a kind of safety net, available in times of emergency. This seminal change became the means of resolving what would become the crisis of the Army's 1929 High Council.

On August 24, 1912, less than twenty-four hours after William Booth's death, at International Headquarters the Army's solicitors opened an envelope sealed by Booth twenty-two years earlier. Under the Deed Poll of 1878, he had nominated his son Bramwell as the Army's second general. Bramwell had never held a rank; he was always referred to as "the chief of the staff." He had been a faithful second in command, the clerk of the works, during the difficult years of mob violence, ecclesiastical and social prejudice, and shoestring financing. William gave the orders, and Bramwell faithfully carried them out.

During Bramwell's generalship the Army continued to thrive, in membership growth, in geographical outreach, and with its growing network of social services. His contribution to the movement as its first chief of the staff, serving for thirty-three years in that capacity, and as second general was second only to that of William and Catherine Booth. William had been the visionary, and Bramwell the organizer. He wrote history as well as made it — his *Echoes and Memories* and *These Fifty Years* are classics in the movement. However, both his autocratic style and its method of succession eventually started to wear thin within the ranks.

The Seeds of Discontent

A group of reformers among Army world leaders made known their conviction for a democratic polity. Commissioner George Carpenter, who served for sixteen years as literary secretary to General Bramwell Booth, had shared with the general the simmering discontent. But due to what was discreetly described as "a conflict of loyalties" in his honest criticism of Bramwell's resistance to abolishing the sealed envelope method of succession, Carpenter was reappointed to Australia, to a position similar to what he had held eighteen years earlier.

As leader of a reform movement, Commander Evangeline Booth recommended to the general in 1927 that he abolish the sealed envelope method of appointing a successor and instead have the High Council elect the Army's new leader. He refused, telling her that the suggestion "aims at canceling the General's most urgent duty — his duty to discern and name his successor." He also reminded her that if the commissioners thought a general was unfit, "they already have the power of deposing him and electing a fit person in his place." Bramwell could not have imagined how soon his hypothesis would become reality.

William Booth had accepted legal counsel that led to the supplementary deed providing for removal from office if a general became unfit. Bramwell's health seriously declined, rendering him unequal to the demands of the office of the general. By November 1928 he had been absent from IHQ for seven months due to illness. On November 13,

1928, Commissioner Edward J. Higgins, the chief of the staff, visited the general at his home and found him to be seriously ill. The following day seven commissioners signed and delivered to the chief of the staff an official requisition for the High Council to be called.

The 1929 High Council Crisis

There was also a growing feeling among some Army leaders that the next general should not be a Booth, and the High Council seemed a good way to ensure a break in the hereditary tradition. Bramwell was intransigent, refusing to abolish the autocratic system of succession, resorting to court action to hold on as general and avoid deposition.

On January 8, 1929, the first High Council convened, composed of sixty-three men and women. After much legal wrangling in the court case with Bramwell's lawyers, with sorrow and reluctance they deposed General Bramwell Booth by 55 votes to 8, bringing to an end one of the most traumatic chapters in the history of the movement.

With the office of the general now vacant, and consequently no sealed envelope for a mandate, this first High Council elected as gen-

General Bramwell Booth

eral Edward Higgins, Bramwell's chief of the staff, by 42 votes to 17. A skilled tactician, Higgins negotiated for the British Parliament to pass the Salvation Army Act 1931. The act secured two fundamental changes. It provided the High Council with sole authority to elect each succeeding general, abolishing the general's right to nominate his successor. Also, in place of the sole trusteeship of the general, a trustee company would hold properties and capital assets of the Army. The Army set the age of retirement for a general at seventy. In recent years the Army policy has set a limit of five years in office (regardless of age) or of reaching the age of sixty-eight.

Amendments and Refinements

England's Parliament further amended and refined the Army's constitution in passing the Salvation Army Act 1980, which outlined the eligibility of High Council membership. It also stipulated election rules: a two-thirds majority on the first three ballots is required for election; when three or more candidates remain on a ballot, the one with fewest votes is dropped; and a simple majority of total votes is required after the third ballot.

Council membership would be further impacted by the 1991 Commission on the Ministry of Women. In addition to changes already cited, it recommended that all women officers married to commissioners hold that rank in their own right. The 1995 Deed of Variation, approved with consent in writing of more than two-thirds of active commissioners, provided for the council to consist of the chief of the staff, commissioners other than the commissioner spouse of the general, and all territorial commanders irrespective of rank or length of office. This provision for the first time included women spouses of commissioners, almost doubling council membership.

High Council Procedure

The High Council was not intended to be representative in the democratic meaning of the word. The intention was to gather senior Army leadership worldwide to discern the will of God and elect the next general. Members of the High Council represent only themselves.

Each council elects a president and vice president, and determines its own procedures, including when and how its proceedings should be published. Time for united prayer is a priority. Nominations are made in secret, with three required for a candidate to stand. The only qualification for nomination is that the nominee be an officer, although it is unlikely that other than one at the High Council would be nominated. Those who accept are called to answer questions in writing, sometimes in excess of 100, recommended by the High Council members and arranged by a Questions Committee. Each candidate also gives a nomination speech, read from a prepared and unalterable text.

All but the 1934 and 1939 High Councils, which met at London's Clapton Congress Hall, have been held at Sunbury Court, the Army's Georgian mansion north of London. This led the wordsmith General Arnold Brown to refer to the members as the "Solomons of Sunbury."

All who attend High Councils give witness that the procedures are bathed in prayer as they seek the will of God for the choice of the Army's world leader.

FIFTEEN

The Generals and Their Legacies

Be shepherds of God's flock that is under your care.

1 Peter 5:2

The generals are both the custodians and the movers of Salvation Army history. They have been, along with IHQ, referred to as "the glue that holds the Army together." Their initiatives and personal impact have had far-reaching influence.

Evangeline Booth

Following Bramwell Booth, sixteen generals have been elected through 2008, serving as leaders of the international movement. Each came to the Army's highest office with proven administrative skills, tested leadership, and godly character. Each also communicated effectively in large gatherings with Salvationists in the expanding multicultural composition of its global membership.

In a day when scandals have rocked even the ranks of Christian leadership, the ongoing roster of the Army's territorial, national, and international leaders has served with an impeccable record of integrity. They acknowledged their commitment to the Army's ultimate Commander in Chief — the Lord Jesus Christ — avowing their allegiance and devotion to him.

Ten of the eighteen generals were of British origin or background. Next is Canada, with three generals, all serving between 1974 and 1993. Nine of the sixteen High Council presidents were Americans.

High Councils Elect the Generals

To Edward Higgins, elected during the crisis of the 1929 High Council, had come the awesome task of maintaining the unity and mission of the Army not only in the wake of its internal crisis but also amid the global economic collapse of the period. We have seen that he skillfully negotiated through Parliament the Salvation Army Act 1931, which replaced the archaic and nepotistic succession by sealed envelope, and the general as the trustee of all capital assets. Higgins earned the sobriquet "Storm Pilot," the title of his biography by William G. Harris. Arnold Brown recorded, "No ship riding so close to threatening reefs could have had a steadier hand on the helm than his. God did indeed provide a *Storm Pilot.*"

In 1934 the first High Council met under the new 1931 provision. Evangeline Booth was elected the Army's fourth general, at age sixty-nine, on the fifth ballot, with 32 out of 47 votes. A daughter of the founder, her thirty years as national commander in the USA were the high-water mark for Army work in that country as she developed evangelistic and social programs, and advisory boards. She blended a flamboyant style with gifts as a skilled administrator, composer, orator, and accomplished musician. Upon election as general, she returned home to New York to a ticker-tape parade up Broadway. Two months later, at a

"National Tribute of Farewell," 20,000 well-wishers thronged Madison Square Garden to hail "America's Gift to the World." Evangeline's term as general, a coda to her illustrious career, was comparatively without distinction. At the end of her term she returned to America to live out the final years in her adopted country. Her death in 1950 at age eighty-four marked the end of an era, and with her died a major family link to William Booth.

George L. Carpenter, an Australian, succeeded Evangeline Booth in 1939 as the Army's fifth general, winning 35 of 49 votes on the fifth ballot. His "banishment" by Bramwell was corrected by Bramwell's successors, who recognized Carpenter's hallmarks of character and leadership. From his position as territorial leader for Canada and Bermuda, he was elected international leader. Upon arrival to his office he was greeted by the sandbagged entrance of the International Training College, to which IHQ had been transferred for safety during the bombing raids. World War II travel restrictions made him a prisoner of his office. Since it was impossible to convene a High Council with a world war raging, by consent of two-thirds of the commissioners Carpenter's term of office was extended by twelve months, until a High Council could be summoned.

Albert Orsborn, territorial commander for the United Kingdom, succeeded Carpenter in 1946, gaining 36 of 46 votes on the third ballot of the Army's fourth High Council. As an infant he had been dedicated by William Booth and reared by officer parents. His stated priorities as general were a continuing emphasis on the gospel of Christ, renewing the Army's world fellowship that had been ravaged by six years of world war, and broadening the base of the administration of the general. In the uneasy peace that followed the war, Orsborn had the sad experience of seeing the Army disbanded in Communist countries, including Czechoslovakia, North Korea, and China. In fulfillment of his commitment to the High Council that elected him, in 1947 he inaugurated the Advisory Council to the General (now the General's Consultative Council), appointing senior leaders to assess existing activity and plan new developments. Under his impetus the International College for Officers in London opened in 1950, with its salutary influence on thousands of officers from around the world who would participate in the two-month study course. In the same year, the International Youth Congress in London brought together 1,200 delegates from all five continents in a demonstration and reinforcement of the international bond of the Army. One of the Army's most compelling preachers, Orsborn is best remembered by succeeding generations of Salvationists as "the Poet General," for his legacy to the devotional treasury of Army songs.

The High Council again convened in 1954 and elected another son of Britain, Wilfred Kitching; he won on the third ballot with 1 vote over the required two-thirds majority, gaining 32 of 46 votes. He, as Orsborn, had held the Army's top territorial position, that of British commissioner, which was responsible for the largest Army membership. His nine years in office were the longest term of any elected general. So that he could be in office for the dedication of the newly constructed International Headquarters in London, which he had spearheaded, his term was extended for three months. He retired following its dedication by Queen Elizabeth in 1963.

Frederick L. Coutts, born in Scotland of officer parents, in 1963 was elected the eighth general with 30 of 49 votes on the fourth ballot. He served in the Royal Air Force in World War I. His service as a Salvation Army officer included eighteen years in its International Literary Department. During his term he introduced advisory boards to the British Territory and launched a record funding appeal to expand social services in the United Kingdom. He presided over the 1965 centenary celebrations in London, which were graced by the presence of Queen Elizabeth II, the archbishop of Canterbury, and diplomatic representatives of some forty countries. A highlight of the congress was the unveiling of a memorial bust of William Booth in Westminster Abbey. He excelled as a scholar and speaker, but off the platform was self-effacing and diffident. His plethora of official Army history and devotional writings would earn him the title of the "Army's Literary General."

A New Geography

Up to this point, with the exception of Carpenter as the fourth general, all the Army's international leaders had been born in the United Kingdom, each with a rich heritage of Army background. A new geography was ushered in when the next seven generals came from other national backgrounds, enhancing the international representation of the movement. Following these seven, the last three elected generals were once again of British origin and Army background, symbolic of the ongoing quality of Army leadership in the land of its birth, even amid recent times of severe attenuation.

Erik Wickberg, elected general in 1969 by securing the necessary two-thirds vote on the first ballot, was born of Swedish Salvation Army officers. He was the first general whose native tongue was not English and the first of non-British stock. Because his service was largely confined to Europe, he was fluent in German, French, and English, in addition to the Scandinavian languages. He instituted a quiet but far-reaching shift of emphasis in leadership appointments, from a "colonial" mode to that of national officers either in charge or second in command in Japan, Korea, four Indian territories, Ghana, Indonesia, Zaire, Jamaica, Nigeria, Pakistan, Zambia, the Philippines, and Sri Lanka. This dramatic development came to reflect more truly the Army's multiracial and multinational character and set the standard for years to come of having a national officer in one of the top two positions in a country. He is remembered as "the Statesman General."

Clarence D. Wiseman, in 1974, became the first Canadian to hold the office of general. In response to his deep concern for those in countries facing famine, disease, and poverty, he inaugurated programs to develop national leadership in these countries. Due to retirement age (seventy), he served for three years less two days, the shortest tenure of any of his predecessors. His term was extended three months to allow him and his wife to complete fifty years as active officers. Evangelistic zeal earned him the title "the Evangelistic General."

Canadian Arnold Brown was elected general on the first ballot in 1977, garnering the popular majority of 35 of 41 votes. The most versatile of all Army leaders, he excelled as speaker, writer, poet, musician, administrator, and visionary. Earlier while in Canada, in 1956 he initiated *The Living Word* television drama that eventually reached an international audience. In 1978 he led the International Centenary Congress in London, which was attended by more than 30,000 Salvationists from over eighty countries. Highlights of his generalship include establishment of the Missionary Literature and Translation Fund for non-English-speaking Third World territories, commencement of a South Asia College for Officers (SACO), and construction of the Salvation Army Act 1980. In 1978 he led the Army's withdrawal from the World Council of Churches, as covered earlier in this book. Responding to the need for a conduit to link the world's "have needs" and "have resources" people, Brown inaugurated the International Planning and Development Department at IHQ in 1978 to facilitate development in Third World countries. This resulted in millions of dollars invested in self-help projects of far-reaching impact in developing countries. It could be said of Brown that "he could not pen a dull sentence." His fluid pen and platform command earned him remembrance as "the Orator General."

Finnish-born Jarl Wahlström was elected general in 1981 with 35 of 44 votes cast on the third ballot. Commissioned a Salvation Army officer in 1938, he was called into the Finnish Armed Forces at the outbreak of World War II, serving part of his five years' service as a battalion chaplain. The 1985 International Youth Congress, which he oversaw, was attended by 5,000 delegates and was the first international congress staged outside the Army's motherland, and the first in the USA. In his initial speech he declared, "The Salvation Army must continue its ministry in evangelism. We must be the Army of the burning heart and the Army of the helping hand." Some who knew him ascribed him the title "the Caring General."

In 1986, Australian Eva Burrows was elected general by the slimmest margin in High Council history, 24 to 22 on the fourth ballot, a margin of one person's vote. Her election set several precedents. At fifty-six she became the youngest elected to the office; she was also the first to have a degree in education, and the first to have served for many years in the Third World (seventeen years in Africa). During her tenure the IHQ took on an increased multinational complexion with her ap-

General Eva Burrows

pointments of Third World staff. Following the fall of Communism, she led the Army's return to Czechoslovakia, Hungary, East Germany, Latvia, and Russia, and to Army advances into Ukraine, Georgia, and Moldova. During her seven years of leadership she set a record of logging over one million miles in visits to the Army's 100 countries, and became the first general to visit China. A daunting undertaking was the revolutionary restructuring of the relationship between the British Territory and IHQ, a knotty issue that had long proved intractable. The results gave birth in 1990 to the new United Kingdom Territory, which was placed on the same level with all other territories in relation to IHQ administration. Her extraordinary interest and openness with people around the world earned her the sobriquet "the People's General." By an almost unanimous postal ballot, the High Council extended her term by two years — the longest extension in the history of the movement — to bring to fruition substantive initiatives commenced during her first five years of administration. Televangelist Robert Schuller invited General Burrows to preach on six occasions on his worldwide *Hour of Power* telecast, and described her as "the most inspiring woman preacher in the world today."

Canadian-born Bramwell H. Tillsley was elected general in 1993 on the fourth ballot by 29 votes to 19. A gifted preacher and prayer meeting leader, he could aptly be titled "the Preacher General." A health breakdown caused him to summarily vacate his office ten months into his generalship, leaving vacant the office of the general until the High Council could again convene more than two months later in July 1994.

Paul A. Rader was elected general in 1994, ending the interregnum between generals. He became the only American-born general, serving a five-year term through 1999. Although Evangeline Booth came to the office from America, she had been British-born. On the first ballot Rader's name appeared along with John Gowans and Earle Maxwell, but his tally fell one vote short of the thirty votes required for the two-thirds majority. In accordance with procedure, Maxwell was dropped. The president then announced that John Gowans had also withdrawn from the ballot. Following consultation with the legal secretary, it was clear that a second ballot would be required even though there was now only one candidate. The president then announced that Paul A. Rader had been unanimously elected, which was unprecedented in High Council history. In an act of personal dedication, Commissioner Rader knelt in prayer, members of the council joining with him.

General Paul A. Rader

Rader in early officership had served for twenty-two years in Korea. His advanced training in theology and church growth, and affirmation of the Army's ecclesiastical identity, led to initiatives that would characterize him as "the Education General." His convening of the International Education Symposium, engaging in ongoing dialogue with the Doctrine Council, and appointing the International Spiritual Life Commission helped nurture holiness and the Army's worldwide mission of evangelism. His vision led to expanded soldier ranks, evangelistic innovation, and mission emphasis. In this dot-com era he also spurred the Army to take full advantage of the digital age by networking computers around the world and establishing an Army presence on the World Wide Web. Rader especially worked in close partnership with his wife, Commissioner Kay Rader, who influenced an expanding role for women officers. The Rader legacy included the upgraded status for married women commissioners, holding that rank in their own right.

Three Unique High Councils

The next High Council, in 1999, was described by one of its members as "an absolute cliffhanger of vote results between Commissioners Earle

Maxwell and John Gowans." It featured the most mercurial of all voting in High Council history. With seventy-four in attendance, and with votes "switching" following the fourth ballot tie of 37 votes each, on the fifth ballot Gowans won 39 votes to Maxwell's 35. Thus was fulfilled one prophetic statement about a High Council, that "the only thing predictable is its unpredictability." Gowans had previously served in England, France, the USA, and Australia. An accomplished and published poet, he wrote the lyrics to John Larsson's music for a number of musicals featured around the Army world. A "Charismatic General," he had a compelling stage presence and initiated major changes in the Army's rank system and officer status.

John Larsson, elected in 2002 in the first round of balloting as the Army's seventeenth general, was born in Sweden and heir to a rich Salvation Army tradition. His paternal grandfather inaugurated the Army's work in Russia in 1913, pioneered the work in Czechoslovakia in 1919, and enabled the Army to remain viable in Sweden and Switzerland during World War II. Larsson's maternal grandfather was in charge of the work in China and the Netherlands during difficult and dangerous periods. His father had served as chief secretary in South America West and East, and was territorial leader in Finland and Norway. His mother was a prolific writer and poet with several published songs and books to her credit. A gifted writer and composer, John Larsson became a household name, along with Gowans, for the ten full-length musicals they wrote beginning in 1968, which were produced around the Army world. Together "the two Johns" composed some 250 songs, 20 of which are included in the Army's official songbook. Prior to his election he served as Gowans's chief of the staff. His emphasis was on the "renewal" of the Army's spiritual life and mission. A gifted writer and leader, exacting in detail, and effective on the platform, his enduring music to Gowans's lyrics has him remembered as "the Musician General."

Shaw Clifton, the Army's international leader at the time of this writing, brings to the position the most extensive portfolio of credits of any nominee in the history of the High Council. Author of several books and many articles, he is one of the Army's premier writers. He practiced and taught law before becoming an officer, and being a theologian and ethicist enhanced his teaching ministry. His career was marked with distinguished service; he was the first to have served on five continents, including time as corps officer and educator in Africa and as an effective leader in the Islamic country of Pakistan. He manifests a deep awareness of the basis of Salvationist faith and practice and holds a rocklike stance on God's Word.

By the time of the 2006 High Council a new star had emerged on the horizon of the Army's international leadership. Commissioner Israel L. Gaither of the USA had already served as chief of the staff for three years, and before that he was in top leadership positions in the States and in South Africa, the first African American to be so elevated. Gaither's impressive credentials of proven leadership, powerful pulpit preachment, and relational and administrative skills highly commended him. Gaither's mantra became "Mission matters most." He had also been a nominee at the prior two High Councils. It was obvious to many that he and Shaw Clifton would be primary candidates for the international leadership of the Army.

In 2006 seven were nominated but two declined, leaving five highly qualified candidates who stood for election. After three ballots there stood Clifton and Gaither, each with strong support but short of the two-thirds majority needed in the first three rounds of voting. On the fourth ballot the two were separated by the votes of but a few members, and Shaw Clifton was elected as the Army's eighteenth general, and ninth of British background.

General Shaw Clifton

None of the candidates viewed the election as a contest, but rather as a searching for the will of God. Clifton invited Gaither to lead his welcome as general in London, and reciprocated by conducting in New York the installation of the Gaithers as national leaders of The Salvation Army in the United States. Gaither became the first African American to hold this position, as he had been in earlier stations of high leadership. At this High Council Salvationists from around the world, via live Web site video, witnessed the bonded spirit of the Army's leaders, transcending the world's human rivalries and ambitions.

Shaw Clifton, who is in his early months of office at the time of this writing, has already set in motion positive initiatives that augur well for the international Army. Besides being an articulate spokesman for the Army's mission, in the brief span of a few months he has appointed a woman for the first time as chief of the staff; established an international Social Justice Commission and office; resurrected the rank of lieutenant, whose demise had been lamented by many; and published the most definitive statement on the Army's ecclesiology and position in the church universal. He early gave evidence that "it would not be business as usual" for the international Army serving in an environment of global change and challenge. Emphasis on holiness has long been a hallmark of Clifton's leadership, and his legacy, among other remembrances, will be that of a holiness teacher.

Sixteen

The Army's Government

So that in everything he [Christ] might have the supremacy.

Colossians 1:18

How does an organization, based in 118 nations, maintain its unbroken unity, administer its vast spectrum of programs and services, retain fiscal accountability and integrity, keep track of and appoint its personnel, and preserve its ethos and mission? Surely a demanding and daunting task! Yet The Salvation Army has for over a century been doing exactly these things.

Through the years it has maintained a strong centralized hierarchical and ecclesiastical structure, with its top appointments and policies emanating from its international headquarters in London. These have effectively filtered down to and networked with the far-reaching tentacles of its national and regional units. The Salvation Army is not a federation of national programs, but a family and union of kindred minds and spirits, bonded in the unity of its Christian faith and purpose.

International Headquarters

The International Headquarters (IHQ) of The Salvation Army serves many purposes. It supports the leadership of the general, promotes the spiritual life of the Army, provides overall strategic leadership, and sets international policy. It gives direction by means of appointments, delegates authority and responsibility with accountability, inspires vision and initiatives, and strengthens the internationalism of the Army in its unity and purposes. It further coordinates the worldwide sharing of financial resources, knowledge, and expertise. It is the spiritual and administrative nexus of the global movement.

The site at 101 Queen Victoria Street, reposing in the shadow of St. Paul's Cathedral in London, was purchased in 1881 by William Booth to serve as the Army's international headquarters. In May 1941 the original building was destroyed in a bombing blitz of World War II, and it was not until twenty-two years later, in 1963, that a new building was constructed to replace it. The International Training College on Denmark Hill in London became the "temporary home" for IHQ in the intervening twenty-two years.

From the outset the site served as headquarters of both the international Army and the British Territory, the latter under the administration of the former. As the Army expanded both within Britain and internationally, this arrangement became awkward and restraining to both headquarters. The possibility of separating the British Territory administration from IHQ had long been viewed as a gigantic task of dismantling the existing structure that over the years found these Siamese twins of administration to be seemingly inseparable. General Burrows initiated research in 1988, and Colonel John Larsson was appointed to undertake this onerous task, looking into the legal, fiscal, and administrative aspects. The Army in Britain needed to be released to fly with new wings, to pursue its mission with greater effectiveness. A separation would also free IHQ from the immediate oversight so it could concentrate more on its true international role as a resource center and facilitator. The long-awaited bifurcation, implemented on November 1, 1990, was hailed as "the Army's most fundamental administrative change in the movement's 125-year history." On that day the international and national administrations in Britain were separated for the first time, and there was born the "United Kingdom Territory with the Republic of Ireland," which took its place under a single command, as was the case in the Army's other territories.

The 1963 edifice had become unsuited for the changes and needs of the new millennium. When in 1998 the new territory moved its headquarters to refurbished premises in South London, IHQ was left occupying only half of the Queen Victoria Street site. IHQ was increasingly uneconomical to operate and inefficient in use of space, and a more practical and dynamic architectural home was envisioned for the headquarters.

The new (2004) International Headquarters, London

A renovated and modernized building emerged in 2004. "A working building, but also a worship building" was how the Princess Royal described the new headquarters when she officially declared it open during a ceremony broadcast live on the Internet. She paid tribute to the Army's stewardship in creating a new headquarters at virtually no cost, due to the enacting of a 150-year lease for two-thirds of the property to commercial tenants to provide ongoing income. General John Larsson described the aims of the new building as "modern in design, frugal in operation, evangelical in purpose."

The crystal-clear-exterior six-story building contains, besides its suite of offices, a chapel, a modern café, and meeting rooms. The end result is a building where "form follows function" in its practical work space, but at the same time it is infused with both architectural and graphic reminders of the Army's spiritual mission. With several million persons each year using the adjoining walkway to St. Paul's Cathedral, the first-floor off-the-street café is open to the public, and an information center enables the public to explore by touch-screen technology the history and worldwide mission of the Army.

Even the architecture of IHQ declares that Christ and his mission are central. Rhidian Brook, award-winning author, tells of a time when he was struggling with a major decision regarding an invitation to visit and record the Army's ministries to AIDS-inflicted villages in Africa and Asia, a daunting and dangerous assignment. He came for his interview at IHQ with his prepared rationale to decline. He "came close to the Scripture-embossed, glass-fronted building . . . and read the words of the one I claimed to follow, written in lasered-glass across the entrance — 'I am the Light of the World. Whoever follows me will have the light of life.'" The reading of that verse became an epiphanous moment, lifting him from his "fog of indecision." He accepted the assignment, sponsored by Rupert Murdoch, and with his family made the journey through a trail of devastation to the HIV/AIDS epicenters in Africa and Asia. His book, *More Than Eyes Can See* (London: Marion Boyars, 2007), bears a searing and stirring witness to the Army's dramatic ministries at the front lines of the dread pandemic that is ravaging and destroying communities and countless lives. Brook's mission had received its impetus from a Scripture injunction engraved on the Army's headquarters, reminiscent of the Bible text "Even the stones will cry out!"

Money to pay IHQ overhead costs comes mainly from the more affluent Army territories. The chief of the staff, a commissioner appointed by the general as second in command, is the Army's chief executive to implement international policy and procedure, and to coordinate liaison between departments.

The General's Consultative Council, established in 2001 to succeed the long-standing Advisory Council to the General, advises on mission strategy and policy. It is composed of all officers who qualify for the High Council, and operates through a Lotus Notes database. Selected members meet four times a year at IHQ with the general in the chair.

Structure

Although The Salvation Army is an international organization with leadership vested in the general, the very nature of its work calls for considerable national, territorial, and local autonomy. While the chain of command starts with the general, actual administration is vested in the territories within each country and their community units.

Shaw Clifton, shortly after his election as general, stated his viewpoint on the blending of the consultative and autocratic system of the

Army. "Salvation Army systems of governance have never been democratic. I welcome the trend towards consultation and the involvement of more people in reaching decisions. But, I still want the Army to retain that distinctive element of autocracy in its systems because that makes for speedy decision when the need arises."

Each country has its own commander, who in larger entities holds the rank of commissioner. Territories operate under the broad general policies established by International Headquarters. The leader of each territory, although with considerable autonomy, is ultimately responsible to International Headquarters. The forty-six territories, ten commands, and two regions come under the administration of five geographical zones: Africa, Americas and Caribbean, Europe, South Asia, and South Pacific and East Asia, headed by commissioners who are designated international secretaries.

The basic worship and service unit of The Salvation Army is the corps community center. Some cities have several centers. They provide a variety of local programs, ranging from religious services and evangelistic campaigns to family counseling, day-care centers, youth activities, and general programs. Corps also supervise community services such as emergency relief, social services, youth services, and sometimes a thrift shop. Sunday school, a major component of every corps, took an innovative step in the USA East under an umbrella called HopeShare, designed to make the Word of God more relevant and exciting for children through second grade, and to reach out to children at risk.

Rehabilitation centers and hostels around the world include residency and recovery programs for substance abusers and others with problems that prevent them from independent living. These come under their departmental leadership within a territory.

Rank System

There is but one general, the international leader of the Army. Soldiers are church members of the Army, officers are full-time commissioned and ordained leaders. More recently a lay membership, "adherents," has been introduced for those who claim the Army as their church but do not take the step of full soldiership with its more rigorous requirements. The rank of "auxiliary captain" was introduced in 1975 to accommodate older recruits, and employees recognized as ministers but not required to undergo cadet training nor have full officer rank.

Through its history the rank system of the Army has gone through a number of alterations. Earlier ranks of ensign, commandant, probationary lieutenant, second lieutenant, senior captain, senior major, adjutant, brigadier, and lieutenant commissioner were abolished in the interest of simplifying. In 2002 General John Gowans initiated major changes that deleted the rank of lieutenant and greatly reduced the ranks of lieutenant colonel; colonel is now reserved for senior chief secretaries, and ranks of colonel and commissioner are limited to territorial and international leaders.

In 2007 the rank of lieutenant was reinstated for commissioned officers by General Shaw Clifton, with cadets commissioned as lieutenants and eligible for captain rank in five years. Promotion to major comes after fifteen years of evaluation and service. Service-year ranks of married officers are now held individually.

Fiscal Management and Stewardship

The fiscal and administrative facets of the Army pose their own challenge to both efficiency and stewardship. How does the Army run a multibillion-dollar-a-year transcontinental movement that serves many millions with a workforce that, by material standards, is vastly underpaid and overworked? The rewards offered are in the spiritual realm.

The Salvation Army has been called "the most effective organization in the U.S." by Peter Drucker, the best-known management theorist in the world. In a book with that title by Commissioner Robert Watson, former USA national commander, he states, "It would not occur to the Army to make that claim for itself, but such a confidence leads Salvationists to pray, 'Lord, please make us worthy of such a trust,' and inspires our effort toward efficient management and accountability." "No one even comes close" to the Army, says Drucker, measured against his five criteria of effectiveness — "clarity of mission, ability to innovate, measurable results, dedication, and putting money to maximum use." On another occasion he described the Army as "venture capitalists," and observed, "Your investment in people gets incredible results."

The Army does not hoard its assets but exhausts them to reach more and more people. In business terms, its supporters are its investors and its service recipients its customers. As with any business, it has to generate revenue and control costs, recruit and train employees, manage properties, and be accountable to its "investors." The "shareholders" and "trustees" of the Army range from those who put a dollar in the Christmas kettle to Joan Kroc, who committed more than a billion dollars to the Army's mission; from community-funding support to government contracts. Its finances are subject to both internal and outside auditing and its balance sheets are a matter of public record. From the start in Victorian England it developed and refined business methods to maximize resources and to expand its response in meeting client needs.

In 1890 William Booth opened a banking department, which later became the Army's Reliance Bank, serving the complicated fiscal needs of the Army both at home and abroad. It provides the gamut of banking services, including personal loans, safe custody of documents, foreign exchange, issuing traveler's checks, transfers of money abroad, and international transactions. It also manages the Army's substantial Overseas Service Funds and Special Projects Fund. It is now known as the Reliance Bank Limited.

In the Western world The Salvation Army became a charter member of federated funding organizations that evolved from "community chests" to United Way, and eventually included government-funded programs. Planned giving programs that cultivate bequests to the Army were introduced into the Army's financial system, providing a vital source of fiscal support. The developing countries of the Army world receive substantial support to carry on their programs and mission. Two-thirds of overseas support are provided by the United States; that total was over $30 million in 2008.

Local budgets and services are supported by internal membership tithes and giving, the Christmas effort, annual appeals, and in some countries direct mail appeals. The *Chronicle of Philanthropy* in 1995 published an extensive survey of the USA's top 400 charitable organizations, listing the Army for the third consecutive year as "America's favorite charity," first and most popular in annual donations. It reported that The Salvation Army received $726 million in private contributions in 1994, more than any other nonprofit. In the same fiscal year the Army also received $199 million from federal, state, and local governments for human services, and reported more than $1.3 billion in total support. That year it helped more than 7 million people at Christmas and Thanksgiving and in year-round social services, besides the 1.9 million people it assisted with emergency disaster service. The Army also was lauded for channeling the major percentage of its donated funds into beneficial programs and less into fund-raising and administration.

The 2006 USA National Annual Report, on its "Financial Highlights" page, once again disclosed that eighty-three cents of every dollar had gone directly to "social services, residential and institutional services, corps community centers, and rehabilitation services," with the balance of "12% for management and 5% for fundraising." The reporting procedure, along with other financial information, is done according to established audit and accounting procedures for nonprofits.

IHQ in 2000 reported a "funding crisis" for its subsidized territories due to out-of-control inflation in those countries and World Services funds reaching a limit. For the Army to stay in the fight it must have the resources needed to get the job done. A vigorous IHQ effort, called "Enterprise Development," emerged to "think outside the box" in exploring and finding new sources of funding projects, including agricultural projects such as farming and the raising of livestock and poultry, thrift stores, and other self-support enterprises. The support of the Army's global mission will be continually challenged by the volatility of the world market and the economic crises that relentlessly loom on the horizon.

The Army's Inviolate Mission

The Army itself imposes certain restrictions on receiving public funds to protect it from compromising its mission. In 1981 in the United States it issued an official statement that "any agency, government or private," that enters into a contract with The Salvation Army should "clearly understand that The Salvation Army is an international religious and charitable movement and is a branch of the Christian Church." The Army receives some $250 million nationally from private and public agencies, using the funds without compromising its basic mission while at the same time maintaining integrity in meeting contract criteria.

In the early 1970s the Army received a $100,000 grant from New York City to feed the elderly in Harlem, a program that had gone on for years. It provided not only nourishing food but also a community fellowship program. One day officials came to the site with a new interpretation of the contract rules that forbade saying grace before meals and the singing of favorite hymns, and said that would have to end. This demand was unacceptable. The Army refused to make the change and the contract was canceled. Most of the folk refused to go elsewhere, and another funding source was found to continue the program.

In another example, the New York Civil Liberties Union in 2004 sued the Army over its employment policy. The complaint involved the employees of the Army's Social Services for children. One of the city's largest private child services groups, it received more than $8 million annually in city and state funds. The Army maintained that their required information for employment was an evaluation of the applicant's "character and fitness to work with children." Jay Sekulow, chief counsel for the American Center for Law and Justice, stated that the Supreme Court has recognized over the last twenty years that religious institutions have the right to define their mission statements and qualifications for hiring and "the fact that they accept some state funding does not put this out of play. I believe The Salvation Army is well within its rights." Army leaders in New York City shared that they had Jewish, Muslim, Catholic, and Protestant employees. The Army did not require them to subscribe to its religious belief, but to accept and abide by its standards and ethos in its service. The Army was ready to sacrifice if necessary the city's funding support rather than compromise its principles. Ultimately its position was upheld by the courts.

In every contract and undertaking the Army keeps its mission and purpose inviolate, its mission statement serving as the template for both its identity and its undertakings.

"Called" to Serve

In the vocabulary of the Army, officers are "called" to service. Theirs is not a career but a covenant, not an occupation but a vocation. Their service is not measured by how much they get, but rather by how much they can give. They are bound by "Orders and Regulations" that impose somewhat stringent rules. Every officer around the world signs the same commitment before his or her ordination, titled "My Covenant."

Called by God to proclaim the gospel of our Lord and Savior Jesus Christ as an officer of The Salvation Army, I bind myself to him in this solemn covenant: to love and serve him supremely all my days, to live to win souls and make their salvation the first purpose of my life, to care for the poor, feed the hungry, clothe the naked, love the unlovable, and befriend those who have no friends, to maintain the doctrines and principles of The Salvation Army, and, by God's grace to prove myself a worthy officer. Done in the strength of my Lord and Savior, and in the presence of the Territorial Commander, training college officers and fellow cadets.

Monetary motivation is not a factor for Salvation Army officers. In an age where executives command six- and seven-digit salaries, officers responsible for thousands of people and multimillion-dollar budgets work happily for a fraction of that. In 1999 the national leader of the Army in the United States and his wife, both serving full time, received a joint salary of less than $74,000, which included the taxable benefits of Army-supplied housing and transportation, an amount for two people far below that of comparative organizations and businesses. In many places in the world salaries and benefits are substandard relative to the local economy. Compensation comes in the satisfaction and fulfillment of a job well done in making a difference in the lives of people and enrichment of community.

A Contract with the Future

Advisory Boards, composed of influential citizens, give valued assistance in promoting and supporting Army projects, including fundraising and fiscal accountability. They provide a link with the businesses and local leadership within the community and interpret the Army's mission and program. Organized in the USA under Evangeline Booth, they now serve in many Army territories and commands. A triennial National Advisory Organization Conference in the USA draws from its over 30,000 members 2,000 volunteers to participate in several days of workshops, presentations by noted speakers, and a concluding inspirational program of worship and dedication.

Like many traditional institutions, The Salvation Army has had to modernize. The black-ribboned bonnets disappeared. The musical diet has been extended beyond the burnished brass to embrace contemporary idiom in some quarters. In The Salvation Army's "contract with the future," what has not been modernized is its unstinting devotion to serve God by serving others, particularly the poor, the lonely, the addicted, and the afflicted.

SEVENTEEN

The Army's Crown Jewels

Therefore go and make disciples of all nations.

Matthew 28:19

The Salvation Army was not initially conceived by its founders to be, or to become, an international movement. From the chrysalis of the Christian Mission there emerged in 1878 The Salvation Army just at the time emigration to the New World was expanding, contributing to the expanding of its world frontiers. The Army's evangelistic mission also led to it taking root in many new territories.

The "crown jewel" of The Salvation Army has become its internationalism that spun out centrifugally from its outreach to the lowest and the lost wherever its members went or were sent. Its mandate was penned in the song by Evangeline Booth, "The world for God, I will do my part, I will give my heart."

During the Cold War years when it was outlawed in Russia, Red China, and all Iron Curtain countries, the Army survived as a global family of nations. In the third millennium it is fighting the good fight in 118 countries, preaching the gospel in 147 languages, both in hovels and among the affluent, and aiding the destitute and wounded of the world. The Army transcends geopolitical, racial, cultural, and language barriers and unites a cross-cultural coalition of diverse ethnic groups under its tricolors.

"Salvos" in Australia and the South Pacific

No two openings of Salvation Army work have been the same. The Army phenomenon of self-seeding took place in Australia in 1880 by two mission converts, John Gore and Edward Saunders, who had emigrated from England. An open-air meeting conducted in the Botanic Gardens in Adelaide, with a grocer's cart serving as a platform, marked the beginning of the Army in the land Down Under; it was officially established in February 1881. Australian Salvationists are affectionately known as Salvos.

Though geographically isolated from the Army's network of nations, the Salvos displayed initiative in Army social work. In Australia prison work had its beginning and served as a model for replication in the mother country and ultimately around the world. The concept of Eventide homes for the aged had its birth in 1901 in Australia.

The Salvation Army in Australia hosts more than 400 corps and outposts; almost 2,000 officers and 30,000 senior soldiers, adherents, and junior soldiers; and over 700 social service and institutional programs. A hallmark of the Army in the land Down Under has been its premier band and songster groups and high-quality corps and soldiership. But the Salvos also reach out far beyond their borders when they sponsor innovative projects including income-generating windmills and 400 self-help groups in India.

In this land of vast distances and open spaces, the outback is served by officers who, as flying padres, minister to over 100 cattle stations — isolated large ranches accessible only by plane. On their visits they conduct worship, weddings, dedications, and funerals, and bring medical supplies and literature. An ongoing aboriginal ministry reaches out to the indigenous population.

In 2007 Commissioner James Knaggs, Australia Southern Territory commander, shared his dream for the Army, titled *One Day*. It was a bold spiritual challenge, calling on "every soldier, young and old, to be sanctified . . . every corps to embrace the gospel for everyone in their community," with a total of thirty-five component visions. Captain Stephen Court recorded: "A spirit of anticipation swept the room as people nudged forward spiritually to the edge of their seats. The Dream is incendiary." This rumbling from Down Under was embraced by soldiers and officers throughout the territory. Their response of commitment is recorded in the unique publication *One Day,* to be used for group discussion and brainstorming. Indeed, the Lord is "doing a new thing" in the Army in Australia.

In Hong Kong, "the Pearl of the Orient," since its inception in 1930 the work has continued to thrive without interruption, with a complement of 19 corps, 52 officers, 20 institutions, 50 social centers, and over 2,500 soldiers. It hosts more than 10,000 students in its 30 schools and nurseries, and 6,000 elderly persons in hostels of residential care. A sheltered workshop provides training for 140 mildly handicapped persons, including 60 in residence.

The Army was reestablished in Taiwan in 1965 by two Salvationists who were serving there in the U.S. Armed Forces. The Army's activities began in Singapore in 1935, later spreading to many parts of Malaysia, and to the Philippines in 1937.

Work in Papua New Guinea was pioneered in 1956 and initially came under the Australia command. The flag that knows no national boundaries was unfurled in New Zealand in 1883 by two young officers sent from England. From New Zealand came extensions to Fiji in 1983 and to Tonga in 1988.

Transplants in Europe

From the Army's native soil in Britain, plantings soon spread across the Channel to European neighbors. A small contingent dispatched to France became the first extension to a non-English-speaking land. It was also the first time a woman was appointed commander of a territory — the founder's eldest daughter, Catherine. The Army flag, the first for continental Europe, was unfurled in 1881 in a little hall in a poor quarter of Paris. The pioneer party received an unfriendly and potentially dangerous response, and not until a quarter-century later did public opinion change to appreciation.

Young women officers were sometimes accosted by men on the streets of Paris. On a boulevard one night a man approached Catherine for a rendezvous. Supposing her silence gave consent, he asked, "Where?" *"Devant le Trone de Dieu!"* *("Before the throne of God")* was her shattering reply. Not only did the man take to his heels but reports of the incident made headlines in France and established the reputation of the women pioneers.

From France the work was extended in 1882 to Switzerland, where again bitter and persistent opposition was encountered. Germany, Italy, and the Netherlands came into the Army orbit in 1886, Denmark in 1887, and the work spilled over into Belgium in 1889.

A postmistress, Hanna Ouchterlony, upon learning of the Army, started its work in her native Sweden in 1882. She held meetings with remarkable results, with official recognition soon following. Ouchterlony ultimately became a commissioner. In 1888 work opened in Norway and spread from there to Iceland in 1895. A Finnish woman, Miss Hedwig von Haartman, heard of the Army while in London, and after being trained in England was sent in 1889 to open the work in Finland.

After the initial explosion of openings, advances slowed, with eastern Europe offering a more promising field. Pioneer parties were dispatched and openings occurred in Austria (1906), Russia (1913), Czechoslovakia (1919), Latvia (1923), Hungary (1924), Estonia (1927), and Yugoslavia (1933). Corps and institutions were opened, but government restrictions during World War II found the Army proscribed, and by 1950 all contact by these countries with International Headquarters had broken down. Many officers and soldiers remained faithful Salvationists, some living to see restrictions lifted and work reopened following the political changes of 1990.

Army Flag Raised in Canada and Caribbean

Eighteen-year-old Jack Addie, an Army convert, emigrated from England to Canada. In London, Ontario, he discovered another immigrant convert, Joe Ludgate. Together in 1882 they started the Army in Canada in characteristic fashion — with an open-air meeting, then indoor meetings. Within a matter of weeks they had enrolled 50 soldiers, and the two young entrepreneurs for God were commissioned captains on the spot. In 1896 Bermuda came under the Army flag, joined within the Canadian Territory.

The Salvation Army in Canada would become one of the Army's most substantial bases of membership and service, with almost 2,000 officers, over 300 corps with some 75,000 soldiers and adherents. Its more than 8,000 employees help maintain 113 institutions, including 170 social service offices, 5 hospitals, 19 senior residences, 14 addiction and rehabilitation centers, and 23 correctional service programs. It meets the needs of homeless men, women, families, and children with 56 hostels and emergency residential shelters, including a 216-unit facility in Vancouver and a 253-bed men's hostel in London, Ontario.

Caribbean countries soon followed. In 1887 a beachhead was established in Kingston, and from there the work spread throughout the island of Jamaica, and ultimately to the fifteen nations that constitute the diverse cultural mosaic of the Army's Caribbean Territory. The territory operates 37 basic schools for over 13,000 students, including its School for the Blind and Visually Impaired in Kingston, where 120 residents benefit from skilled and compassionate care. Provided are social services for the homeless, Eventide homes for seniors, and hostels and shelters for women and children. Its fifteen independent island states render it the most fragmented territory in the Army world, but five languages and multiple currencies have not been able to dampen the zeal nor fragment the unity of Salvationist fellowship.

Elsewhere, in Central America the Army flag was hoisted in Mexico, Panama, Costa Rica, Honduras, Guatemala, Belize, and El Salvador. Countries of South America soon fell to the Army's invasion and now include Brazil, Argentina, Uruguay, Chile, Peru, Paraguay, Bolivia, Brazil, Ecuador, Venezuela, Colombia, and Guyana.

A Beachhead in India

Judge Frederick Tucker was a highly positioned and well-paid civil servant of the British Indian Civil Service in India, fluent in Sanskrit, Hindi, and Urdu. A convert of Methodism, after reading of Booth's Army he renounced his position and generous pension, and traveled to London to offer his services as a full-time officer to Booth, with a plan for the Army to work in his adopted land. "I am now penniless," he told Booth. "You must take me." Booth could only agree. At his request he was sent to commence the Army's work in India, the first expansion to a non-Christian culture.

Tucker and his party of five landed in Bombay on September 19, 1882. The small party was arrested several times, and only Tucker's intimate knowledge of Indian law freed them. Rather than try to Westernize the Indians, they chose to live as the lowest caste in India, adopting Indian food, dress, customs, and even names. Meals of curry and water were eaten in Indian custom, cross-legged on the floor.

Major and Mrs. Tucker with early officers in India

An incident occurred in Gujarat where Tucker and a coworker had initially been turned away by the people. Having walked for miles, barefoot over the burning sand, Tucker and his companion settled down in the shade of a tree to rest, where both fell into an exhausted sleep. This soon caught the attention of the men of the village. Seeing the "sahib" asleep, they were amazed to discover that Tucker was barefooted like them. They felt the soles of his feet, finding them, unlike theirs, soft and with sores and blisters. It was then the men realized that Tucker and his associate had come to them at physical sacrifice. Seating themselves at a respectful distance, they waited until the sahib awoke. When Tucker awoke, he began reading the Bible, and soon noticed the attention of the men fixed upon him. He invited them to come nearer and he explained the love of God as revealed in Christ. As a result they were invited to meet with the entire village that night to share the gospel. In later referring to this incident, Tucker would say, "I preached my best sermon with my feet!"

India's rigid caste system did not take well to their living on equal terms with Indians. But the Army's indigenous approach brought results in what turned out to be one of its most successful overseas ventures in both evangelism and a broad array of social services.

In addition to evangelistic work, various social programs were inaugurated for the relief of distress from famine, flood, and epidemic. Educational facilities such as elementary, secondary, and industrial schools were provided for the poorer class. Medical work originated in Nagercoil in 1893 when a dispensary was set up at the Army headquarters.

India became the Army's oldest, most costly, and largest missionary field, ultimately to boast over 5,000 centers of work and almost 3,000 officers. As had his spiritual mentor, John Wesley, Booth was coming to see the world as his parish.

Gandhi once said it was impossible to know India. But The Salvation Army seeks to know the people and their needs in this enormously populated country of nearly a billion people — one-sixth of the world's population — who speak more than a thousand languages and dialects. This "nation of nations" today hosts six territories of the worldwide Army, more than any other country. Responding to the demographic changes, the Army in India in the twenty-first century will increasingly be reconfigured to the urban context, from the villages to the cities. In 1990 a national organization was established, administered from India's territorial offices, to support and coordinate work in the six territories.

India became the gateway to other Asian lands. From there the Army flag in 1883 was carried to Ceylon (now Sri Lanka) and to Lahore (now Pakistan). Burma was opened by officers from India in 1915. The Army was introduced into Indonesia in 1894, and in 1895 the Army carried its flag to Japan. From its beachhead established in India, the Army rapidly expanded on the shores of Asia.

Undaunted in Korea and Myanmar

Following the visit and survey of William Booth to Korea in 1907, the following year Colonel and Mrs. Robert Hoggard "opened fire" in Seoul. The first converts accepted Christ in the Hoggard home even before a hall had been opened. The ready response to the gospel by the Korean people, with a hundred converts in six weeks, resulted in a permanent work being set up in the country.

The rubric "the Land of the Morning Calm" did not apply to the Army's work there in ensuing years. The story of the Army in Korea has

Prayer response at 1992 Korean Congress with General Burrows

been a saga of courage and tenacious faith amid a century of uncommon turbulence. During the Korean conflict in the 1950s the youth band attached to the Boys' Home in Seoul was marched northward and disappeared, never to be heard from again. One Korean officer was martyred for his faith, and others were listed as missing with the Army shutdown in North Korea. The Army in South Korea has remained alive and well; it has doubled since the 1970s and is vibrant, celebrating its centenary in 2008 with an emphasis on church growth and strategic church planting and, above all, fervent prayer. Recording over 60,000 members in more than 250 centers, and over 100 institutions and social programs, Korean Salvationists meet as early as 4:30 in the morning throughout the year for an outpouring of thanksgiving and petition. The Army's multicultural ministry continues with new plantings of Korean corps in the USA, Canada, Australia, the United Kingdom, Argentina, the Philippines, and Russia.

The Army's work in the isolated land of Burma (now Myanmar) has survived persecution since it began in 1915. The story is recorded of adjutant Saw Kedoe of Rangoon who, when no longer allowed to wear his uniform, still bore the Army crest tattooed on his left arm and the crossed flags on his right. Such was the undauntable spirit of Salvationists during war years, with many later surfacing as heroes who kept the faith and loyalty to the movement to which they had dedicated their lives. Today in Myanmar the Army operates a growing corps, three children's homes, a day-care center, and a School for Officer Training.

The Wind of the Spirit in Africa

The wind of the Spirit was blowing in Africa when a party of three officers in 1883 "opened fire" in Cape Town, South Africa. Today The Salvation Army, largely under African leadership, has a robust membership on the continent, with work in Zimbabwe, Mozambique, Nigeria, Kenya, Ghana, Zambia, Uganda, Namibia, Tanzania, the two republics of the Congo, Malawi, Angola, and Liberia.

Africa, its fifty-three nation-states culturally complex and linguistically diverse, through the years has constituted one of the Army's major missionary fields. The continent has also been notorious for its civil wars, overwhelming poverty, and pandemics of disease. But in recent decades Africa has exploded with burgeoning and dynamic Christian

Commissioner Israel L. Gaither

growth, as 46 percent of Africa's population has become Christian. The fastest-growing segment by far of the global Salvation Army has been in Africa. Its largest corps is in Nairobi, the capital of Kenya. At the time of this writing almost half of the senior soldiers of The Salvation Army are in Africa, with Kenya (173,234 members) and Zimbabwe (117,263 members) accounting for the largest number and exceeding by far any other Army territory. Overall, African countries now constitute almost half of the Army's over one million world membership.

December 4, 2001, in Johannesburg, became a red-letter day for The Salvation Army in South Africa. Commissioner Israel Gaither, territorial commander (later USA national commander), arranged to hold discussions with Nelson Mandela, along with General John Gowans and Commissioners Eva Gaither and Gisele Gowans. The world-renowned leader exhibited an extremely warm and gentle humility. "You know you are in the presence of greatness," reflected Israel Gaither, "when in the presence of Nelson Mandela." When it had seemed that cataclysmic confrontation over apartheid would erupt between black and white, he was the one who helped turn the nation back from the precipice and led the long walk to freedom and democracy. In 1990, following twenty-seven years in prison, he played the decisive role that led to South Africa's first democratic election, and retired as president in 1999 to serve as senior statesman. The president spoke warmly of his appreciation for the work and mission of the Army, saying, "South Africa needs The Salvation Army." He invited continued contact on specific matters, including ongoing emergency relief efforts. Israel Gaither shared the sentiment of Billy Graham, who upon meeting Winston Churchill said, "I felt like I had just shaken hands with Mr. History." Two days later the Army leaders were graciously received by South Africa's president, Thabo Mbeki. It was evident that the Army had a friend in both the past and current presidents, which augurs well for the forward movement of its mission in South Africa.

William Booth's Deathbed Plea

William Booth, in his final words to his son Bramwell, confided, "I have been thinking very much during the last few nights about China. I want you to promise me that you will unfurl our flag in that wonderful land." Father and son clasped hands in assent, and prayed together.

The founder's deathbed plea was heeded when work commenced in North China in 1916. Many converts were won, and day schools and night schools and a home for boys were established. Captain Hal Beckett pioneered the work in North China and served there with his wife from 1917 to 1924. In his book, *Save the World Army* (name of Booth's Army in China), he said he was appointed to "have 800 square miles to evangelize, to be the father and mother of a children's home, to secure properties and open corps." By 1928 The Salvation Army in North China had 212 trained men and women officers, and work started in eighty-four centers. But on the horizon were the bitter setbacks and incarcerations in the Sino-Japanese War and the Army's heartbreaking 1951 expulsion from Red China.

Political upheavals often brought the Army into their turmoil, leaving danger, disruption, and sometimes even death in their wake. The first cracks in China's bamboo curtain allowed a dialogue in the 1980s with former Salvationists of quiet heroism in that vast land. Heroes and heroines of resolute faithfulness emerged from settings of long-term persecution and suppression.

Since 1989 Lieutenant Colonel Check-Hung Yee (USA) has journeyed fourteen times to China, renewing links with former Salvationists, including trips to bring relief to thousands of disaster victims. Today The Salvation Army is in China, but in a different role. It has a beachhead of social services in mainland China, which it launches from its China Development Department in Hong Kong. Since 1993 it has initiated over 100 social service programs in twelve provinces of China, including disaster relief and community development projects. The Army's intervention that targeted critical areas of food, health, farming, education, and income generation has helped many communities to move from dire poverty to breaking the cycle of poverty. One project provides training in agriculture and husbandry and creates job opportunities. Also, HIV/AIDS workshops were conducted for pastors and seminary students in Kunming, Yunnan.

The Army has remained strong in Hong Kong, which since becoming part of China in 1997 has supported social projects within mainland China. In July 2004 the China Development Team conducted two teacher-training sessions, during which it introduced new materials to some 100 teachers in the Guangzi and Yunnan provinces, ultimately to benefit the students. Army music groups and summer youth mission teams visit China as goodwill ambassadors of God's peace. In this vast land that today hosts one-sixth of the world's population, William Booth's deathbed plea is being implemented in ways he would never have imagined.

The New "Missionary"

The Army's traditional overseas programs and policy did not escape the winds of change and trends. Medical ministries transitioned toward community development, direction-setting consultations on health, healing, and wholeness. The 1990s witnessed an openness to a wider interpretation of health and healing in the total ministry of the Army.

Missionary service had been an integral part of the Army's overseas work since its earliest days. Its worldwide work was often initiated, nurtured, and maintained by missionary officers. But paradigm shifts overtook the Army's overseas work, and by the early nineties the international Salvation Army no longer had "missionaries." Officers serving overseas were termed "reinforcement officers," the change in name also designating a change in philosophy, policy, and practice.

In many places the shift was determined by external circumstances. As early as the midseventies, the chief of the staff, Commissioner Arnold Brown, was informed by the Zairean government that if the Army did not appoint a national as territorial leader, it would be proscribed. In response, Colonel Mbakanu Diakanwa in 1976 was appointed territorial commander of Zaire, a position he held for twelve years. Commissioner Brown was told by the British ambassador in Bombay: "The key words today are indigenization and Indianization." General Rader in 1997 observed, "In some countries the involvement of expatriates in the future may be on a consultative or an occasional task-oriented basis."

Governments of the newly emerging countries tightened their rules or set quotas, limiting the number of visas for missionaries. In some countries the doors completely closed to the missionary, for example, in Indonesia. Salvation Army leaders also came to increasingly recognize that the church flourishes best when it is self-governed, self-supported, and self-propagated.

A shift in geography also took place with expatriates no longer exclusively moving "from west to east" or "from north to south." Developed territories more frequently requested reinforcements to relate to their own exploding ethnic populations. Salvationists from Korea have come "on loan" to the USA to open corps where Korean populations have developed, and have enriched the Army's culture with their emphasis on pastoral ministry, stewardship, prayer, and Bible study.

In 1994, 75 percent of the Army's numerical strength was in the developing world. In that context Army leaders acknowledged that to have participated in a seventy-fifth anniversary of a territory in that part of the world that still had never had a national leader, quickened the sense of urgency to address the identifying, preparing, and training of future leaders.

The Salvation Army, along with other churches, has learned that the pluralism of our global village legislates for an indigenous presentation of the gospel. Today it seeks to present its message in the idiom of each culture that Christ is the true template for abundant and eternal life.

The chief of the staff in April 2008 announced: "The Salvation Army has 'opened fire' in the African nations of Namibia and Mali. The Army previously worked in Namibia from 1932 to 1939. Now, 69 years later, the re-establishment of a presence in the country has been warmly welcomed by both the Church and non-governmental organizations." Contacts have led to official registration in the country. Namibia is part of the Army's Southern Africa Territory, which also oversees Salvation Army work in Lesotho, St. Helena, South Africa, and Swaziland.

Following an invitation for The Salvation Army to establish a presence in the predominately Muslim nation of Mali, a local response was undertaken with help from the Army in Nigeria and IHQ. Mali is the most northerly part of the African continent in which The Salvation Army has a presence. Attendance at meetings has grown steadily, and official registration in Mali has been granted to "labor for the progress of Christianity, to struggle against poverty." Mali is attached to the Army's Nigeria Territory.

General Shaw Clifton in 2008 announced that following intensive research and visits, an official presence was established in Mongolia, overseen by the Korean Territory. The Arabic Gulf State of Kuwait also joined the Army's roster of nations, its work located in the Protestant compound with allocated space for meetings, administration, and residence for its officers. Over 300 Salvationists are among the immigrant population in Kuwait. And lastly, in 2009 as this copy is being prepared for publication, the Army's flag was hoisted in the demo-

cratic country of Nepal, the work there to be overseen by the India
Eastern Territory.

Familiar words of John Oxenham find expression in the Army's
global family:

> In Christ there is no east or west,
>   In him no south or north,
> But one great fellowship of love
>   Throughout the whole wide earth.

EIGHTEEN

Invasion of the USA

The boundary lines have fallen for me in pleasant places.

Psalm 16:6

Booth's Army without guns dared to invade and to seek to bring into its domain the United States, which a century earlier had successfully resisted British forces. This time providence favored the invasion.

James Jermy, of African descent and a Christian Mission convert, migrated to Cleveland, Ohio. There in 1872 he planted a seedling from the mother plant that sprouted a replica Christian Mission. But this initial American enterprise withered and died when Jermy returned to England in 1876.

In 1879 a seventeen-year-old Salvation Army officer, Lieutenant Eliza Shirley, sailed to America with her mother to join the father of the family in Philadelphia where he had emigrated to find work. Soon after arrival the two Shirley women, at their own expense, acquired the use of an old chair factory and converted it into a mission hall.

They began with the first street-corner meeting held in America, at Fourth and Oxford Streets, where a plaque marks the spot. Unsupported, they pressed on with nothing but a love for God and their fellow sinners. After four weeks the turning point came when one night some boys set fire to a barrel of tar nearby. The fire brigade turned up, and most importantly a large crowd appeared. With a crowd of people on their doorstep, and a blazing flame as a dramatic backdrop, they launched a meeting, singing a hymn and preaching a sermon. The town's notorious alcoholic, Reddie, showed interest, was invited into

Invasion by Railton and the seven lassies in 1880 *(Petrie art)*

the factory, and was followed by hundreds of people. Reddie was converted, and from that point the Army in Philadelphia established a firm beachhead in America.

The Shirleys had unofficially begun the work of the Army, inauspiciously in that abandoned chair factory on October 5, 1879. Upon hearing reports of its success, William Booth sent George Scott Railton with seven "Hallelujah lassies" to open the work officially. The invading party landed in Battery Park at the southern tip of New York City on March 10, 1880. Of the invasion, historian David Bennett observed, "Nearly a hundred years before England had failed to hold on to its American colonies with trained troops. Now a General with quite a different mission was sending an army of eight, six under the age of twenty, to 'capture America for God.'"

Two weeks later, on March 24, 1,500 people gathered in Philadelphia, with over 200 uniformed soldiers on the platform, for the ceremonial presentation by Railton of the Army flag sent by Catherine Booth to Eliza Shirley. Two months later Railton cabled William Booth that the Army in the States totaled sixteen officers, forty cadets, and over 400 soldiers.

A Breach in the Ranks

Initially, Railton's successor in charge of the Army in the States, Major Thomas Moore, zealously moved the Army ahead with good success. In 1884 Moore asked Booth for permission for Army properties to be incorporated in the States. Booth, as titleholder of all properties, rejected the idea. In the same year Booth's international auditors reported Moore's accounts in disorder. A transatlantic dispute erupted between them, prompting the general to replace him, appointing him to the command of South Africa.

He defected from the movement, and having become an American citizen, had all Army property deeded to himself. He took the property and personnel, and assumed the title of General of America's Salvation Army. Evangeline Booth later brought legal action against the American Salvation Army, and it was banned from using the title. Moore's remnant was renamed the American Rescue Workers, and still exists, primarily in the northeastern United States.

When Major Frank Smith arrived as replacement in November 1884, he found a decimated Army, with only 17 of the 100 original officers remaining in Booth's Army. All property and equipment had been impounded by Moore. Not long after, the trustees of Moore's army deposed him for mismanagement, and appointed the defected Colonel Richard Holz in his stead.

In late 1886 William Booth conducted an eleven-week whirlwind campaign in the States that helped restore order. In the next turn of leadership, Booth replaced the ailing Smith with twenty-seven-year-old Ballington Booth, the general's second son, who took over a force of 654 officers working in 312 cities and towns. Later, in 1889 Holz returned to the ranks, bringing a large contingent of the officers who had defected. The Army in America had weathered its first major crisis. But another dark cloud and storm loomed just over the horizon.

Tension between William and his lively progeny, characteristic of the Booth family dynasty, broke out first with Ballington in the United States. In 1896 Ballington and his wife, Maud, seceded, denouncing their general's "despotism." But did the other American leaders feel the same way? Ballington called a meeting at the headquarters, now in New York, and behind locked doors presented to them the reasons for his resignation.

Evangeline, in New York at the time of Ballington's resignation, had been given temporary command of the American territory, but found herself locked out of the meeting. Her concern for what was going on inside the building made her determined to gain entry. So she walked from the Fourteenth Street main entrance into the Thirteenth Street doors, went up the fire escape, and climbed in through a window, despite the inconvenience of her long skirts. She made her way to the meeting hall and mounted the platform. The assembly gasped at her unexpected appearance, and then went silent. She fixed her piercing eyes upon her surprised brother. "I wish to speak, Ballington," she said firmly. He knew to defy her was ill advised. "You may," he consented. Orator of the Booth family, her speech was fiery, her words persuasive. She did not denounce her brother, but made it clear that to resign en masse from The Salvation Army would be a disaster. She had the rapt attention of her hearers. Ballington had been outmaneuvered. Following the meeting, the majority of American Salvationists remained loyal to William Booth. A few joined Ballington and Maud in their breakaway organization, giving birth to the Volunteers of America.

At this critical junction, Frederick Booth-Tucker and his wife Emma, another Booth daughter, were placed in charge of the Army in the States. The work prospered under their competent leadership; they even received access to the newly elected President McKinley. The general finally acquiesced to allow the Army to be incorporated in the United States in 1899, with The Salvation Army (capitalized article, as part of the official title) defined as a "religious and charitable corporation."

Mission Accomplished

When General Booth returned to the States in 1895, he traveled 18,453 miles to hold 340 meetings in 86 cities, speaking to 437,000 people and seeing 2,200 coming to the Army's "mercy seat" for salvation. During a visit in 1903 he opened the Senate in prayer and dined with President Roosevelt, and met with the president again on his 1907 visit.

William Booth appointed in 1904 as commander of his Army in the States his thirty-nine-year-old daughter Evangeline Booth, who would hold that position for thirty years. Unmarried, charismatic, and highly talented, she was described by historian Ed McKinley as "a phenomenon of historic proportions." She had an innate ability to creatively respond to the crisis of the moment, whether to those stranded in Alaska during the 1898 gold strike, to victims of the 1906 San Francisco earthquake, or most prominently to the doughboys in the trenches of World War I. She also had the ability to move in elite circles, garnering both a high profile and substantial support that pushed the Army to great advances. When she had arrived in New York, Army property was valued at $1.5 million; when she left that figure had risen to $48 million plus a capital account of $35 million.

In 1930, for the Army's jubilee in the United States, Commander Evangeline Booth dedicated its new national and territorial headquarters on Fourteenth Street in New York City, comprising a large auditorium, headquarters offices, and a women's residence in the rear. This classic property hosted the Army's national and territorial offices for over fifty years, and still serves a valued administrative and service purpose.

The worldwide Army would ultimately become a heavy debtor to its sibling in the States. From there came the concepts of music camps for thousands of budding and proficient musicians, annual Brengle Institutes for teaching holiness, advisory boards for community support of its social services, and program components that became replicated around the Army world. Perhaps the greatest contribution of the Army in the States, in addition to valued leadership for overseas posts, has been its generous support for the work in less developed countries, millions of dollars annually; it has carried over three-fourths of the fiscal burden for the Army's supported territories.

Since 1922 the highest level of leadership in the USA has been the Commissioners' Conference, chaired by the national commander. It is unique in the Army world, composed of the five U.S. commissioners, the chief secretaries, and in recent years the spouses. It convenes three times a year to provide a forum for discussion and resolution of questions of national import and common concern, and to formulate policies and procedures to protect the interests and advance the program of the Army.

Today The Salvation Army in the States has become the "flagship" branch of the Army world in its galaxy of social services. Nationwide more than 32 million persons are touched by the Army, one in every ten Americans. The States host 855 institutions providing social and emergency services, transitional housing, adult rehabilitation services, child day care, correctional services, substance abuse services, and medical services, besides 3,800 service units and countless social service offices. The equivalent of a small city, with a population of 65,000, sleeps under Army roofs every night. Its vast network of trained emergency and disaster workers and equipment renders it an ever-ready Army for response when disaster strikes.

The proclamation of the gospel and the network of community service go forth from over 1,300 corps community centers with 130,905 soldiers and adherents, led by a fighting force of over 5,400 officers — almost one-fourth of the worldwide number.

Under the leadership of Commissioner James Osborne, the USA national headquarters achieved an enhanced status, including its relocation to Alexandria, Virginia, strategically placed near the nation's capital to facilitate relations with government programs, and for the first time amalgamating all its national departments in one building.

Indeed, the former "colonies" this time capitulated with open arms to the invasion from their mother country!

Nineteen

Serving the Armed Forces

*Endure hardship with us like a good soldier of Christ
Jesus.*

2 Timothy 2:3

Service to those in the armed forces was early launched when in 1874 at
Portsmouth, England, more than 300 men about to embark for the war
front were served refreshments and sent off with prayer. Both practical
and spiritual help was offered to servicemen as far back as the Ashanti
War of 1874 and the Zulu War of 1879. William Booth established the
Naval and Military League (NML), which came into its own with the out-
break of the Boer War in 1880. With the motto Love Conquers All the
NML became a unique expression of Army ministry.

The original work among troops owed an immense debt to outstanding women, who rendered a motherly and spiritual concern for every man. The Army provided recreational needs; good, inexpensive
food; winter clothing; writing paper and envelopes; a letter-writing service; and round-the-clock visitation of loved ones at home. A young Salvation Army lieutenant, William Warwicker, kept a personal journal
during the Second Boer War (1899-1902). By the spring of 1901 he had
visited 2,111 sick and wounded servicemen, and counseled another
1,800 on spiritual matters. His military pass gave him access to all military camps in South Africa. His exemplary service paved the way ultimately for Salvationists to serve as fully accredited military chaplains.

In years to follow, through its Red Shield program, the Army would
serve armed forces personnel in many countries and even on the battle-

field, through its chaplains and frontline ministry. General Shaw Clifton writes, "Today our chaplains are the custodians of a distinguished heritage."

The Salvation Army in the USA Goes to War

When President Wilson declared war in 1917, Evangeline Booth, USA national commander, swung into action by summoning a National War Council to respond to the needs of American soldiers. She appointed national, territorial, and provincial war secretaries, placing the entire Salvation Army in America on a war-service basis. Service centers and hostels were set up adjacent to military camps. But Evangeline wanted to do more than serve the military at home. "American boys are going to France," she said. "We must go with them."

The American commander sent her emissary, Lieutenant Colonel William Barker, to France to ascertain how Salvationists could best serve the troops there. He was graciously received by none other than General John J. Pershing, head of the American Army in France. Pershing shared how The Salvation Army had once helped him when a fire swept through his San Francisco home, killing his family. Even though other organizations were already involved, Pershing gave permission for Salvationists to serve in the militarized area.

Evangeline led her Army's effort to send immense quantities of hospital supplies and provisions to the troops. Barker quickly discovered that homesickness was the scourge of the troops and the presence of American women would boost their morale. He cabled Evangeline, and she issued a call for young, single, female officers. She would send only her best officers. "Quality is its own multiplication table," she said. "Quality without quantity will spread, whereas quantity without quality will shrink." She charged them: "You are going overseas to serve Christ. You must be examples of his love, willing to endure hardship, to lay down your lives for his sake."

After receiving Pershing's permission, Salvationists set up "huts" as close to the front as possible. Sometimes this was a tent staked to the ground, or a deserted, ramshackle building. But the spirit of warmth and love inside made it the closest thing to home for the soldiers.

The First 24/7 Doughnut Shop

In August 1917 fighting raged near Montiers, France, as soldiers huddled, hungry, weary, and drenched by thirty-six consecutive days of rain. In a tent near the front lines, Salvation Army lassies made dough with ingredients on hand and used a wine bottle as a rolling pin. With a baking powder tin for a cutter and a tube for making the holes, they fried doughnuts in soldiers' steel helmets on an eighteen-inch stove.

The water-soaked tent finally collapsed. However, the 100 doughnuts made that first day were an immediate success. Soon as many as 500 soldiers stood in mud outside the resurrected tent waiting for the sweet taste of doughnuts. Before long, 9,000 doughnuts a day were being made around the clock. The tent became the first 24/7 doughnut shop in the world.

The Army lassies attended the burials, singing, praying, and leaving wildflowers at the grave. On Mother's Day of 1918 the "Sallies," at the request of American mothers, decorated 1,000 graves with flowers and flags. They "mothered" the American troops, never proselytized, and

Supporting those at the outposts of freedom

Veterans' Day—November 11

A letter to home from the "foxhole"

"Home Delivery"

The most popular chow line

expressed their faith through action. When the simple service for an American soldier was over, the girls would say, "Now, friends, let's go and say a prayer beside our enemy's graves."

The Salvation Army became endeared for giving its kits and many needed practical items, all without charge. Religious services were held for those who chose to attend — simple gatherings with well-known hymns and Bible homilies. Men joined in hymn sings accompanied by a cornet. Faced with death on a daily basis amid the horrors of war, some asked for prayer or made a confession of faith.

The Sallies won over both soldiers and war correspondents, whose dispatches described their tender ministrations. The Salvation Army "Doughnut Girls" in World War I became legendary for their service to the "doughboys" at the front lines in France and Belgium. They served in the rain and knee-deep mud, in the cold, amid lack of bathing opportunity, during gas attacks, living close to the mutilated and the dead. They mothered the troops by the thousands, doing every useful, kindly act that came to hand. They darned socks, sewed on buttons, wrote letters home. Sometimes they had to break bad news, such as when one had to tell a seventeen-year-old soldier that his mother had died back home. They wrote letters to mothers describing sites where their sons were buried.

And they baked. Above all, they baked. With no stoves, proper pans, with only a bit of flour, lard, baking power, and sugar, with makeshift utensils they made doughnuts by the thousands. Word spread, and before long Army lassies were making doughnuts wherever the war was being fought. The word went around: "If you're hungry and broke, you can get something to eat and free at The Salvation Army." It was reported that some pilots dropped notes asking for doughnuts for their troops.

Army lassies followed the troops to the front lines, at times coming under fire as they carried hot food to the men in combat, sometimes even into the foxholes, placing the Army's huts and field kitchens as close to the fighting as allowed. Sallie Chesham has written, "The Army lassies in France were safe unchaperoned." The fragrance of the Army's cup of coffee and the taste of a freshly made doughnut lived on in the memory of innumerable servicemen.

Returning servicemen could not say enough about the Sallies. They were celebrated on magazine covers, on stage, in song and poetry, with a "tin hat for a halo." Their wholesome womanhood had given soldiers uplift in the lonely and dangerous trenches. Soldiers praised these maternal surrogates and their huts as the closest thing to home. One of the odes to the doughnut, probably composed in the trenches, regaled:

> A doughnut's just a doughnut, boys, 'til you're "over there"
> And day and night you're in a trench away in France somewhere;
> You get a fresh-made doughnut, seems it comes from
>   heaven above,
> That doughnut, boys, reminds you of a slice of mother's love.

A Noble Heritage

Official records show that The Salvation Army sent thirty-eight contingents consisting of 253 Salvationists to France between August 1917 and November 1919. As death loomed over the soldiers in the trenches, Sallies recorded, "Being killed makes a serious question arise and the men seem to realize the need of being saved. They listen as we tell them of salvation, and many are being saved."

The best-selling author Grace Livingston Hill was invited by Evangeline Booth to write the story of the Army's heroic and dedicated frontline service in the war. In the foreword of the book, Evangeline wrote, "Service is our watchword, and there is no reward equal to that of doing the most good to the most people in the most need." Her words "Doing the most good" became the Army's national slogan in the USA in 2006. She ended her foreword: "With them in the blood-soaked furrows of old fields; with them in the desolation of No Man's Land; and with them amid the indescribable miseries and gory horrors of the battlefield."[1]

The Sallies served, preached, modeled the gospel. The legendary service of the Sallies at the front lines of World War I became a turning point for the Army in the States, catapulting it to the front ranks of respected American charities and philanthropies. The Army's service in France and amid the battlefields of Europe was one of its most shining hours.

Evangeline Booth in 1919 was awarded by the United States government the Distinguished Service Medal. Professor Herbert Wisbey, in his doctoral dissertation on the history of the Army, concluded that World War I probably marked "the climax of Salvation Army history in the United States."[2] Some 250 Salvationists were in war service in France. Women served with such distinction that they retained a special place in the heart of Americans long after the war ended.

But far more than coffee and doughnuts was offered to those serving in the trenches, as illustrated by the following story. An example from half a world away was that of William McKenzie, a Salvation Army officer of Australia (later a commissioner) who had volunteered to serve as a chaplain. He visited the sick, became the confidant of any man in trouble, and dug trenches with the men. Strong in physique, when necessity arose he did not hesitate to descend on the local house of ill repute and drag his men out. In 1915 on the Gallipoli beaches, McKenzie was with his men as his battalion suffered 600 casualties in eight weeks. His was the sad duty to identify the dead from some fragment of clothing or personal item and then write to the loved ones. Moving across the shell-pocked slopes of Gallipoli, he heard a young soldier, wounded and near death, faintly calling: "Padre, do you know a Catholic prayer?" "I think I do, my boy," came the answer. "Say after me: 'God — be merciful — to me — a sinner. I lay — all my sins — on Jesus.'" Such were the final words of prayer on the lips of those visited by this padre who knew no lines of demarcation.

A Joint Enterprise

In 1941 The Salvation Army invited six organizations to join in a cooperative war effort. As a result The Salvation Army, YMCA, YWCA, Jewish Welfare Board, Catholic Community Service, and Traveler's Aid Society provided joint welfare, recreational, and spiritual services called the United Service Organization, or, more popularly, the USO. The largest interfaith program ever undertaken, the USO set up service centers near military bases around the country. It strove to be a home away from home by offering such provisions as books, music, games, coffee, doughnuts, mail, and social services as needed. Salvationists also operated mobile canteens, opened Red Shield clubs, and provided emergency lodgings in the nation's larger cities. In World War II the Army in the United States provided thirty-two chaplains and officer personnel for its 219 Red Shield clubs and 200 USO clubs.

This army of "soldiers without swords" served valiantly, its weapons of compassion and practical support freely offered to those in the service of their country and often in harm's way. There was neither a defense nor an offense against the effective weapons this army deployed.

TWENTY

Global Outreach

The kingdom of the world has become the kingdom of our Lord and of his Christ.

Revelation 11:15b

Each advance into a new country was an epic of its own, a venturesome start and establishing of a foothold. However, not all would survive. In some places the seed would sleep beneath the snow, awaiting a new springtime.

A New Springtime

In transcontinental Russia, where eastern Europe and northern Asia meet, the Army's work had commenced in 1913. But after Communism took over, it was proscribed in 1923, with all contact lost.

But a springtime did occur, with the collapse of Communism. The 1990s witnessed the stirring saga of the Army's return to nations where its work had been abolished by Communist dictators, including Russia, East Germany, and several eastern European countries.

Mutations spawned by global politics of the 1990s launched the Army into a new world of challenge and response. The fall of the Berlin Wall in November 1989 released twenty-six satellite states out of the USSR's orbit of atheistic Communism. As the grip of Communism gave way to freedom in eastern and central Europe, the reopening in Russia and new openings in other CIS (Commonwealth of Independent States) countries sparked epochal events in the Army's history.

With barriers removed there came the reunion of Salvationists living in the diaspora of East Germany. As the Communist system imploded, The Salvation Army along with the country bore the wounds and scars of over four decades of oppression. One event illustrates the poignancy of separation.

In May 1984 a ten-day international conference of 116 leaders of twenty nationalities, from the then eighty-four Army countries, met in West Berlin. They addressed economic concerns with devaluation and inflation, the response to crises of refugees, the fostering of unity in a divided world, and evangelism as a priority. The miracle of the Army's internationalism and unity was reaffirmed.

The delegates passed through notorious Checkpoint Charlie on a bus driven by an East German into East Berlin, and were stirred by its symbolism of division and separation. They had come from all over the world, in their varied uniforms of blue, gray, and white, in saris, and in many hues of skin — obviously a very international company in the midst of the divided city. One described that moment as filled "with an inexpressible sense of unity, our togetherness in Christ all the more dramatic in this setting."

On the street some of the older people recognized the uniform and exclaimed "*Die Heilsarmee* — oh, how we loved you." Then it happened, as the delegation gathered in a church sanctuary — a spontaneous and eloquent expression of what they were all feeling, as described by Commissioner George Nelting, one of those present. "The strains of *O Boundless Salvation* started to echo our deep feelings through the sanctuary of that great church, irrepressibly pouring forth from the sanctuary of our hearts. All our diversities and differences in that moment were transcended by our union in Christ eloquently expressed in the words penned by our founder and inspired by his world vision for God and the Army. It was truly an electrifying and memorable experience." He also recalls that "As the bus was returning following the meeting, the guards checked under the bus with large rolling mirrors." This first postwar incursion of the Army to East Berlin left its deep impression.

As the monolithic force of Communism withered away, the Army made a dramatic return to lands where it had been persecuted and proscribed. April 1990 ushered in a new springtime in Prague as the Army returned to Czechoslovakia after an absence of over forty years. The following month a cable was received at IHQ from an early Salvationist in Budapest that read, "As of today our flag is officially flying again in Hun-

gary. Hallelujah!" The Army commenced work there in 1924, and following the fall of Communism it was again recognized as a church by
the Hungarian government. At the return to Latvia in November 1990,
the head of the Department of Religious Affairs commented, "The Salvation Army is needed in Latvia. We need you because you have shown
that you are prepared to act and restore in people your faith in the value
of man. Welcome back!"

To Russia, with Love

Of all the returns to former Communist-dominated countries, the return
to Russia stood as the pinnacle of these epochal events. The Salvation
Army in 1923 was expelled by the Communist government. Russia's policies of *glasnost* and *perestroika* gave the first promise of a breakthrough.

"Mission accomplished" was experienced when General Burrows
officially reopened the Army in Leningrad (St. Petersburg) in July 1991,
after an absence of sixty-eight years. Captains Sven and Kathleen

**Front row, left to right: Lt. Colonel Betty Evans, Lt. Colonel Howard Evans,
General Burrows, Commr. Schurink; back rows: Russian cadets**

Ljungholm (USA) and Lieutenant and Mrs. Geoffrey Ryan (Canada), under the oversight of Lieutenant Colonel and Mrs. John Bjartveit (Norway), led the dramatic return of the Army as a new day dawned. Lieutenant Colonel and Mrs. Howard Evans (USA) came out of retirement to train the first Russian cadets, who were commissioned by General Burrows in June 1993. The return to Russia and the Soviet bloc countries was a meridian on the landscape of Army history. Within The Salvation Army the cross was replacing the Communist symbol of the hammer and sickle, and the liberty of the gospel the oppression of Communism.

But the Army's initial welcome back to Russia did not proceed without hurdles and a major setback due to the entrenched and restrictive bureaucracy of the Russian government. The Army in Moscow initially registered with the state in 1992. After a restrictive Law on Freedom was passed in 1997, Moscow's city government rejected the church's reregistration application and accused the Army of being a "militarized organization." In a significant challenge to Russia's 1997 religion law, the European Court of Human Rights in October 2006 ruled that Russian officials wrongfully denied legal status to The Salvation Army in Moscow and levied a fine of 10,000 euros (U.S. $12,700), payable to the Army in Moscow, every euro of which the Army used for the benefit of the poor. "This allows us to get on with the vital ministry of reaching out to the lost and serving the poor and suffering," stated the Army leader. This historic landmark decision by the highest court in the Russian Federation assisted not only the Army in Russia but also other churches registered in Russia prior to 1997. The Army's work in Russia since its return continues to meet with good growth and success, particularly with recruitment of capable and dedicated Russians as soldiers and officers. From Russia further advances and openings were made in the former Soviet bloc nations of Ukraine and Moldova.

Russia, Ukraine, Moldova, Georgia, and Romania constitute the Army's Eastern Europe Territory. Not only has Army membership been expanding in these countries but the countries are sending out missionaries "presented as a gift to the international Army," initially to the Czech Republic, Taiwan, United Kingdom, and Poland. Four youth mission teams from the countries of the territory in 2000 made a multinational impact conducting open-air meetings and children's ministries in Moscow, summer camps in Georgia, evangelistic meetings in Ukraine, and evangelistic meetings and day camps in Moldova. Lieutenants from Russia in 1999 opened the Army's work in Romania, start-ing in Bucharest and overseen from Moldova.

In Europe Today

"Europe today is a mission field," stated Commissioner Thorleif Gulliksen, international secretary for Europe, in 2006. "People seem to turn away from Christianity." General Larsson frankly admitted at a leader's conference in 2004 that "It's tough in Europe. Salvationists must use creative ways to draw people to Christ." He cited an event in Norway when a troop of motorcyclists roared into a stadium for an evan-gelistic meeting, resulting in the winning of converts.

In recent years the Army has suffered serious attrition in the land of its birth as well as in its European posts. The rise of secular humanism has taken a heavy toll on the church in general in Britain and Europe, as its people have left the churches to espouse a secular philosophy.

The Salvation Army is today the largest social institution in France, and is known as that, and not as a church. In 2000 government regula-tions separated the Army's religious and social services into two identi-ties. The social work became almost 100 percent funded by the govern-ment. The work includes rehabilitation centers, day care and Eventide homes for the elderly, a cybercafé for youth, emergency housing and as-sistance, and forty-five social centers that employ 1,700 people. With challenges evaluated and resources identified, the work of the Army in France presses forward.

In Germany the Army operates the largest and most professionally developed social institution in the field of rehabilitation for homeless people. The large complex of fifteen buildings houses more than 200 men and women with social problems. As part of an ecumenical out-reach at the 2006 World Cup staged in Germany, seventy Army dele-gates from four continents shared the gospel in varied ways, including the distribution of 75,000 copies of a special edition of the German *War Cry*. In the same year the message of Christmas was presented to mil-lions of TV viewers in a nationwide broadcast by the German staff and territorial commander.

In Italy an open-air witness was conducted at the historic site of Rome's Coliseum during Easter in 1999, led by General Paul A. Rader. The territory's theme in 2007 was "Strengthened by the past, we are certain of the future with Christ." In October of that year the Army opened work in Greece, administered from Italy.

Commencement of work in Warsaw, Poland, in 2005 was coordinated by a team from IHQ. "We won't start anything we can't afford," said team leader Colonel Vibeke Krommenhock. Consequently, all corps activities took place at the officer's quarters and on Sunday the Army rented a hall for its meetings. The Army there started as church and not as a social service agency; the latter is planned for the future.

In Spain groups of Salvationist youth regularly seek out the homeless, the destitute, and street prostitutes to offer hot drinks and food and to witness to the power of Christ. The life of a young man in Madrid named David was turned around when he was found lost in drink and depression under the bridge where he slept. The Army officer approached him one night, not only with hot soup, but also with compassion and an invitation to the corps the next day. There he had his first hot shower in months, and a clean change of clothes. The following Sunday David found himself in the worship service, and he never left again. "My life has come full circle," David explains. "I once received clothes from the clothes room, now I give clothes to others. I once took showers at the corps, now I supervise that ministry for others. I once lived under the bridge, now I minister to others living under the bridge. I was offered soup, soap and salvation, and now, I offer the same to others." The "Gateway to the Sun" in downtown Madrid, near where the Salvationist found David, became David's "Gateway to the Son."

In Switzerland, since 1999 Salvationists have been dispensing to people who live on the streets not only food but also friendliness, practical support, and Christian witness. Fellowship meals are also served in the St. Gallen corps to the hungry and homeless.

In the midst of Stockholm's throbbing life, a local corps outreach is a spiritual oasis. It is a place for recuperation, relaxation, laughter, love, and above all, it is a place filled with God's presence. It is but one expression of Sweden's and Latvia's 168 corps, twenty-two institutions, centers for deaf and blind and community and family services, integrated with its spiritual focus.

In Amsterdam an Army corps is next door to where young women offer their services to men walking by. Loud music comes from the bar at the other side of the building. At the Army center a cup of coffee is offered, a wholesome and friendly atmosphere prevails, and the liberating gospel of Christ and the true purpose of life is communicated.

Since 1888 The Salvation Army has reached out to the Norwegian people with the message of God's love and a practical ministry. The territory consisting of Norway, Iceland, and the Faroe Islands vigorously seeks new ways of telling the gospel story. The Army's thrift stores constitute one of the country's largest companies for occupational rehabilitation, training 850 people. In addition to forty-five shops countrywide, it has thirteen work rehabilitation and recycling centers and a blanket factory. The Oslo Harbor Light Center had 62,000 visitors in 2005; many homeless persons and drug addicts came to take a shower, get clean clothing, consult with a nurse or social worker, or consume one of the more than 30,000 hot meals that the center has served.

USA journalist Sue Schumann Warner, on the basis of her two-week visit with the Army in Europe in 2006, reported,

> Europe today is not the Europe of the Reformation, nor is it the Europe of William and Catherine Booth. God and faith are in question, and for many, both tilt towards irrelevancy. Most of Europe also has reasonable, functioning welfare systems. In this environment Salvationists are learning more of lifestyle evangelism, living their faith in a tangible way, providing compelling reasons for friends and neighbors to ask of the hope that is within them. In Europe Army attendance is down, corps are closing, and finances are tight. Some of these comments are heard in the Western world as well. But there are encouraging signs that William Booth's valiant soldiers in Europe will forge ahead in the spirit of Christ.

Kenya on the Grow!

In Kenya, where growth has been exponential, in one year thirty-five new corps were opened and over 10,000 new soldiers added. The more than 350,000 senior and junior soldiers in Kenya make up the largest membership of any Army territory.

In Kenya's capital city of Nairobi, the Central Corps is the Army's largest, in 2008 reporting 3,419 senior soldiers and 1,201 junior soldiers. In the space of one year the corps enrolled 150 new soldiers into its fellowship.

When corps halls in Kenya become too small to accommodate such growing congregations, the East African answer is to build another hall

Nairobi Songsters in vibrant praise with song, dance, drum, and timbrel

around the old one and, when the new hall is completed, knock down the former walls. The project involves not only the raising of money, but also the making of bricks, the gathering of stones, and the cutting of wood, with soldiers providing the labor.

When Kenya opened a new officers training college in 1991, seventy-three cadets arrived to train as officers, the largest session at the time in the Army world. This fastest-growing territory was mobilizing its program and leadership to meet the needs of its dramatic expansion. The massive numerical growth and geographical spread, with its administrative challenges, resulted in March 2008 in a subdivision into two territories, Kenya East and Kenya West.

Recognition of the Army's spiritual ministry in Kenya was given by the government, which authorized it to appoint an officer chaplain at all airports and ports. Also, a major sugar producer invited the appointment of a chaplain for the spiritual needs of its employees. A corps subsequently was founded on the premises.

Elsewhere in Africa

A 2004 Army convention in Ghana reported: "There was a tremendous movement of the Holy Spirit in all meetings, when seekers were so great in number that they crowded the large area in front of the altar and back into the aisles." Besides its evangelistic outreach, the Army implemented a major education thrust by operating 217 schools for over 20,000 children, in addition to other social centers. Also, in one year (1983) there were 2,455 infant deliveries at Army clinics, and despite transport problems, 389,026 outpatient treatments given. The Community Rehabilitation Programme, in its specialized schools and clinics, has helped over 6,000 physically disabled and deaf children, enabling them to live independently in their homes and community.

In southern Africa, where the Army maintains a vital spiritual ministry, it has made a frontal assault on the HIV/AIDS scourge. Its outreach to thousands encourages abstinence and fosters faithfulness, and includes home-based care and orphan and vulnerable child support, including a home for babies with AIDS.

The 7,000 delegates made history by attending the first All Africa Congress in 2005 in Harare, Zimbabwe. The gathering, led by General John Larsson, was punctuated with exuberant music and praise by the Salvationists, who came from all the Army's African territories, commands, and regions.

In Zimbabwe the Army operates four boarding schools besides quite a number of day secondary schools, including a high school with an enrollment of over 1,000 students that offers a Christian-based, high level of education. Originally there were hundreds of primary schools, but the government turned them over to local councils. Health authorities in Zimbabwe report that there are more than 450,000 orphans in the country as a result of the HIV/AIDS epidemic. A training camp was established to assist orphans in coping with the trauma and grief process in their loss of parents and to provide training in nutrition, hygiene, marketing skills, vocational issues, and traditional and cultural practices. The training camp is committed to maintaining and strengthening the traditional African concept of the extended family in the care of AIDS orphans. Thousands of children have participated since the start of the program in 1998. Other Salvation Army territories in Africa have replicated the program. Also introduced are group loans given in the form of cattle. When the cow gives birth, the calf is handed on to the next member of the group, until all members have received a cow.

Overshadowed by war in the Democratic Republic of the Congo in 1998-99, Salvationists in areas of combat were forced to take refuge in the forests or in neighboring states. As much as possible they reached out with aid and hope to two million refugees and displaced persons, carrying meager baggage on their heads. Nearly two million lost their lives as a result of the war, including many Salvationists, like Major Eugene Nsingani, a divisional commander, who was murdered along with other religious leaders. Reinforcement officers had to be evacuated from the country. As normality slowly returned to the country, Salvationists regrouped. A report stated: "These events have not obstructed the primary work of evangelism and pastoring, even though some were living in camps in the bush, in terrible conditions and under threat from roving armed bands."

With order restored, in 2004 more than 10,000 Salvationists of the Congo and Angola Territory gathered for the seventieth anniversary congress led by General Larsson. The Army in that area addresses the scourge of AIDS with programs and centers for persons in both urban and rural areas, providing social and medical ministries and bringing hope to orphaned children. Expanded services included a new dental unit opened in 2005 at its medical center.

In Nigeria the Army has committed itself to bring people from darkness to light, from sickness to wholeness, from illiteracy to being literate, and from poverty to abundance in God. It seeks to build bridges across gender, illiteracy, and poverty gaps, and above all the sin that separates man from God. Vocational training centers, schools, and

Refugee families are part of Captain Mwanza's parish in Malawi.

medical and health centers serve major cities, as well as an HIV/AIDS Action Center. In 2004 a center opened to give support to victims of child trafficking and prostitution. In its efforts to establish medical work in the territory, the Army recently opened a training center for auxiliary nurses and health workers, funded by Norway. Women from rural areas were being trained to strengthen the staff of Army health centers and clinics.

The description of Malawi as "the warm heart of Africa" is embodied by the devotion and service of Salvationists in the country. In 2004 a corps officer reported, "We are caring for 4,000 orphans in my area." The officer covers 138 villages on his bicycle, ably assisted by 500 volunteers who are keen to spread the message of salvation through this practical method of evangelism. Also, in partnership with World Food Program, a "food for work" project has a positive impact on several rural communities by repairing existing roads and building new ones. The working day starts at 5 A.M. when corps officers pray with the 7,000 participants in the project.

Malawi's "warm heart" opened in 1991 to allow the Army to host 10,069 refugees — 2,000 families — who had fled across the border from the war and terror in Mozambique. Salvationists, serving in this barren wasteland and lonely outpost of human suffering, established a school in tent classrooms, conducted a daily feeding program, and offered training for the building of 6,000 huts.

During and after Liberia's fourteen-year civil war that ended in 2003, the Army provided support for internally displaced persons, giving food, clothing, seeds, and tools to rural communities and commencing a piggery scheme. The country's civil strife brought unspeakable violence; hundreds of thousands were massacred and children were left desolate. The Army's feeding program for malnourished children met an urgent need, as did efforts to combat high illiteracy rates by reopening schools that had been closed during civil strife. Amid the strife a faithful and ever-growing membership and expression of evangelism have been maintained.

The Legend of Chikankata

The name Chikankata has through the years been synonymous with the legendary mission work of The Salvation Army in Zambia, revered in the

The Army's medical ministry to Africa's outlying areas

hearts and history of Salvationists. The name conjures up images of dedicated missionaries, compassionate ministry among leprosy patients and the destitute, medical and educational services, animal husbandry, and vocational training — a myriad of ministries rendered to thousands in rural Africa.

Chikankata, in the vanguard of Christian missions, provides 30 percent of the total health services for Zambia, with 50 percent of that going to rural areas. More than 1,000 persons have been trained to deliver health services to a rural community of 100,000. Mobile units make monthly visits to a network of thirty community-based village health centers.

How has Chikankata defied the tendency for a movement to abandon its founding purpose after a generation or two? What is the magnetism that brings young couples and singles to serve there, and that keeps an Army major there for twenty-seven years? No one can fully explain these intangibles. In this complex, within a landlocked nation bordered by eight countries, working and living by candlelight becomes a common experience for residents during the recurring periods of "no power, no water."

The Salvation Army compound at Chikankata is a self-sustaining community of up to 2,000 people in its schools, hospital, clinics, and vocational training programs; it also provides outreach to the villages and bush, and a host of other practical ministries. There the mission of the Army is expressed as compassion in action, where education and health care on a large scale go hand in hand with spiritual ministry.

When this writer visited in 1991, the compound included a 260-bed hospital, a maternal and child health clinic, a secondary school for over 700 students, a nurses training school, a nutrition center, staff housing, a training center for laboratory technicians, and a new conference center; staff also made monthly primary health care visits to rural villages in the catchment area. Farming and tree planting were also part of the extensive services, along with aquaculture; classes in blacksmith skills, metalworking, carpentry, and tailoring; and such unique services as a grinding mill for maize shared with neighboring villagers. The health team in areas remote from the hospital inoculated over 19,000 children against the common infectious diseases of childhood. The multiple ministries of the complex assume a proactive as well as a reactive stance to the challenging health, educational, and vocational needs of the people.

A unique and significant ministry emanating from Chikankata has been its Salvation Studio, a radio recording unit established by Lieutenant Colonel Damon Rader, OF, a pioneer in Christian radio ministry in Africa, when he served in Chikankata in the mid-1960s. The radio tape ministry reaches populations in southern, central, and eastern Africa. This mass media ministry expanded to include not only radio programs but also television, cassette recording, and stereo music recording. Christian groups from all over Zambia record their offerings and seek technical advice. The weekly programs are heard on Zambian radio and over Trans World Radio from Swaziland.

Chikankata Hospital, having moved from its long tradition of service to leprosy patients, now gives compassionate ministry to those suffering with and dying of AIDS. Not content to rest on its laurels, Chikankata in 2007 added to its health services a biomedical college of sciences for thirty young men and women.

The consolidation and continued updating of the wide spectrum of activities in the compound, and in outreach to those in the surrounding villages, continue to be a legend and legacy to countless who otherwise would be without hope and help.

Around the Army World

From India to Indonesia, from Ukraine to the USA, God is using The Salvation Army to change people's lives. The following cameos tell only a very small part of the story of the Army's dynamic and multifaceted ministry taking place around the world.

Since 1984 the Army in Brazil has operated as a national religious entity by presidential decree. The ever-increasing problem of street children and those in favelas (shantytowns) elicited Army support centers and drop-in shelters for children, as well as a twenty-four-hour counseling center, with results of hope and faith replacing the hopelessness of poverty and destitution.

The 2008 *Army Year Book* reports, "Throughout its history, The Salvation Army in Pakistan has never stopped growing." It celebrated its 125th anniversary in that year by reaching a landmark membership of 60,000 senior soldiers in addition to thousands in its varied programs who call the Army their church. Besides its "heart to God," its "hand to man" was stretched out in 2002 to the frontier town of Peshawar that had become home to over 3.25 million Afghan refugees. The Army's International Emergency Services provided a feeding program serving 1,200 refugee families and 700 locally based families, with over 15,000 people receiving food every week.

In Papua New Guinea, where many children do not reach adulthood, the Army installed a solar-powered refrigerator and provided essential vaccines and drugs through its social services. Families are praising God for this healing ministry at village corps. Social services also include implementation of water projects and literacy programs.

In Portugal, a soup run in the capital, Lisbon, twice a week brings many homeless and hungry people under the Army's umbrella, along with a spiritual ministry at a homeless shelter.

Enterprising officers in Ukraine launched a sawmill business along with a farm rehabilitation program for substance abusers. Clients assist a trained supervisor in moving rough-sawn lumber to a drying kiln and then selling it for a good profit that supports the program. One client had been an alcoholic living in the alleys of Kiev. After he came through the training scheme, his mother said, with tears in her eyes, "I cannot thank you enough. You have given me back my son. I thought he was dead but look at him now."

In Taiwan, Salvationists responded with practical aid and ministry following the devastating earthquake of September 1999, which claimed more than 2,500 lives and left 200,000 homeless. A relief team was mobilized to the worst-affected areas and distributed food, medical supplies, tents, and sleeping bags.

In China, in the Hua Shan Village, women are trained in various animal husbandry techniques so that they may qualify for a loan to commence raising and selling livestock, improving family income and raising the living standards of the community.

Australian mission teams undertook creative ways to reach the spiritually lost, through barbecues, car washes, knocking on doors, praying for people in their homes, and handing out *Jesus* videos. In Sydney a facility for homeless women opened, providing for fifty-five women in apartments. During the 2000 Sydney Olympic Games, mission team members witnessed to more than 50,000 spectators and athletes and distributed literature; at the Paralympic Games that followed, they gave out over 400,000 cups of cold water to people passing by their mission tents.

The Salvation Army invaded Iraq, with gas, on April 22, 2003! The first Salvation Army convoy of its peace force carrying propane cooking gas arrived in Umm Qasr, Iraq, where clean water and cooking fuel were desperate needs. Representatives from the World Food Program (WFP) had asked the Army to provide cooking gas to war-damaged cities in the region. Major Mike Young (USA), one of the first to be deployed, found the setting not only difficult, but dangerous. Army staff had to hire guards and find a place to stay, and often slept on the ground in sleeping bags — never out of harm's way. However, the distribution proceeded successfully in partnership with the Save the Children Fund that coordinated the humanitarian effort. In 2004 eighty Salvation Army personnel undertook short-term deployments in Iraq and Kuwait. Along with skilled Iraqi personnel, they built schools and clinics, developed vocational training and adult education, and provided housing and support to returning families. Ongoing service to Iraqis resulted in 1,200 young girls and women successfully completing sewing courses at ten centers in southern Iraq, in a vocational training sponsored by New Zealand.

Forgotten people in Sri Lanka comprise part of an Army parish served by forty-two community worship centers and a caring ministry in children's homes and in hostels, and in child care. An expanded physiotherapy center and AIDS program serve more than 5,000 patients a month. In response to sexual trafficking, the Army is housing Chinese children who had been used as prostitutes. The Philatelic Bureau in Colombo issued a 1999 commemorative stamp acknowledging the 116 years of Army work in the country.

In Bangladesh the Army has a knitting factory that offers training and employment to people in need of rehabilitation.

A new corps hall in Haiti was built from scratch in 1999 by thirty-one persons from USA Central Territory's Global Missions Team Project.

In Prague a conference was held for twenty-five delegates from seven former Communist countries to aid the Army's continuing ministry in central and eastern Europe, by sharing experiences and exploring future strategy.

Annual summer Bible conferences have been major events in the USA. Old Orchard Beach, Maine, has in recent years added a pavilion to enhance its over-100-year-history of camp meetings that attract several thousand persons each summer. The Southern Territory also has a rich history attracting more than 1,000 delegates each summer at its annual Bible conference at Lake Junaluska, with notable speakers and musicians.

The USA South sponsors *Wonderful Words of Life,* an award-winning worldwide radio program of The Salvation Army. It presents a fifteen-minute weekly program with lively dialogue, Army music in various styles, and inspirational teaching. On the air for over fifty years, the program is distributed to more than 1,200 stations worldwide, touching the lives of millions of listeners with the gospel message. In 2002 it became available on the Internet. A divisional commander in Australia contacted the Atlanta office to share his delight at how the radio program reached a person in the outback and visited "people we can't reach any other way."

The lines from a song by Salvationist William Pearson trumpet the movement's outlook:

With salvation for every nation,
To the ends of the earth we will go,
With a free and full salvation,
And the power of the cross we'll show.

TWENTY-ONE

Global Gatherings

*And he has made from one blood every nation of men to
dwell on all the face of the earth.*

Acts 17:26 NKJV

After leaping the seas in its conquests, the Army's mosaic of nations became further bonded through its international congresses. William Booth convened the first in 1886, as a series of meetings with the following purpose: "become better acquainted, lay down new methods and plans of action, and that there might be a great Pentecostal baptism of the Holy Ghost that should spread salvation to the uttermost parts of the earth."

Reports of the Army's work in its then nineteen countries were shared, as were testimonies by "trophies" — outstanding converts — and a grand parade was staged in London, highlighted with addresses by William and Catherine Booth. From the five continents of Army stations "They came, they saw, and they went forth to conquer" the world for Christ.

The second international congress in 1894 witnessed a dramatic exhibition of General Booth's *Darkest England* scheme. At the third of these mammoth gatherings, held in London in 1904, an estimated 50,000 filled London's capacious Crystal Palace. Delegates from the Army's forty-nine countries, of ebony, yellow, and white complexions, in their multicolored national uniforms, invaded London as a human kaleidoscope, described as "one of the greatest religious assemblies that the world has ever known."

The fourth international congress in 1914 was marred by the greatest tragedy in the history of The Salvation Army. One hundred twenty-four Canadian Salvationists en route to the festivities perished at sea when their vessel, *Empress of Ireland,* sank when rammed by another ship. Only 26 were saved. Among those lost were the territorial commander and most of the Army's Canadian Territorial Staff Band; the band did not re-form until 1969.

Centenary Celebration

In June 1965 the Army celebrated its centenary in London. Queen Elizabeth II, in addressing the capacity crowd in Royal Albert Hall, eulogized:

> The service conducted by William Booth in a tent on a disused burial ground in the East End of London in July 1865, was the start of one of the great worldwide religious organizations, supported and respected everywhere it works. The secret of its success lay in William Booth's complete self-dedication to the will of God and to His service, and in passionate love for the souls of men and women. In the past century The Salvation Army has grown from a small mission in a London side street, with no permanent base, into a religious and humanitarian organization which encircles the world.

Archbishop of Canterbury Dr. Michael Ramsay added his plaudits to the century-old movement: "You of The Salvation Army do show us how to care and inspire us to care. At the same time, putting first things first, you also show how the caring Christian has to care about man's greatest predicament and greatest need, namely, the estrangement of his soul from God. There is one gift that I believe every Salvationist has in a wonderful measure — and that is the gift of joy. I have seen many odd things in my time but I do not think I have ever seen a gloomy Salvationist."

In historic Westminster Abbey, a ceremony was held for the placement of a bust of a once itinerant street preacher in London, and the tricolors of his worldwide movement flew atop the Abbey tower. The Saturday gathering at the Crystal Palace Park brought an estimated 50,000 to celebrate the Army's centenary.

Across the ocean, the speaker in the legislative assembly of Alberta announced that an unnamed peak in the Rockies should henceforth be called Mount William Booth. Soon thereafter the celebration of the centenary in the United States drew a record meeting of thanksgiving in America's largest Protestant cathedral, St. John's in New York City, where an estimated congregation of 10,000 heard General Coutts preach from its honored pulpit.

Congress Fever

Other international congresses followed, each serving as "an outward and visible sign" of a movement with a worldwide outreach. The fifth, in 1978, celebrated the 100th anniversary of the naming of The Salvation Army. The sixth, in 1990, adopted the theme "With Christ into the Future"; General Eva Burrows presided over more than 3,500 overseas delegates, augmented by almost 9,000 Salvationists from the United Kingdom. The final program was held in two venues, the Royal Albert Hall and Wembley Arena, concluding with a service of consecration.

The seventh international congress, in 2000, was held in Atlanta, the first venue outside London. Some 23,000 delegates made light of distance

Each congress features its grand parade; this one is from 1990.

as they traveled from 107 countries. Defining the international movement, General John Gowans declared, "What makes us united is our concern for the lost, our desire for God to work in us through the power of the Holy Spirit to make us like Jesus in his caring and compassion, and our desire to celebrate Christ and his redemption." This festival of cultural, ethnic, and worship diversity, all under the unifying love of Christ, epitomized the Army's strong international bonding and fellowship.

These congresses, coming together over the years, could easily have become a reconstruction of Babel. Rather, they exhibited skilled organization and dignified management, which became a hallmark of the Army. One London newspaper reported that "the admirable discipline of its component parts was passed off with a distinction and a picturesqueness which would scarcely have disgraced the Horse Guards Parade." The spirit of William Booth was present at each gathering, and at one he was referred to as "this Caesar of evangelism, this Napoleon of the penitent-form." These gatherings, with their grand parades and dazzling ceremonies, dramatically witnessed to the global presence and membership of this Army with its successful invasions and spiritual coups around the world.

Zimbabwe Celebrates 100

The latter part of the twentieth century gave rise to centenary celebrations in many parts of the world. Let one notable example suffice.

"Welcome home" was the greeting to General Eva Burrows in Zimbabwe, where she once served for seventeen years. An aggregate attendance of over 95,000 came from the cities and the bush for the 1991 centenary congress in Harare. Inspired by the ministry of the general and the participation of the Zaïre Territorial Band and the Soweto Songsters of Southern Africa, exuberant Salvationists danced and sang their way through the weeklong celebrations. Thousands of seekers were recorded and 100 soldiers enrolled during the congress.

In what seemed an unending stream of serried ranks under the warm African sun on a brilliant Easter morning, 10,000 smartly uniformed Salvationists, with bands and banners, songs and salutes, marched past their general and territorial leaders. Their sprightly steps symbolized the Army of Zimbabwe marching into its second century with Christ.

Some of the crowd at the Zimbabwe congress; new soldiers are in front.

The congress showcased the variety as well as the verve of African Army music. Included among the 30,000 gathered in Harare's stadium on Easter Sunday were massed units of 1,800 timbrelists, 800 songsters, and 600 hosho (hollow gourd with seeds that rattle) players. In pomp and ceremony two services of thanksgiving in the Anglican cathedrals of Harare and Bulawayo launched the celebrations. Memorable renditions of the Zimbabwe Territorial Songsters in Harare, and the Soweto Songsters in Bulawayo, matched the Gothic cathedrals' noble proportions.

At a more favorable time for the country and his leadership, President Robert Mugabe gave a private audience with the general, and spoke for fifteen minutes in the Saturday evening program. He lauded the Army's work in Zimbabwe: "The Salvation Army has rendered to Zimbabwe a service we can never forget, and that service has been truly, and I say this genuinely, immaculate." He related that many in important positions in his country "were educated in Salvation Army schools and now the Army is developing the lives of their children."

Besides this tour de force in Zimbabwe, the Army's 100th birthday was being celebrated in small communities as well as nations around the world. Centenaries became the order of the day, not only to celebrate the past, but also to inspire the march into the future.

A Literary Landmark

In April 1994 there came to Alexandria, Virginia, 162 delegates from sixty countries for seven days to the Army's first International Literary and Publications Conference. A kaleidoscope of uniforms and nationalities turned the Army's national headquarters into a mini–United Nations scene as delegates toured the Army's expansive facilities. Delegates took advantage of the venue's proximity to the resources of personnel and technology of the National Publications Department and the historic ambiance of Washington, D.C. Under the cochairmanship of Commissioner Arthur Waters of IHQ and Colonel Henry Gariepy, USA national editor in chief, its forty workshops and fourteen plenary sessions led by editors and writers of the Army world were designed to launch the Army's literary ministry into a new era of change and technology.

Major Victoria Devavarum of India summarized: "This conference will bring a revolution to the Army literary ministry." Some delegates returned to organize similar conferences in their countries. Sue Schumann Warner, professional editor with the Army in the USA West, later wrote, "I keep coming back to that first international literary conference — it really opened avenues and networking around the Army world, and is a major contributor to the ease in which we SA journalists now communicate."

Workshops showcased the impact of the electronic age upon publications, and state-of-the-art equipment enhanced the effectiveness of presentations. A highlight was the Sunday morning message by General Arnold Brown (retired), elder statesman of Army writers and editors, who defined a writer's vision as "that inner incandescence that happens when a person feels himself united with something beyond himself."

The historic conference concluded in hallowed moments of dedication that sealed a renewed dependence on the ultimate source of their inspiration.

Partners in Mission

In 2003 a scheme called Partners in Mission was launched, in which territories became donor partners to Army work in developing countries. The intent was not only to channel financial resources but also to enhance the givers' awareness of the people they were supporting, and the social and cultural context of their needs; prayers and mission teams would also be targeted for the designated countries. Commissioner Lawrence Moretz, a major supporter of the program, writing on its reciprocity, stated, "All territories will be givers and all territories will be receivers. No territory in the world has a monopoly of practical experience, of human resources and wisdom, of spiritual energy. How good it is to be part of that wonderfully gifted and diverse family of God called Salvationists!"

The lengthened shadow of William Booth had fallen across five continents and, as with the apostle Peter, men and women found healing in its shade.

TWENTY-TWO

Addressing the Issues

Speak up for those who cannot speak for themselves.

Proverbs 31:8

We have already seen the Army's strategic attack on poverty in 1880 with William Booth's *In Darkest England,* and the victory in 1885 in the continuing war against human trafficking. Confronting the issues that afflicted human beings was in the DNA of The Salvation Army, passed on from William Booth to future generations of Salvationists. His Army was irrevocably committed to serving in the front lines of human need and suffering.

Issue of Apartheid

Apartheid, or "apartness," was the gross evil underlying the philosophy and political system that had guided South Africa since 1948. This diabolical and oppressive system enshrined inequality in scores of laws that regulated every aspect of life according to race, based on the concept of white supremacy. Years of exposure to the inhumanities of apartheid had reduced all people of color to the status of nonpersons, abetted by centuries of colonial and white rule. Oppressive racism was inflicted on Salvationists along with their countrymen in the violence of this oppressive and dehumanizing system. Many experienced forced relocation due to the Group Areas Act, which compelled the movement of blacks.

Toward building a bridge over the great racial divide that had traumatized Salvationists under apartheid, in 1986 there was inaugurated an integrated cadet-training session in Soweto. But the Army, which had to submit to government rules in South Africa, had difficulty confronting the issue.

After Eva Burrows, who had served in Africa, was elected general, she soon made her official statement on the issue. "We find the South African apartheid system unacceptable and express our strong hope that the present apartheid system will be completely abolished in South Africa and a truly non-racial society established. The Salvation Army reaffirms its long-standing policy that Army leaders will conduct gatherings anywhere in Africa only if they are open to all citizens of that country." She further made what became one of the strongest statements issued in the history of the Army against a social evil backed by political power, declaring, "Apartheid is anathema! It's a philosophy of life that is contrary to the teachings of Christ."

Her words resonated worldwide in Army publications as well as in the hearts of those suffering under apartheid's evils, and hope was encouraged for a new day in this tormented land. There was no doubt that God's Army had thrown down the gauntlet on the evils of apartheid.

Criticized for violating the Army's nonpolitical stance, she declared, "I believe we should speak out about social injustice. If 'political' means speaking out on issues such as prostitution or abortion, poverty or homelessness; if 'political' means speaking out to quicken the consciences of the government on the needs of the people, then I'm political."

Burrows had discerned that issues in the modern world had become politicized. She established a Moral and Social Issues Council to study issues in the world at large and to help the Army respond appropriately. Positional statements were prepared for distribution on such topics as abortion, alcoholism, euthanasia, capital punishment, unemployment, debt and easy credit, homosexuality, embryo research and biotechnology, the priority of the family, and nuclear disarmament.

The Army was putting into practice the scriptural injunction: "Speak up for those who cannot speak for themselves."

Taking on the Moral Issues

In the arena of film media, *The Last Temptation of Christ* received a vigorous protest from General Burrows, who described it as "morally offensive to the extreme, with blasphemous claims and sick distortion." Salvationists reviewing the film pointed out that it portrayed Jesus as weak, neurotic, a liar, a hypocrite, and plagued by guilt.

Burrows, along with her predecessors and successors, during her visits to various countries was usually invited to meet with the head of the nation. These visits with kings, queens, prime ministers, and heads of state afforded opportunity to discuss the Army's response to the needs in that country, and to bring into focus some of the issues that contributed to the poverty and suffering of the people. She always ended her visit with prayer for the nation's leader, its people, and its needs. The pressing business of the country's leader was suspended in those moments, as the Army's international leader acknowledged and called upon the ultimate source of wisdom for the needs of that nation.

The Army's addressing of issues reached all the way into the Gen-

General Eva Burrows prays with USA President Reagan in the Oval Office, accompanied by, left to right: Colonel Ernest A. Miller, Commissioner Norman S. Marshall, Commissioner Andrew S. Miller.

eral Assembly of the United Nations. There was perceived the grave danger posed by the nuclear arms race, with weapons of massive destruction not only apt to be used in warfare but also possibly coming into use by accident or misunderstanding. The nightmarish growth to monstrous dimensions of nuclear arsenals imperiled the survival of our planet and the human race. The Salvation Army was constrained to raise its voice in opposition to this global insanity. In 1988 Commissioner Andrew S. Miller, USA national commander, represented General Burrows before a General Assembly session devoted to disarmament and peace, urging it to "save succeeding generations from the scourge of war." Representatives of the nations of the world listened as there resonated through their historic venue this clear call from a leader of God's Army for relief from the escalation of terrifying weapons of mass destruction.

The Salvation Army had asserted its belief in the sanctity of life, founded on biblical teaching that a life commences before birth, that each life is of infinite value, and that God has compassion for the defenseless. The Army's pro-life position was buttressed by new medical evidence concerning development of the human fetus. It accepts that termination of a pregnancy may be justified when competent medical staff judge that it poses a serious threat to the life of the mother or could inflict irreversible physical injury to the mother. Its position statement on abortion concludes: "A serious commitment to the protection and care of the unborn calls us equally to promote and work for a society in which all those born into it find loving acceptance and the resources necessary to enable them to reach their fullest potential."

Some years ago the author, while speaking at a family camp meeting series in California, was approached by a young woman. "Are you the speaker here this weekend and the editor of the *War Cry*?" she asked. In response to my affirmative reply, she pointed to a beautiful six-month-old baby girl in a stroller and said, "She is here because of your *War Cry*!" She then told her story. Pregnant and unmarried, counseled by family and friends to have an abortion, she had decided she would have an abortion. She added, "Then I read your *War Cry* and that changed my mind." She referred to a special edition published on the theme "Alternatives to Abortion." Needless to say, that became a sacred moment and spot for the editor in chief who had produced that edition.

Pandemic of AIDS

While the pandemic of AIDS (acquired immunodeficiency syndrome) led some religious leaders to celebrate the disease as divine retribution, the Army avowed its standard for chastity and extended Christian love and its fellowship and worship to all.

AIDS became the number one health concern in many countries of the world. First documented in 1981, AIDS, caused by a virus that attacks and destroys part of the body's immune system, leaves those infected without defense against infections and certain cancers; there is no known medical cure. AIDS had become the new leprosy of the modern world, and every Army territory was asked by General Burrows to respond to the crisis.

It was estimated in the year 2000 that over 10 million children under the age of ten in Africa had been orphaned as a result of AIDS. The Army's approach there became twofold: belief that AIDS is best dealt with not just through the traditional medical model but also through behavioral change; and that the solution is linked to mission through caring relationships, community, and society.

Army medical care entered a new phase as Salvationists in Africa reached out to help hundreds of thousands of people afflicted with HIV. By 1986, with one in ten persons affected in Zambia, the Army's hospital at Chikankata that for many years had served people with leprosy, the number of which had greatly declined, revised its emphasis. It reorganized to serve people with HIV in both care and prevention, with outreach to the homes and community as well as providing hospital care.

Army medical staff at Chikankata perceived that any successful prevention program would have to build on the strengths of the family. The challenge was to make use of the family network before an entire generation of young adults was lost. They responded with a home-based care and prevention team to visit and conduct counseling sessions with AIDS patients and their families in their villages and, where possible, in the wider community.

The team quickly developed innovative approaches that proved influential regionally and nationally in Africa, and internationally. Chikankata's AIDS teams, in their counseling, aimed to transfer the responsibility for AIDS prevention from health workers to individuals, families, and the community. "They are the only ones who can change their behavior and stop the spread of the virus," said the hospital's project manager, Salvationist Bram Bailey.

In Soweto, South Africa, in August 1993, the Army's Bethesda House opened a home for the abandoned babies of HIV-positive mothers, the first facility of its kind in the country. Faced with the dramatic increase in the number of children in need of this type of care, the Army opened a second home for forty babies. Even though the deaths of children in these two homes were an ongoing tragedy, care continued undeterred.

The AIDS pandemic ushered in a new era of ministry. Army staff both host symposiums and participate in concerted efforts to address the issue, including International Aids Conferences. Partnerships with government and agency funding sources substantially increased resources for operations in developing countries, as well as fostering shoulder-to-shoulder efforts with other Christian relief and humanitarian agencies.

Anti-Suicide Ministry

The World Health Organization reports that one million people take their own lives each year. Suicide in William Booth's day aroused concern, leading him to write, "The act of self-destruction is on the increase in every land and among all classes. Statistics of suicides are alarming. Can anything be done to prevent the suicidal tide from rising? It seems to me that we must supply the friendless, the dazed, bewildered creatures with a guide, and above all lead them to the One who is still saying, 'Come unto me, all you that labor and are heavy laden, and I will give you rest.'"

Booth established in 1907 an Anti-Suicide Bureau. Soon afterward a standing order was placed in every police station in London to hand over certain categories of would-be suicides to the Army for sympathetic remedial treatment instead of punishment. During the first three years of the Bureau's work, more than a thousand persons, from nearly all ranks of society, called at the London office. Three years later the number had risen to over five thousand, and of all who had applied for counsel, the Army knew of only five who had carried through their intention to commit suicide.

An application of the founder's idea was soon thereafter made in the area of Sydney, Australia, where along the coastline there is a break known as the Gap. Its precipitous cliffs, with surf boiling over the rocks, seemed to have had a fatal fascination for suicides. That is, until a notice was posted at the site inviting all who were in trouble to get in touch with The Salvation Army. In the initial days as many as sixty people every week called for counsel at the Anti-Suicide Bureau in Sydney.

The Army in Australia is still in the forefront of the Army's ministry in this field, through the dedicated service of Envoy Alan Staines. In 1983 Staines felt called of God to establish a twenty-four-hour help-line counseling service from his home, and later that year left his work as a builder, was commissioned an envoy, and set up his service in Sydney. He recalls, "The program grew like 'topsy.'" On December 1, 2007, Staines was recognized for his devoted work with conferment of the Order of the Founder.

In 2007, in Ireland, at a conference of the International Association for Suicide Prevention, of which Staines is a member, The Salvation Army was recognized for the centenary of its anti-suicide ministry and as the first global organization to commence suicide prevention programs.

Today, through its multiple ministries, the Army helps persons to link up with the spiritual resources that will enable them to get through life's difficulties. It renders practical counseling in times of natural disaster, personal trouble, and traumatic circumstance, and continues on all fronts of human need to provide support to those at risk of suicide and to family and friends who have been bereaved by suicide.

Social Justice Commission

On July 1, 2007, a new arm of International Headquarters came into being, known as the International Social Justice Commission. Its importance was identified with the appointment of the highest officer rank as director, Commissioner Christine MacMillan, a skilled administrator with extensive experience working with social issues. Although administratively linked to IHQ, the office is located in New York City just four blocks from the United Nations.

General Shaw Clifton announced it as "a new global initiative with regard to issues of social justice," to serve as an advocate and adviser on social, economic, and political issues and events relating to social injustice in the world, and to assist in addressing social injustice in a systematic, measured, proactive, and Christian manner. The commissioner was also appointed the Army's representative to the United Nations, the Army having a long-standing position within the NGO (nongovernment organization) structure of the United Nations, and with a consultative status with its Economic and Social Council.

MacMillan stated that "social justice can be interpreted broadly — including topics of human trafficking, climate change and caring for God's creation, and religious freedom — but focuses on standing on behalf of the marginalized." She encapsulated her philosophy: "I believe that The Salvation Army needs to stand up and be counted, but I would rather have a meeting with the head of a country than to stand outside of his office with a megaphone."

William Booth's compassionate vision a century ago continues as a beacon on the dark and difficult paths of life, to be a friend to the friendless, a hope for the hopeless, and a means of God's grace to all who will seek his salvation and strength.

TWENTY-THREE

Human Services

For I was hungry and you gave me something to eat, I was thirsty and you gave me something to drink, I was a stranger and you invited me in.

Matthew 25:35

The Salvation Army's birthright is that of serving as the Good Samaritan on the Jericho roads of life, where people are wounded and in need of life support. Billy Graham once described its mission: "The Salvation Army serves with the cup of cold water in one hand, and the Gospel in the other hand."

Art by Karen Yee Lim

Both space and concession to reader interest limit this account of the vast network of Salvation Army social services around the world. Human needs vary in both the countries where the Army serves and the various periods of its more than a century of operation. This chapter presents but a representative sampling of what could fill several volumes of accounts.

"Go and Do Something!"

Bramwell Booth recalled a defining moment in the Army's history when he had called at his father's house early one morning in 1887. "No good-morning-how-do-you-do here! 'Bramwell,' he cried, when he caught sight of me, 'did you know that men slept out all night under the bridges?'"

William Booth had arrived in London very late the night before and had to cross a bridge to the city to reach his home. What the founder had seen on that midnight return accounted for this morning's tornado. Bramwell replied, "Did I know that men slept out all night on the bridges? Well, yes. I replied, 'A lot of poor fellows, I suppose, do that.'"

"Then you ought to be ashamed of yourself to have known it and to have done nothing for them," he went on vehemently.

"I began to speak of the difficulties, burdened as we were already taking up all sorts of work for the poor. My father stopped me with a peremptory wave of his hands."

"Go and do something!" he said. "We must do something."

"What can we do?"

"Get them a shelter!"

"That will cost money."

"Well, that is your affair! Something must be done. Get hold of a warehouse and warm it, and find something to cover them. But mind, Bramwell, no coddling!"[1]

The founder's now famous command, "Go and do something!" was destined to alter the future of The Salvation Army. Within a year, in 1888, the first facility for food and shelter was opened in London with accommodations for some 70 men. Soon more than 2,000 persons were being fed daily, including more than 700 hungry children who came for soup. Pressing need and success led to more being established.

On the continent of Europe and in other overseas stations, Salvationists were quick to follow the lead of Britain. Today, in the world, 11 million lodgings are provided each year for people in need who sleep under Salvation Army roofs each night. Such a statistic would be the envy of any hotel chain, but of course, none of the major chains can rival the Army's rates, nor its personalized service!

The Social Reform Wing

The "Food-for-the-Million" shops were the Booths' first entry into the social service sphere, with which The Salvation Army's name came to be unalterably associated. There were five such shops in London in 1872, open twenty-four hours a day and catering to the poor, offering hot soup and a three-course meal. These shops closed down in 1874, due to inadequate fiscal support.

The social service efforts of the Army, at first tentative and experimental, soon proved their worth and quickly expanded in number and quality of service provided. By 1890 the launching of Booth's *In Darkest England* scheme had given birth to what became known as the Social Reform Wing. These services were destined to become an integral part of the still-nascent Salvation Army.

William Booth early came to the conviction that God required his followers to be concerned for the temporal as well as spiritual welfare of others. At a 1911 gathering of Salvationists, one year before his death, he said, "Our social operations are the natural outcome of Salvationism, or, I might say, of Christianity as instituted, described, proclaimed, and exemplified in the life, teaching, and sacrifice of Jesus Christ. Social work harmonized with my own personal idea of true religion from the hour I promised obedience to the commands of God, as well as comply with the commands of my Lord, who had expressly told me that I was to feed the hungry, clothe the naked, care for the sick, and visit the prisoners."

He at that time admitted, "For a long time, however, I failed to see how this work could be done in any organized or extensive manner." That would come later with his *Darkest England* scheme.

When it started, Booth likened the social work of the Army to an ambulance picking up at the foot of the precipice of human failure those who had fallen. But the better method, he claimed, would be to erect a fence at the top. First he organized the ambulance brigades, with centers where the "wounded" would be cared for. But while the "ambulance" remained available, it was superseded by a vast network of medical, educational, institutional, welfare, and vital ministries to keep people from going over the brink of the precipice.

Social work was in the spiritual DNA of the founder. But there was no doubt of what he saw as the foundation of the Army's human services: "All the social activity of the Army is the outcome of the spiritual life of its members. All social service must be based on the spiritual, or it will amount to little in the end."

Inside Prison Walls

Australia's first Army leader, James Barker, commenced in 1883 the Army's prison ministry, working in the opium dens and with released prisoners. At first Barker could interview prisoners only from behind bars and in the presence of a guard. With perseverance he obtained the right of every prisoner to be visited in private by his minister, including Salvationists, to render more effective the Army's postrelease work with prisoners.

In 1884 "the mother emulated the child" as London started its own Prisoners' Rescue Brigade. Prisoners were visited privately in their cells, and some were converted in Army meetings within the prison walls. Ex-convicts were aided with counsel, housing, and employment. The Army believed that a "new start in life" was based on "a new heart," and its double-pronged strategy rescued many from the pitfalls of their former life. "One sinner saved by grace," said William Booth, "will outlast the British Empire." The saying now dated, its truth remains.

The founder had charged his troops, "Go for souls and go for the worst!" General Booth himself spoke to convicts on several occasions, including women prisoners. Starting in 1916 an annual Prison Sunday was observed.

Correctional ministries spread with varied approaches around the Army world. Ministry takes place outside prison walls for newly released prisoners and ex-offenders, and includes halfway houses, employment services, parole and probation supervision. In the 1980s the Army took over the misdemeanor probation services for thousands of clients in the state of Florida. For more than ten years retreats were held for women inmates and their children at The Salvation Army's USA camp in New Jersey.

In June 2000, at the Army's International Congress in Atlanta, one of the recipients of the Order of the Founder was retired Major Kathryn Honaker Cox (B.S., M.S., criminal justice), honored for her years of dedicated prison ministry. She still coordinates the USA Southern Territory's Bible correspondence courses for over 30,000 inmates and counsels the families of condemned prisoners, as well as the prisoners themselves on death row; she has witnessed twenty-one executions. On that occasion it was announced that she had recently enrolled a death row inmate as a Salvation Army soldier.

The Army takes seriously the words of Jesus: "I was in prison and you came to visit me" (Matt. 25:36).

Health and Medical Services

In 1889 the Army opened its first maternity home, where unwed young women and their infants would be cared for until able to go out into the world again. In years to come many such homes would be opened around the world, providing the best obstetrical care along with counseling and social service as needed.

Early rescue homes for prostitutes were soon followed by a wide variety of homes for women and children in desperate situations. The maternity homes and hospitals before the turn of the century had become the havens for unmarried mothers. Care provided reached a high standard, and also included private patients who sought the expert and compassionate care provided in the Army hospitals. The branch of what became the Women's Social Service Department, inaugurated in 1884, at its peak oversaw numerous maternity homes and hospitals operating at nearly full capacity throughout the 1950s. Many women would look back and express their gratitude for that time of vital care that made a difference both for them and for their child.

The United States moved into the health field in a major way, developing a chain of more than thirty homes and hospitals. India had its leprosaria as well as its general hospitals. Japan opened twin hospitals in Tokyo that became major centers for the nation's health and healing. Maternity homes and hospitals served in a number of European countries, and clinics, dispensaries, and hospitals opened in a number of countries including Australia, Canada, Ghana, India, Indonesia, Japan, Korea, South Africa, the United Kingdom, the United States, and Zaire.

The 1960s were marked by changing social mores including more common birth control methods; abortion was legalized in the United States in the early 1970s. In Western countries society developed a tolerance for pregnancy outside of marriage, and the unwed mother became mainstreamed. Anonymity became passé; society became increasingly litigious; exorbitant liability insurance and spiraling hospital costs, along with the Army's anti-abortion stance, required the Army's maternity hospitals to review their focus. Some institutions moved into geriatric care, such as both the Mothers' Hospital and the Booth Hospital in South Africa. The converging of these social, economic, and cultural factors resulted in the closing of most homes and hospitals in the 1970s.

Through program redesign many health centers had become outward-looking instead of remaining institutionalized. The Harry Williams Hospital in Cochabamba, Bolivia, in the early nineties developed a community health program with a training program for community health volunteers. The goal was to provide clinical care, but within the context of counseling, pastoral care, and interaction with community in its capacity to make decisions. Thus care and prevention came to be seen as indivisibly linked. This fundamental integration of the Army's health services included a multidisciplinary approach, networking between government and nongovernment agencies, and linking policy initiatives from the community to higher levels. The Army's tradition of health work was making a major transition in vision and direction, from being a "provider" to being a "participant" with the core concepts of care, community, change, and hope. Also, as hospitals in the West began to close or transition in recent decades, mission hospitals endured and added large networks of health facilities and programs.

The Army's health services in Africa have changed as rapidly as the nations in which they exist, being affected by politics, economics, wars, and internal liberation struggles. With malnutrition the number one cause of death in some African countries, the Army developed nutrition programs in Zaire, Congo, and Zambia. Primary health care with growth monitoring, oral rehydration for diarrheal disease, breast-feeding and immunization in Bangladesh were demonstrations of ways in which health issues became entry points to community development.

In the field of social-medical service, The Salvation Army established leper settlements, beginning in Indonesia in 1908. Two leper hospitals were opened in South India, along with care facilities in Africa. The advent of multidrug therapy in the 1980s, together with the emphasis on community rehabilitation, led to a reduction in the number of persons with leprosy under the Army's care. Consequently Army treatment centers transitioned to caring for those with AIDS.

Paradigm Shifts

Paradigm shifts in the 1990s impacted the Army's worldwide health ministries. Its institutions that had cared curatively modulated into promotive and preventive health care. The Catherine Booth Hospital in Nagercoil, India, designed an outreach from a hospital resource center so that home care and counseling could lead to attitude and behavior change by individuals, families, and communities. The approach included clinical care but also counseling, pastoral care, and education.

In the 1940s The Salvation Army had more than sixty medical facilities around the world, focused primarily on maternity services. The Army's Mothers' Hospital in London (1913), and its sister hospital in Manchester (1919), trained more than 600 officer-nurse midwives to staff Army institutions around the world, until those programs were incorporated into the British Public Health Service in 1986.

Its coast-to-coast Grace Hospitals had been the flagship of the Army's social service in Canada, with 75,000 patients admitted each year to the eleven hospitals, two of which had nurses training programs that graduated over 100 persons annually. Nearly 25,000 children were born in Army hospitals in Canada in one year, with Halifax Grace Hospital averaging as many as twenty births a day. The "Grace" in Vancouver was the largest maternity hospital in the country; it also had a prenatal and diagnostic treatment center. However, in 1994 the Army brought to a close its sixty-seven-year administration of Vancouver's Grace Hospital, as it became no longer possible to meet the expectations of the public and government within terms of reference established for hospitals in Canada. The winds of change also led to closure in 2002 of the seventy-seven-year service by St. John's Grace Hospital, and services modified at Calgary Grace and Halifax Grace Hospitals. The Winnipeg

Grace Hospital, a 250-bed general hospital and one of Canada's most successful, traces its roots to 1891.

Salvation Army health programs began to move into the field of palliative care. In Japan in 1989 a 30-bed hospice in Kiyose for the care of the terminally ill and their families was dedicated.

The William Booth Memorial Hospital in Covington, Kentucky, was sold in 1990 when Army operations ceased at this facility after seventy-five years of medical service. The Booth Hospital in Chicago joined the retired ranks of Army hospitals that had rendered a valuable service for many years. The Booth Memorial Medical Center in New York, a 417-bed hospital that admitted over 20,000 patients annually, and another 100,000 through emergency services and outpatient clinics, and had an annual budget of over $200 million, was the Army's largest single institution in the world. Its comprehensive program of patient care had received the highest level of recognition in the medical field. But hospital administration became increasingly complex, beset with spiraling medical cost, costly equipment having an early obsolescence. After extensive evaluation the difficult decision was made in 1992 to sell this last of the Army's hospitals in the USA, closing a chapter of valued and noble ministry.

Alcohol had long been regarded as a significant problem affecting those under the care of the Army. The need for greater emphasis on prevention and the early treatment of those with an alcohol addiction became apparent. Among new programs was a model in holistic treatment started in Costa Rica. The Salvation Army ultimately initiated a two-pronged thrust in its spiritual and social rehabilitation to alcoholic men.

A specialized program, initiated in the USA, called Harbor Light was extended to skid row (down-and-out) residents and now boasts thirty-eight centers. Work therapy became an essential ingredient both for the recovery of the men and for help in defraying the large overhead cost for such a program.

The Men's Social Centers, now known as Adult Rehabilitation Centers, host 191 addiction dependency resident programs worldwide. They adopted modern retailing techniques by refurbishing furniture and selling it at retail stores, along with low-priced clothing, antiques, and all sorts of knickknacks. These centers have become one of the most effective and successful frontline ministries of the Army, providing resident care and comprehensive social service ministries. Clients are aided with prevention, alleviation, rehabilitation, treatment, guidance, education, and opportunities for personal development. Overcoming addiction to substance abuse and becoming stabilized in the community are major goals, with clients often being recognized for one year or more of sobriety. Over 10,000 seekers — those who profess salvation in Christ — are annually recorded by these centers in the States. The history and panoply of these ministries have been recorded by Salvationist professor Edward H. McKinley in his book *Somebody's Brother* (Harper and Row, 1980).

The Army's substance abuse treatment programs in recent years have adapted to the new demographics with an increasing number of women clients, and have dealt with the problems of drug addiction and the spread of AIDS.

A Galaxy of Ministries

In response to its founder's dictum "Go and do something," Booth's Army today works around the globe and around the clock. Its holistic ministry has spawned a galaxy of global services, including hospitals, Eventide homes, hostels for the homeless and for those recovering from addictions, nurseries, children's homes, and schools that now serve over 300,000 pupils. Dynamic overseas projects in less developed countries continue to alleviate poor health and widespread unemployment; provide clinics, health education, and nutritional support; train medical personnel; and sponsor agricultural projects and animal husbandry, vocational training, homes and institutes for the blind and handicapped, and missing persons bureaus. The Army's caring ministry is found at the front lines of tragedy around the world, including in the refugee camps, among those struck by natural and man-made disasters, and amid the burgeoning population afflicted with AIDS.

The first Eventide home for the elderly was introduced in Australia in 1901 and was soon duplicated in other advanced countries. Besides Australia, they sprung up in Norway, Sweden, France, Canada, and Kenya. They offered an alternative not only for poverty but also for loneliness.

Since the 1970s in the USA West, multistory apartment buildings for low-income elderly persons, known as Silvercrest Residences, became a major development. Capital funding and rental subsidy were provided by the government's Department of Housing and Urban Development (HUD). Upon construction, the residences, with up to 257 units, were turned over to the Army for administration. It may seem strange to find the Army in the apartment business, but the concept is to provide more than just housing. They were designed to provide clean, safe, and comfortable housing in an environment responsive to the needs of the individual residents. They were operated in concert with adjacent corps community centers, providing a range of supportive services to sustain independent living and to enrich the quality of residents' lives through opportunities for social fellowship, personal growth, and spiritual nurture. The USA Western Territory has thirty-nine such residences — thirty-five subsidized by HUD and four Army-owned — with a total of 3,258 units. In recent years fiscal and administrative concerns halted further expansion.

The Army's missing persons ministry, one of its oldest social services, was established in 1888 in London. One hundred years later missing persons departments were found in virtually every Army territory. Dramatic encounters ensued, such as twin sisters separated at birth with each put out for adoption, and some forty years later being united for the first time by the Army's missing persons ministry. Now called the Family Tracing Service in London, it received some 3,728 inquiries in a recent year; 85 percent of them were concluded successfully, and every working day an average of 10 persons were successfully traced and reunited with their families. In England, Elsie May Ashford of Southampton met her brother William Pring at his home, the first time they had set eyes on each other for eighty-one years. The reunion was recorded in *The Guinness Book of Records* as a new world record for length of separation of family members before coming together. For the Army, it was another day's work of the type it had been doing for more than 100 years.

Salvation Army Farming

Feed a man today and he will return hungry again tomorrow. But give him the means to produce food, and he will be able with dignity to look after himself and his family. Agricultural programs by the Army are an important feature in developing countries. Small farms produce most of the food crops in these countries, and the Army assists families with such programs as forming a cooperative, providing seed, setting up a marketing system, giving guidance on improved methods of agriculture, encouraging young people to stay in the rural areas. The Army also sponsors animal husbandry as an aspect of self-support and food supply.

At its institute in Zimbabwe, an agricultural program trained farmers in improved practices, including the use of fertilizers and crop variation. Livestock farmers worked with poultry, rabbits, goats, and bees, with the harvest of honey becoming a good source of income.

In response to the plight of rural poor, young farmers' clubs were initiated in Zaire, the project funded by Salvation Army World Service Organization (SAWSO) and United States Aid for International Development (USAID). Projects in Zambia included the growing of maize, a staple food there, and aquaculture with ponds that spawned a large harvest of fish. In India, buffaloes were loaned to poor farmers, who used them to work in their rice fields and to supply milk for their families. Over a period of two years the cost of the animal was repaid from income gained; the funds were used to purchase another buffalo to repeat the assistance to another family.

Child Sponsorships

A young boy for whom home was a cardboard box in Manila ate what he could beg or scavenge. Most nights, ten-year-old Carlos fell asleep hungry. His story was not unusual. Over 75,000 abandoned children wandered Manila's streets, easy prey for dealers in child prostitution. But Carlos's story did not end there. He was given his own bed at The Salvation Army Joyville Center in the Philippines. Meals, often made with food he had helped to grow, were shared with other children of the streets. What mattered even more was the love that enveloped him through the special Overseas Child Sponsorship Program. Directed for over fourteen years by Major Hildred Schoch of the USA, it enrolls over 1,000 individual sponsors who contribute a monthly donation, supporting over 3,000 children in more than twenty territories.

Since 1977 The Salvation Army has assumed the role of parent for nearly 9,000 orphaned or abandoned children in 220 Army homes for

**Major Hildred Schoch with
sponsored children in Teajon, Korea**

children around the world; sponsors hail from Australia, Canada, Great Britain, New Zealand, Norway, and the United States.

Addressing the Perennial Problems

The underlying premise of The Salvation Army's philosophy of social services is that the movement is simultaneously and inseparably both a religious and charitable organization. It is of one fabric, not two distinct, loosely joined parts. However, recipients of social services are not required to accept the Army's religious beliefs. They are helped simply because they need help. In some programs, such as substance abuse facilities in the Adult Rehabilitation Centers, clients understand that the spiritual program is one of the required therapies. These centers, fully

self-supporting, are free to be intentional in their evangelistic emphasis, including the requiring of chapel attendance.

General Shaw Clifton, in a *New Frontier* interview by Sue Schumann
Warner, May 2006, stated his view of the Army's current approach to its
social work.

> Some needs never change; they are perennial. They are constantly
> with us — poverty, homelessness, fractured families, and the conse-
> quential impact upon children. With the sophistication of the 21st
> century, we are still having to hand out food, even in the richest coun-
> tries of the world. We still have to feed people, and clothe people, and
> house people. So there is inherent in our societal structures a deeply
> entrenched inequity.
>
> The Army needs to be in the forefront of doing something about it.
> When I say doing something about it, I'm talking about causes, not
> just addressing the consequences. The Salvation Army needs to re-
> discover its voice of advocacy for those who have no voice. We have to
> recognize the deep assault that is taking place upon the exploitation
> of women — and also children — for sexual purposes. The Army, of
> all Christian bodies, perhaps with the exception of the Roman Catho-
> lic Church, is beautifully poised to use its network and its structures
> to do something meaningful in addressing these issues.

The Army's major weapons continue to be "the cup of cold water in
one hand and the Gospel in the other."

TWENTY-FOUR

At Front Lines of Tragedy

Whatever you did for one of the least of these brothers of mine, you did for me.

Matthew 25:40

"The front lines of The Salvation Army run through the tragedies of our world," declared the Army's former international leader General Arnold Brown.

The Formidable Challenge

The Army's mission statement presents the challenge: "to meet human needs in his name without discrimination." In today's global village our TV screens project images of the extremity of human needs, of individuals and families struggling to survive amid poverty, war, and ongoing crises.

Disaster wears many masks, and the Army over the years has responded to the onslaught of every kind of human misery, both man-made and natural. To be prepared for response, substantial training programs have been designed for Army personnel — full-time workers, lay personnel, and volunteers — including certification upon completion of courses. Dedicated Salvationists and volunteers stand ready, around the calendar and around the clock, to serve in the trenches of human need.

Army leadership identifies four related dangers to avoid when responding to disasters: (1) failing to grasp the opportunity to improve the lives of those impacted as we care for them at times of crisis; (2) allowing the least resourced to remain marginalized as they seek to recover; (3) permitting bureaucratic obstacles or failings to hamper the recovery program; and (4) failing to prepare for the next major disaster.

The Army could well be considered "seismographic," responding spontaneously to the tremors of tragedy, the devastations of floods, fires, hurricanes, typhoons, tsunamis, and earthquakes. In response to the outcry of anguish and suffering, it has responded in full force to global disasters, with trained personnel and equipment quickly on the scenes. It has often worked in concert with government-funded programs, the Army providing the personnel, expertise, and service, taking advantage of its infrastructure with staff and facilities already on location. The Indonesian tsunami, Hurricane Katrina, and other names associated with widespread human tragedy have become a part of its lexicon of disaster service.

The Earthquake and the Gold Fever

In the foreword of Evangeline Booth's *War Romance of The Salvation Army,* she writes of the Army's response that she initiated to two crises. "At the time of the wild rush to the Klondike in the 'gold rush' of 1898, the Salvation Army was with the only women amid tens of thousands of men upon the mountainside of the Chilkoot Pass, saving the lives of the gold seekers, and telling those shattered by disappointment of treasure that 'doth not perish.'"[1]

In Skagway was Soapy Smith, a desperado and local saloon keeper, who became a legend of Alaska. As a boy he had attended Army meetings that attracted his interest in Evangeline's visit to this outpost of civilization. Soapy made a late-night visit to Evangeline, where she spoke of a salvation from sin in this life and from death in the life to come. Five days after she and Soapy Smith had knelt in prayer, a rival gunned him down.

Those seven Salvationists mustered by Evangeline Booth in April 1898 had set out from Skagway, Alaska, over the dangerous Chilkoot Pass to Bennett, British Columbia. Evangeline writes: "They journeyed not for gold or gain, but for God. Somehow on June 22 they reached Dawson City, Yukon Territory, bursting its seams with 20,000 men, lured by the gold-rush. Those Army women served where none other of their gender had dared to go, and brought a message of hope to those whose dreams for a better life met a dismal end caught up in the Klondike fever."

Evangeline writes of another crisis to which she led her Army's response, when at 5:12 A.M. on April 18, 1906, San Francisco was jolted awake by an earthquake registering 7.9 on the Richter scale. While damage from the temblor was severe, the ensuing fires were catastrophic. As many as 3,000 people died and 225,000 (over half the population) were homeless. Salvationists met survivors fleeing the fire by boat at the opposite shore with round-the-clock shelter, hot meals, and needed clothing, and helped them communicate with their families and find missing children. Evangeline recorded in her book, "When that beautiful city of the Golden Gate, San Francisco, was laid low by earthquake and fire in 1906, the Salvationists were the first upon the ground with blankets, and clothes, and food, gathering frightened little children, looking after the elderly, and rescuing many from the burning and falling buildings." The Army's unique response to this crisis exemplified an accolade once accorded it: "The Salvation Army meets the need at the point of need."

Refugee Crises

In early 1981 General Arnold Brown announced, "We are confronted with a magnitude of displaced persons as never before addressed." The number of refugees in the world had mushroomed to over 20 million, the majority being women and children fleeing terror, famine, and genocide; they had often seen their loved ones suffer violent death. He described one setting with "a half million refugees starving on an arid piece of land, families with handcarts loaded with their life's belongings, walking from hole to hole, from furrow to furrow." Brown had seen Salvationists serving in the spirit of Christ on the borderland between Thailand and Vietnam, where he heard parents, knowing they could not keep a child alive, in anguish pleading with Salvationists, "Please take my baby."

Medical aid, both preventive and curative, became one of the Army's major components in responding to those exposed to the world's worst horrors of suffering.

In the late 1970s wave after wave of boat refugees fled to Hong Kong from mainland China; in one camp some 9,000 people were housed wall to wall. Salvationists provided an ongoing program of education, recreation, and spiritual care as families waited for their turn to move on to a new country.

In January of 1993, nearly 2 million Ghanaians were expelled from Nigeria. The Army was the first agency on the scene, responding with a worldwide outpouring of supplies and services. The government asked the Army to provide penicillin and liquids to combat dehydration; these were flown in. Medical supplies and basic necessities, including 53,000 servings of high-nutrient protein instant soup and biscuits from the USA, and more than 300 tons of food were received to alleviate hunger and malnutrition. Emergency relief services were provided to mothers and children who were without basic survival needs; liquid supplies were given to over 100,000 of those afflicted.

Famine, disease, and hopelessness descended in the winter of 1993 upon refugees in the battle zone of the country of Georgia; the refugees multiplied to more than 200,000 according to the United Nations. Tbilisi, the nation's capital and a city of 1.5 million people, was without heat or electricity. The Salvation Army became the primary humanitarian aid agency in Georgia, led by Captains Ronald and Linda Lee, USA officers stationed in Tbilisi. Through provision made possible by SAWSO, the Captains Lee directed a network of twenty-two feeding stations that provided hot meals to over 25,000 persons a day, averaging 340,000 persons a month in a United States Department of Agriculture "Food for Peace" program. For refugees trapped in mountain valleys, the Army provided food staples that were air-dropped by government helicopters. In Georgia, life was fragile; it had to be handled with prayer, and with practical aid.

Also in eastern Europe, led by Captains Geoff and Sandra Ryan (Canada), the Army took on the major task in 1994 for Chechnya refugees — serving malnourished and war-injured children, providing supplemental nutrition and emergency feeding of infants and child refugees. Dispensed were 79,525 items of supplementary food distributed to 8,638 children, and 70,000 units of supplemental food, including baby formula, oatmeal, baby rice, canned strained fruits, and bottled juices. Following the second Chechen war, some 225,000 Chechens fled from their homes, grabbing shelter wherever they could find walls and a roof, including abandoned train cars. A woman named Heda gave birth on a roadside near the border, where Salvationists found her and the baby, and took and nourished them both to health. "Help stations" in refugee settlements provided basic medical supplies, child facilities, bedding, cooking wares, client advocacy, and education and recreation opportunities.

Other crises laid claim to the Army's medical ministries, such as in 1990 and 1991 when cholera broke out in Zambia. Teams from the mission hospital at Chikankata and area corps supplied medicines, food, water, blankets, powdered milk, and comfort to the afflicted people.

The Army's compassionate ministry was a work done in the name of the One who, as an infant, was himself a hunted and harassed refugee. For Salvationists the world over, there was no bifurcation of faith as it presented a whole gospel in the name of the One who said, "Whatever you did for one of the least of these, you have done for me."

The Gigantic Afghan Refugee Project

In the aftermath of Russia's invasion of Afghanistan in December 1979, and during the ensuing nine years of conflict, more than 3 million Afghan refugees made up the largest refugee community in the world. In beleaguered Afghanistan, more than two-fifths of its 16 million people were either dead or in exile. In response to the mounting refugee problem on the Afghan border, with approval from the Pakistan government and an initial grant of $255,000 from the U.S. government, The Salvation Army was allocated three camps, and in 1982 its ministry among the Afghan refugees began.

As Afghans continued to stream across the border to escape the conflict between Soviet military forces and resistance fighters, the Army's work was extended following successive requests from the Pakistan government. It mushroomed from 21,000 refugees initially to 41,000, then to 76,000 and to 96,000, and ultimately to over 100,000, after which the Army had to decline requests for more refugees. The extensive project was made possible by substantial funding through SAWSO and support from USAID and other U.S. government grants.

Medical teams were assigned areas in which to provide extensive relief to the refugees. In the Afghan refugee camps of northwest Pakistan in the 1980s, The Salvation Army was the sole provider of medical care and vocational training for over 100,000 people — the most substantive single undertaking in its history. For over a decade, children who had become the innocent victims of war, with their families, received care and hope for the future from Salvationists who gave sacrificially of themselves in a compassionate and practical ministry.

The project developed a strong vocational training program, including leatherwork, metalwork, carpet weaving, embroidery, tailoring, and quilt making. All young trainees participated in literacy classes while learning their new skills, which emphasized the development of income-generating projects, enabling the employment of thousands in a tannery and leatherwork production center, a quilt-making factory, and a recently opened soap factory. Among personages to inspect the Army's work were, in one year, the president of Pakistan, the prime minister of Turkey, and Princess Anne of the United Kingdom. General and Mrs. Jarl Wahlström visited the program in 1985, and General Eva Burrows in 1990.

In 1991 the Army's sponsorship came to a close as the Pakistan territorial commander signed a memorandum of understanding with the newly formed Afghan Development Agency, created from the vocational training and income-generation department of the Army's program. The document effected the transfer of administration, allowing this agency to become independent and to manage its own affairs and raise its own support. Totally managed by Afghans, it was the first of its kind in Pakistan and attracted attention from other donor governments and agencies.

The program was a landmark in the Army's work among the dispossessed of the world, and was documented in the definitive book *A Task Accomplished* (1992). The documentary spoke volumes about a compassionate and practical ministry that impacted a beleaguered nation and people.

The task accomplished, the Army withdrew from the North-West Frontier Province. Some nine years later a Christian congregation in Kohat asked to become part of The Salvation Army, having observed the corps in Lahore. The pastors expressed a desire to train as Army officers. Undertaking a training course, they became auxiliary captains. A property was bought and soon a corps was established there with uniformed soldiers. Following the American invasion of Afghanistan in 2001, a new and smaller refugee relief project was set up, based in Peshawar. A property was purchased and served as a base for food distribution. Pakistani officers were appointed, together with relief workers, resulting in the Army, after the second refugee project, becoming established in two cities in the province.

When in 2004 General John Larsson visited Pakistan, a large number of Afghan refugees, to whom the Army had ministered at the most crucial time in their lives, made the twelve-hour journey from northern Pakistan to be at the special gathering, greeting the general and expressing appreciation to the Army.

Billy Graham in SA Uniform

The devastation wrought by the earthquake in northern California in 1989 brought Salvationists to the front lines of tragedy and human need. The violent shifting of earth reduced thousands of residences to uninhabitable, tomblike shells. Critical assistance was provided to thousands of victims, police, firefighters, and relief workers in the aftermath of what was declared the costliest disaster in U.S. history.

Billy Graham and Commissioner Rader visit disaster workers.

Nearly 600 officers, cadets, and volunteers managed twenty tent cities and provided assistance to the estimated 25,000 people sleeping in the improvised shelters.

Billy Graham spent more than two full days with Commissioner Paul Rader visiting the trenches of human suffering, praying with and encouraging those devastated by the quake. He walked with Salvationists through the mud and in the pouring rain to speak and pray with families whose homes had been destroyed and who were temporarily sheltered in the tents provided by the Army. Dr. Graham, who donned the Army's relief team cap and jacket, said, "I regard it a great honor and privilege to wear this Salvation Army jacket and to be associated with their work in this disaster. I have always wanted to wear a Salvation Army uniform!" Following his visit, a donation of $100,000 was given by the Billy Graham emergency relief fund.

Salvationists provided grief counseling and encouraged rescue workers searching for survivors. In the months following, nearly a quarter-million people received direct assistance from the Army's thirty-six centers of operation and scores of mobile canteens. Long-term relief efforts continued throughout the winter and spring. Their full-scale effort to aid the victims of the earthquake was described by Commissioner Rader, USA Western Territory commander, as "a great story of courage, compassion and creative response, of cooperation and coordination by community leaders, volunteers, agencies and our own officers and soldiers."

SAWSO Spells Hope

In 1977 USAID bestowed a grant that resulted in the Army establishing SAWSO (Salvation Army World Service Organization) at its U.S. national headquarters near Washington, to serve as a conduit for government and internal funds sponsoring aid and self-help projects in developing countries. SAWSO would become one of the most dynamic and far-reaching developments in the history of the Army. It engages to find long-term solutions and to promote self-help initiatives that address underlying causes of poverty in developing countries. As a vehicle for the effective delivery of development services and emergency relief, SAWSO has no peers. Its diverse programs would ultimately touch the lives of hundreds of thousands of people with new hope and enablement.

SAWSO's aim has been to help people help themselves through programs that improve living conditions, raise skill levels, increase productivity, and instill self-confidence.

It carries out its program through the Army's international network of facilities and personnel. Over 50,000 indigenous Salvation Army officers, employees, and professional staff form the teams working in developing countries. Since its inception SAWSO has channeled more than $100 million in goods and services, obtained through donations, contributions, and government grants, to developing countries around the world. It opened the way for the Army to partner productively with government agencies in channeling assistance to the most critical needs through sustainable programs that release the energies and preserve the dignity of those assisted.

SAWSO also provides material assistance in the immediate aftermath of a disaster, and promotes and supports longer-term assistance such as health services and income-generation projects for those affected by disasters. For many people around the world, "hope" is spelled *SAWSO*.

Rwanda Genocide

In 1994 the horrors of genocide that took place in Rwanda made worldwide news. In one of the world's worst atrocities, the country holds the world record for the most people killed in 100 days — an estimated one million, done with machetes. Army leaders reported that some churches long after the killing still had pyramids of bones and skulls inside, a ghoulish reminder of entire generations wiped out.

News releases from Rwanda showed poignant scenes of refugees walking among the dying and dead, desperate to get a cup of fresh water; of living children lying next to their dead mothers. A generation of Rwandan children were ravaged and traumatized; more than a third of a million were orphaned by the war. As this African country convulsed in genocide, God again called his infantry to the front lines and into the trenches of this human devastation, to serve with a heroic commitment and compassion.

The Army's response to the country's civil war and resulting genocide was launched with a team of seven officers commissioned into action by General Rader at his installation in London on September 1,

**Rwandan refugee children meet a new friend,
the Army's "first lady," Commissioner Kay Rader.**

1994. The officers, representing several countries, included experts in health, agriculture, education, nutrition, water, and community development. The team was to serve a three-month term, after which a follow-up team would be assigned. Their mission to the refugees' colossal suffering in that war-ravaged land was to establish villages for an estimated 100,000 abandoned children and unaccompanied minors. The general's appeal for $750,000 to support the project was met with quick and generous responses.

The team proceeded to Kigali, Rwanda, to initiate relationships with other relief agencies, both government and church-related. They assisted in the establishment of clinics and nutrition programs, the development of fresh water facilities, and the distribution of agricultural implements and seeds so that people could grow their own food. IHQ maintained contact through a satellite phone system.

This international team of Salvationists ministered especially to children left without parents, distributing food and other essentials, arranging sponsorships. A United Nations report estimated that 75 percent of all Rwandan children had witnessed a brutal murder, most often the murder of a relative. Army team members met the distressing sight of some of the 350,000 refugees, mostly members of the Tutsi tribe, housed in shelters made of plastic sheeting or canvas. Lieutenant Colonel Bjørndal reported, "I was appalled by what I saw. The only possessions the refugees own are the clothes they have on. To come here and see 350,000 people traumatized by an incredible situation, we realized that we are fulfilling the words of the Lord when he said, 'I was naked and you clothed me.'"

November 24-28, 1994, Mrs. Kay Rader visited the Army's relief team to encourage and further assess the Army's mission at that front line of human tragedy. As Mrs. Rader observed the Army's dedicated team, working tirelessly amid such an overwhelming scene of human suffering and devastation, she thought, "So few, doing so much, with so little, for so many, in so little time. Truly this is a miracle of God."

For years after the Rwanda holocaust, the Army was challenged not only by the immense material needs but also in dealing with the psychological legacy of the genocide. The great unseen was the damage done to people's minds and emotions, to their spirit. Never was the Army's holistic mission more greatly needed and applied to a suffering nation and people.

Without the genocide Rwanda would have been a priority for relief; with it, it was frontline. The team had managed to supply food, clothing, and medical supplies to approximately 80,000 people in two remote villages, contributing significantly to the rehabilitation and restoration of the refugees. When completing her term, Lieutenant Lisa Brodin was presented with a card by a Rwandan national. It read, "God alone carries our burdens. Yet he has carried mine through you, and the rest of the Salvation Army team here in Rwanda. I am trying to start my life over again because you have supported me in my sorrow."

Major Roland Sewell, Most Excellent Order of British Empire, reported that ultimately in the commune of Kayenzi, 36,000 people were supported with food aid for four months, until the seed distributed with the first food ration yielded a harvest. A total of 267 destroyed homes were rebuilt, 201 water sources rehabilitated, cattle and goat stocks revived, roads and bridges repaired, and orphaned children fostered by 1,500 families. When the immediate relief was completed, a holistic mission of development continued.

On the first Sunday of Advent, Mrs. Rader and Army staff were asked to attend a meeting with the people of the village, held in a large tent. Soon 3,000 persons had gathered, spilling over onto the hillside, to express their thanks for what the Army had done. A rousing hurrah was given to the team from whose hands they had received so much assistance and blessing. In tribute, the village *bourgmestre* (mayor) said: "Today we have received among us the representatives of the worldwide Salvation Army. The population has been plundered, and those still here would have died of hunger if The Salvation Army had not intervened. We no longer starve. Our dignity is restored. You brought hope to our people. You are our shield, our protector against all the disease, famine and poverty. You came, you stayed, you touched us. You are Jesus Christ's soldiers indeed."

The Army's mission met with such an overwhelming response that in the aftermath of war it was asked to retain a presence in the war-ravaged land. The groundwork for a corps was established, and later more than 560 people gathered to celebrate the opening of the Army's first corps in Rwanda, with Captains Bamanabio from the Congo appointed as corps officers.

In a short period a thriving corps program hosted 500 senior soldiers, 400 junior soldiers, four corps and two outposts, a women's home league, and trained, native Rwandan officers. The Salvation Army corps rose as a phoenix from the ashes of suffering, providing an ongoing nurture of the soul as well as the body. Many found Christ as the answer for the rebuilding of their lives and nation. Once again, God's soldiers of peace had the opportunity to place arms around a people shattered by war, disaster, and disease, to bring the compassion of Christ to men, women, and children in their moment of crushing tragedy.

Earthquakes, Hurricanes, and Floods

The "seismographic Army" responded to the tremors of tragedy, to the devastation of floods, fires, hurricanes, typhoons, and earthquakes. As the outcry of anguish and suffering was heard throughout the world, basic human needs and counseling services were provided around the clock.

The Salvation Army was established in El Salvador in 1987 as a response to the earthquake that nearly leveled the capital city of San Sal-

**Captain William Cundiff carries
a U.S. flood victim to safety.**

vador. Again, in February 2001 an earthquake destroyed 3,500 homes
and left 257 people dead and 2,500 injured. The Army cared for 3,400
refugees at its centers, and built sixty temporary homes for poor families whose homes were destroyed. Large amounts of food and medicines were rushed in and distributed.

When the great flood of 1993 deluged the heartland of America, as
the onslaught of the flood waters could not be stopped, neither could
the spirit of Salvationists in serving the thousands of victims traumatized by the disaster. The flood took forty-eight lives, displaced 70,000
people, and left more than $10 billion in damages. Emergency service
was provided, as officers, soldiers, and volunteers from all over the USA
Central Territory responded to the call for help by offering more than
800,000 volunteer hours. The Army established comprehensive case
management services and programs for rebuilding old homes and con-
structing new ones for flood survivors. Philanthropist and friend of the

Army Ross Perot gave a boost to the Army's relief effort by contributing $2 million in a challenge program where his gifts were matched by others, with contributions from around the country totaling more than $29 million, enabling the Army to maintain a long-term constructive relief program.

On August 29, 2005, Hurricane Katrina made landfall along the Louisiana and Mississippi Gulf Coast, leaving incredible havoc and devastation in its wake. Coastal towns were inundated; homes were torn from foundations by a storm surge that in some locations reached twenty-seven feet. Thousands of residents were evacuated, 1,330 persons killed, over 300,000 homes destroyed, 770,000 persons displaced, and 2.5 million people left without power.

Katrina unleashed a savage storm in the USA southland, but in its wake was also unleashed an unprecedented response of goodwill and compassion to the victims who suffered its catastrophic effects. The Army responded with an overall $362 million recovery effort used for reconstruction, housing development, volunteer programs, and job-readiness training. To implement the plan, the Army signed agreements with a number of organizations.

As part of the long-term recovery plan, relief was provided at Community Assistance Centers. In partnership with Habitat for Humanity homeownership assistance grants, survivors unemployed as a result of the hurricane received job training and skills certification. Team members of the Army prepared over five million meals, and provided over four million articles of clothing, 737,778 gallons of water, 39,731 blankets, 12,549 items of furniture, and 91,363 nights of lodging.

One young captain lost his life while serving the afflicted. Salvationists counted it a privilege to house the homeless, feed the hungry, clothe the naked, and put their arms around those who were hurting. What Katrina did was an act of nature; what The Salvation Army did in response was an act of God.

9/11 Foot-Washing Servants

On September 11, 2001, an unimaginable tragedy struck with the terrorist attack in the United States, with a destruction of life and property beyond human comprehension. Eighteen Army canteens, hundreds of Salvationists, and more than 1,000 walk-in volunteers responded, both

Salvationists in the trenches of 9/11

at the time of the tragedy and in the aftermath months of recovery and healing. The first Army canteen was at the scene within an hour, and ultimately some 8,000 Salvationist personnel and thousands of volunteers toiled around the clock, providing meals, lodging, and counseling, and distributing over 300 truckloads of donated goods that came from across the country.

The rubber boots of firemen melted as they worked in the smoldering debris, and the leather boots of police blistered. Major Carl Schoch, the divisional commander who led the Army's response to the tragedy, describes an extraordinary ministry on-site:

> It was here that Major Molly Shotzberger with others rendered a most remarkable ministry. As weary and distraught men sank in chairs, the Major would kneel before them, unlace boots or cut them away, pull away the "sooty waterlogged" socks, and gently place the feet in basins of cool water. She washed the swollen feet of the men, dried them with soft towels, dusted foot powder and drew on clean socks

and new boots. With a word of encouragement, a prayer, and frequently a tearful hug, she released the men to return to the hell that awaited them. In days and weeks that followed, Salvationists serving around the clock exemplified the ministry of "the basin and the towel." And I am certain that upon them was the benediction of the One who said, "As you have done it unto the least of these my brothers, you have done it unto me."

Said one New York firefighter, "The Salvation Army wasn't just about food and clothing, it was about a lot more. It was about caring. It was about somebody there to give me a hand up when I was starting to feel down, to help me go on."

Captain B. Bryan Smith, working "in the pit at Ground Zero," was approached by a doctor who asked if he was a minister. When he replied yes, he was asked if he would perform last rites for two firemen. Such a moment and request knows no ecclesiastical boundaries. The major quickly made his way up a high ladder leaning against the debris that led to where the firefighter lay dead. Rescue workers went about the task of taking the body out of the rubble, placed the man in a body bag and on a stretcher, and brought him to Captain Smith. Some thirty firemen and rescue workers, with helmets removed, solemnly stood around the captain. With one hand on the bag, he prayed and quoted Scripture over the hero who sacrificed his life that day and went to meet his Maker. The captain also prayed for comfort for the family and loved ones left behind, and for the caring men who stood around him. A short time later a second fireman, also now dead, was brought to the captain for his prayer. This requested ministry was repeated over and over again, with Army officers serving as chaplains in the early hours of the tragedy.

Other Salvationists served at the morgue where they met, prayed with, and counseled families of victims. That day, remembers the captain, "People just walked up to me because I was in uniform."

Gordon MacDonald, well-known minister and author, and his wife were among the volunteers serving and ministering at the site. The following is his testimony:

More than once I asked myself — as everyone asks — is God here? And I decided that He is closer to this place than any other I've ever visited. The strange irony is that, amid this absolute catastrophe of unspeakable proportions, there is a beauty in the way human beings are acting that defies the imagination. Everyone — underscore, everyone — is everyone else's brother or sister. Tears ran freely, affection was exchanged openly, exhaustion was defied. As much as I love preaching the Bible and all other things I have been privileged to do over the years, being on that street, giving cold water to workmen, praying and weeping with them, listening to their stories was the closest I have ever felt to God. Even though it sounds melodramatic, I kept finding myself saying, "This is the place where Jesus most wants me to be."

Gail and I spoke in a worship service at The Salvation Army College. When I began my talk I held up my Army cap that says, "Disaster Services." I told the officers and cadets that of all the hats and caps and helmets I'd worn during my life, this one brought me the most pleasure. I would keep it, I said, for the rest of my life as a symbol of an extraordinary experience where I felt I saw the Spirit of Jesus at work like never before. Life at the pit boosted my already strong reverence for The Salvation Army. No group has worked harder to balance the two calls of the gospel: the salvation of the soul and the salvation of society, the proclamation of the Saving Christ and the cup of cold water.

At the three major disaster sites from the 9/11 terrorist attack, the Army served more than four million meals and provided counseling or social service to more than 100,000 persons. A ministry of grief counseling continued to reach out to families more than two years following the tragedy as the nation mourned the death of over 3,000 innocent people.

Tsunami in Indonesia

Indonesia, a necklace of some 14,000 islands strung out over an equatorial ocean, is the world's largest archipelago and its fifth-most-populated country with almost 200 million people. The Salvation Army commenced work in Indonesia, along with India and Sri Lanka, over 100 years ago.

On December 26, 2004, in one of the most destructive tsunamis in history, a fatal wall of water struck the coastlines of these three coun-

The Army was on the scene for the 2004 tsunami.

tries, leaving death and destruction in its wake. The Indian Ocean tsunami response highlighted the value of the Army's worldwide presence. As with many disasters in these countries, local corps members, cadets, and officers were on the scene within hours, providing essential relief. Reports of damage to Army property did not deter the Salvationists and volunteers working to enable families to move from dependency to self-sufficiency, and to provide long-term solutions.

On February 6, 2005, the prime minister of Sri Lanka laid the foundation stone for the Army's housing project. Located in the Galle district of that country, it was designed for a community of 1,000 families and included houses, community centers, a medical clinic, and playgrounds. Standards incorporated into houses constructed in Indonesia and Sri Lanka meant families moved into new homes that were better and stronger than the ones they so tragically lost.

The Army's Front Lines

In 1996 an Emergency and Refugee Service (ERS) department was established at IHQ, coordinated by Major Roland Sewell (U.K.), a professionally trained engineer. Its mission statement summarizes the Army's philosophy in its response to disasters: "Moved by compassion and in obedience to the example of Jesus Christ and commanded to love and care for those who suffer, the Emergency and Refugee Service of The Salvation Army strives within its power to provide support, training and resources to respond to the needs of those affected by the disasters and emergencies without discrimination." With this mandate the role of the ERS was to coordinate the Army's response to international disasters and to increase capacity, preparedness, and procedures for dealing with them.

Indeed, the front lines of The Salvation Army will continue to run through the tragedies of our world.

TWENTY-FIVE

History Makers

These were all commended for their faith.

Hebrews 11:39

To those knowledgeable of Salvation Army history and biography, the list of persons explored in this chapter will be noted for its omissions as well as its inclusions. This roster is intended to be representative, not exhaustive. The Salvation Army has been served by countless men and women, both the known and the obscure, who have been its heroes, heroines, and history makers. Such stalwarts on its landscape define a movement — its ethos and its compelling mission that lead them to rise above personal interest and comfort, at times even sacrificing life itself. May this representative chapter not only help define The Salvation Army, but also serve as a memorial to the courage and service for God of both the named and unnamed that have made a difference within this God-ordained movement. The lives of its saints are the heritage of the church.

We have already met in earlier chapters some of the Army's history makers. Seventeen-year-old Eliza Shirley pioneered the Army in the States, Frederick Booth-Tucker took the Army to India, Samuel Logan Brengle left his stamp of holiness teaching on the movement, Evangeline Booth had a courageous vision. Other names add luster to its ranks.

We have also noted the impact of the dominant personalities of William and Catherine Booth, Bramwell Booth, George Scott Railton, and some of the early pioneers. They nurtured the tender sapling of a movement that would eventually grow into a towering oak spreading its branches over the world, paving the way for an illustrious succession that would follow in their train.

The names that follow belong in the pantheon of the Army's heroes. Their story both defines The Salvation Army in their time and place, and serves as a reminder of its mission today.

Order of the Founder

Some of the names inscribed in this chapter will be identified as having received the Order of the Founder. In 1917, on the fifth anniversary of the founder's promotion to Glory, General Bramwell Booth instituted the Order of the Founder, the Army's international and highest honor for distinguished service. It was "intended to acknowledge such service, on the part of an officer or soldier, as would have specially commended itself to William Booth." The honor is rarely given; it involves a rigorous selection process with every nomination scrutinized by a panel of senior leaders at International Headquarters. Its recipients most often come from the rank and file of Salvationists. Recommendations are required from all levels of leadership under which the nominee has served. The proposal is forwarded to the international commissioners constituting the Chapter of the Order with a request for their recommendation. The general makes the final decision and usually presents the award. General Eva Burrows has called it The Salvation Army's "aristocracy within its democracy — an elite that has no connection with rank, status, or official responsibility — its heroes of the faith."

In addition to the Order of the Founder, in 1941 there was instituted the Order of Distinguished Auxiliary Service to mark the Army's appreciation of distinguished service rendered by non-Salvationists who have furthered the Army's work in a variety of ways. Mrs. Joan B. Kroc (USA) was admitted in June 2002, cited as "a woman of vision, compassion and commitment who has contributed by personal endeavor and financial generosity to the development of Salvation Army services and facilities to allow individuals of all ages to pursue excellence in mind and body." Her surname would ultimately enter the Army's lexicon in a major way, as will be noted later in this volume.

A third award was added — the Certificate in Recognition of Exceptional Service. It is awarded to Salvationists and friends whose work has been of outstanding value and should be placed on permanent record.

Communicator Extraordinaire

Gunpei Yamamuro as a student had been greatly impressed by the aims of Booth's *In Darkest England*. He enlisted in Japan as the first Salvationist and the first officer of Japanese nationality. He was appointed editor of the *War Cry* and was also a key member of the pioneering group that was attacked in 1900 when invading the brothels of Tokyo to offer freedom to the geisha women. Yamamuro became the first Japanese commissioner and territorial commander of his native country. He attended the 1929 High Council and was among the group of seven who visited Bramwell Booth during that time of crisis.

To Gunpei the Lord gave a shining and far-reaching vision — to present the Christian gospel in the everyday vernacular of the common people. This led him to write his classic *The Common People's Gospel*, a simple story of the life and teaching of Jesus that sold more than three million copies in more than 500 editions. It first appeared in 1899 and is still in print. He drew upon Japanese history, Buddhist teaching, and Confucian ethics to illustrate the truths of the Christian gospel. In a country where but 1 percent are Christian, his book, sold in bookstores throughout Japan, was to many a lone voice proclaiming the gospel. Kagawa, Japan's noted Christian reformer and receiver of the Nobel Peace Prize, called it his favorite book, "a masterpiece of religious literature."

The young Japanese student who had been called to enlist in Booth's militant Christian Army, who had marched on the streets to oppose prostitution, who had written the best-selling Christian book in his native country, and who had risen to the highest rank of Army officership was twice decorated by the emperor of Japan, and in 1937 was admitted to the Order of the Founder.

Helping the Blind to See

Captain (Dr.) Vilhelm Wille, a young Danish doctor, a specialist in diseases of the eye and in midwifery, upon becoming a Salvationist fulfilled his life desire to be a missionary. In 1907 he and his wife were appointed to Java in response to the government's request for the Army to take charge of a "beggars" colony where many were stricken with eye disease. Dr. Wille, from 1908 to 1913, in most difficult surroundings directed the healing of more than 5,000 sufferers, including performing 2,705 eye surgeries that saved many from blindness.

One of the most serious afflictions in tropical countries is blindness. It is caused by accidents at birth in which skilled attention is lacking, or by glaring sunshine, dust, and infection, which local conditions favor. The Army has not only maintained institutions for the education of those hopelessly blinded, but its officers combat conditions that cause this terrible affliction.

In 1915 Dr. Wille's work led to the opening of the William Booth Eye Hospital in Semarang, the capital of Central Java, Indonesia, where thousands were saved from blindness. In 1920 he was on the first list of admissions to the Order of the Founder, and received national recognition by Queen Wilhelmina of the Netherlands and, later, King Christian of his native Denmark.

"Queen of the Barge"

Women achieved a legendary role in the Army's mission. In Paris, one woman who alone had served over a million meals became part of the tour on the river Seine. As the tourist boat passed her venue, the guide commented: "And moored there, *mesdames et messieurs,* you see the barge of *l'Armée du Salut (The Salvation Army),* where every night more than a hundred poor men are given free lodging by Major Georgette Gogibus." The major's floating hostel was for many homeless of Paris an ever-present refuge in their time of trouble.

Professionally Georgette was a university-trained chemist who met the Army through offering volunteer service at a social service center in Paris. Once involved, she felt her personal lifestyle challenged by the realities of human need that confronted her. She accepted Christ as Savior and turned away from her promising career to serve her fellow men and women.

After serving in several appointments, she found her destiny in the floating night shelter moored on the Seine, a barge donated to the Army. An average of between 150 and 200 men slept on the boat every night. Gogibus, the only woman on board, lived in a sparsely furnished room in the bow of the barge, a simple latch the only fastening to the door. Creature comforts were few, but Christian care abounded. In charge of the barge for twenty years, she was affectionately known as "Queen of the Barge" and, to many, L'Admiral.

In 1958 she was awarded the Order of the Founder by General Kitching. Of her it was said, "If our Lord's blessing rests upon a cup of cold water given in his name, then surely the bed and hot meal offered to her nightly guests was an authentic Christian sacrament."

"The Angel of Amsterdam"

When the Germans occupied the Netherlands in 1940, Captain Alida Bosshardt was working in the Army's Children's Home in Amsterdam, situated in the middle of the Jewish quarter. In 1941 the Germans forced the closing of the home, at which time the Army made a transition into private residences. When the Germans cracked down on these homes, Captain Bosshardt, working to keep safe the eighty children in her charge, many of whom were Jewish, fled with them to the northern part of the city of Amsterdam and sheltered them in ten homes. At risk

Lt. Colonel Alida Bosshardt

to her own life, she would cycle past the Nazi soldiers with Jewish babies hidden in the wicker basket on her bicycle, taking them to safe houses to be cared for by Dutch families.

She went out to collect food, although it was forbidden. She was betrayed and captured by the Germans, but after two weeks the person who questioned her "forgot" to lock the door behind him and the captain was able to walk out onto the street. With help from the Dutch resistance, she managed to find homes for more than seventy-five Jewish children.

After the war, in 1948, Senior Captain Bosshardt was given responsibility for all social service work in Holland and set up her headquarters in the inner city of Amsterdam, where she was already known for her work before and during the difficult days of Nazi control.

For many years a one-room living area served as her bedroom, business office, counseling room, and place for any other function connected with her work. In the dangerous and debauched section of that great city, on many nights she was awakened by a knock on her door and a despairing cry for help. In his biography of Bosshardt, *Here Is My Hand,* Denis Duncan comments on her commitment: "It meant constantly dealing with drunks and the derelicts of human society at any hour of day or night. It meant living with the sin and evil of this world to the point of descending into other people's hells."

On an October night in 1948, in company with two women officers, she began to make her first contacts by distributing the Dutch *War Cry* in the district where 3,000 registered, and almost as many unregistered, prostitutes plied their trade. She came to know the prostitutes by sight and most by name. Always in full uniform and bonnet, with indefatigable energy and love, she was the chaplain and social worker to the diverse population of the red-light district.

While she was teaching courses at the School for Social Work at the University of Amsterdam, one of her students expressed an unusual interest in learning more about her work. To see and discuss the problem firsthand, the student was invited by Bosshardt to accompany her on one of her midnight patrols. As they were making their rounds in the pubs, a newspaper reporter spotted them, and the next day the escapade made the headlines. That student had been recognized by the reporter as none other than the young Crown Princess Beatrix, who had worn a disguise as they moved together in the red-light district. From that day Major Bosshardt's ministry with the prostitutes became "high profile." The princess was to become the reigning HRH Queen Beatrix, and a lifelong supporter of Bosshardt's ministry.

On April 14, 1962, The Salvation Army, under Bosshardt's leadership, opened its Goodwill Centre, serving the most needy in Amsterdam's inner city. On that same day she was awarded the Army's highest international award, the Order of the Founder.

When commissioned to start her work in Amsterdam's red-light district in 1948, she had been given 100 guilders (approximately $35) by the divisional commander and told she was on her own. Thirty years later at her retirement, she handed a jar to the general that contained 100 guilders, saying she no longer needed the money, as her budget was now $12 million a year. The center continues to serve in the heart of the notorious district, providing a safe haven for those who choose to leave the life of prostitution.

Her home country recognized her by naming a KLM Airlines Boeing 757 *Major Alida Bosshardt*. Her car had the city of Amsterdam crest on it, enabling her to park anywhere. The queen invested the colonel as an officer in the Order of the House of Orange-Nassau. One press release reported, "She is not a woman in a thousand, but one in a million."

In 2004 the Holocaust Memorial Organization recognized Lieutenant Colonel Bosshardt as Righteous among the Nations, the highest honor the State of Israel awards to non-Jews, in recognition of her efforts in saving Jewish babies and children during World War II.

On June 30, 2007, the major made her last visit to the city where she had worked for over fifty years. The country mourned and the media wrote of the death of a great hero. Her Majesty Queen Beatrix expressed her esteem for and sense of loss of this great woman, with whom as a princess she had visited bars and prostitutes and poor families in the red-light district. Madame Tussaud's also joined the remembrance, displaying in its window the wax figure of Bosshardt, holding a Bible and with a Salvation Army flag draped behind her. More than one million viewers watched the funeral live on television and heard the mayor speak of her as "the Angel of Amsterdam." A message from General Shaw Clifton eulogized, "We salute and honor Alida Bosshardt for her deep devotion to the cause of Christ, for her selflessness in serving others, for her example of Christlikeness, and for the wonderful inspiration of her discipleship."

In June 2008 a set of nine postage stamps was produced in the Netherlands to celebrate the life of Bosshardt, one of its best-loved citizens. The commemorative stamps feature a variety of illustrations of her in her famous Salvation Army bonnet. The Royal Post also produced a booklet portraying the new stamps and photographs of Bosshardt through the years. On the cover is her life motto: "To serve God is to serve people and to serve people is to serve God."

Salvationist Extraordinaire

Commending him as a "role model for all Salvationists as a unique combination of a man of vision, spiritual influence and leadership, an innovator, a teacher and a good Salvationist," General Eva Burrows admitted Dr. Robert Docter to the Order of the Founder in 1992. That same year Docter celebrated his fiftieth year of soldiership at the Pasadena Tabernacle Corps in California.

His local officership included corps sergeant-major, Sunday school teacher, and institutional visitor. His open-air leadership for many years at a busy crossroads was so unique and faithful that it became legendary. He played solo cornet for decades, marched in the Army's annual Tournament of Roses Band, and in 2008 was recognized for sixty-two years of uninterrupted service as a bandsman.

Dr. Docter was a principal architect of lay involvement in founding the Territorial Laymen and Officers' Council (TERLOC) and its divisional counterpart, DIVLOC, and served on multiple Army boards. He continued the work of his father in writing and producing the territory's "Army of Stars" musical program distributed to 1,500 radio stations across America and made available in compact disc and cassette tape to thousands of SA supporters. In 1983 he became founding editor of the territory's pacesetting newspaper, *New Frontier.* As a practicing psychotherapist, Dr. Docter worked for years with drug- and alcohol-abuse cases at the Army's Adult Rehabilitation Centers and social services. He is a retired professor of educational psychology and counseling at California State University and a past president of the Los Angeles Board of Education. His six children and grandchildren are all active in the Army. "Sergeant-Major Bob Docter" has helped shape Army history and has well earned the title "role model Salvationist."

A Noble Legacy

Colonel (Dr.) William A. Noble left his homeland of the United States to serve for forty years at the Catherine Booth Hospital in Nagercoil, India, expanding it from 40 inpatients to 500, from a primitive station with no telephone or electricity to an adequately equipped complex of more than forty buildings and many departments. He also developed thirteen branch hospitals, founded the 200-bed Evangeline Booth Hospital for lepers, organized and developed a government-recognized nurses training program, and supervised at government request a 500-bed leper hospital. For twenty years he was personal physician to the maharajah of Travancore, and was a member of the state medical board. He was a fellow of the American College of Surgeons and the International College of Surgeons.

The Salvation Army conferred on Colonel Noble its highest honor, the Order of the Founder, in 1957. The citation reads in part: "His 36 years' ministry brought healing to countless multitudes. Whether ministering to the prince or to the poorest of his people his Christian character has been expressed in his entire ministry."

Colonel Noble retired in 1961, but after a few months' rest returned to India to take charge of a hospital. His personal battle with cancer brought him back to Atlanta for radical surgery in 1963, from which he lost the use of his left arm. After forty-five years in India, Colonel Noble began a whole new career of service to humanity as medical consultant.

"Descent into Greatness"

As a newly commissioned lieutenant, Ruth Schoch was appointed to the Army's Chikankata Hospital in Zambia, which had a long tradition of outstanding ministry to the people in rural Zambia. In 1991 she shared with the doctor in charge a vision the Lord had given to her.

For years she had supervised the nursing program at the hospital. But in 1986 God clearly laid on her heart a burden for the increasing number of patients suffering with AIDS. "I'll gladly give up my position to work with the terminal ones," she explained. "They need to be given a chance to die in hope, to know that they are loved for Jesus' sake. God is asking me to do this."

"You can't do it. We cannot spare you as the nursing supervisor."

Major Ruth Schoch with AIDS baby

The harried administrator of the Army's Chikankata Hospital in Zambia was adamant. But Major Ruth Schoch held her ground. A Swiss Salvation Army officer nurse and midwife, and qualified in nursing administration, she had already given more than twenty years to the Army's acclaimed center of healing.

Stepping down from her position as matron in charge, Ruth joyfully made her own unassuming "descent into greatness." She saw her ministry as helping patients in their final days by "changing the face of death into something purposeful in preparation for eternity."

Her vision resulted in establishing at Chikankata the Bethany Ward for the terminally ill with AIDS. The inpatient program she began augments a community-based initiative that addresses the AIDS pandemic through education and evangelism, behavior change, and visitation outreach in the surrounding villages.

The doctor in charge shared his problem during the author's visit there in 1988. "When our patients meet Major Schoch, they no longer want to be released to go home. They want to remain here to die under her care." Many were ushered into the next life as the major held their hand and prayed the final prayer for them, enabling them to die with loving care and with hope for the better life to come.

Upon her retirement in 1998, she was recognized for her lifelong dedication by admission to the Order of the Founder.

God's Pioneer

At the time General Burrows was leading the Army's return to Communist bloc countries, on the high tide of that moment of history she looked for a leader with vision, energy, and devotion to the Army's mission. She found such a person in Commissioner Reinder Schurink, a dynamic leader in the Netherlands who, implementing new initiatives, had achieved outstanding results in that territory. In 1987, at the Army's large Centenary Congress gathering in Amsterdam, Queen Beatrix had bestowed on him the Order of the House of Orange-Nassau, the country's highest civilian honor.

His first appointment as a young and newly commissioned officer had been to a new corps in his native country of Holland. Now, years later, he was given responsibility for reopening the Army's work in a country, in its return to Czechoslovakia. His efforts gained support from the government and President Václav Havel. Following the good success of that venture in 1992, he was placed in charge of the Army's reopening in Russia. He, with Colonel Fred Ruth (USA), established a strong foundation that ultimately would result in the Army's most successful return to a former country in which it had been proscribed.

But there were still more frontiers to conquer, awaiting the abounding energy and vibrant spirit of this pioneer. After returning work to the Czech Republic and leading the Army's work forward in its dramatic reopening in Russia, he then ventured to oversee the Army resume its mission in the former Soviet republics of Ukraine, Georgia, and Moldova. All this historic undertaking away from his homeland, in which he served beyond normal retirement age, took place at the time his wife was suffering with Alzheimer's back in the Netherlands. Their separation was part of the high cost he paid for his devoted service to God and the Army.

Such was the heroic devotion that moved the Army forward to its new frontiers as political oppression gave way to new doors of opportunity opening for offering both the "cup of cold water" and the gospel to those in need.

For His Kinsmen's Sake

In 1949 Check-Hung Yee fled China just ahead of the bullets in the Communist takeover of his homeland. While in Canada as Salvation Army soldiers, he and his wife Phyllis were encouraged by the territorial youth secretary, Major Arnold Brown, to consider Salvation Army officership. They entered the Army's training school in California and, upon being commissioned in 1959, were appointed officers in charge of the San Francisco Chinatown Corps. They served their kinsmen in that capacity for the entire thirty-five years of their officership. During that period Yee designed and had constructed a new modern facility, conducted over 900 weddings, dedicated 1,000 babies, and developed a prospering corps with over 1,000 participants.

In 1978 his corps inaugurated a fifteen-minute weekly religious television program, the only such program in the Army world, and through it raised hundreds of thousands of dollars for recovery projects

Lieutenant Colonel Check-Hung Yee

in flood-ravaged districts in China, including a school and later a hospital. He became one of the first corps officers in the States honored by promotion to the rank of lieutenant colonel. Following ten trips to China and reuniting former Salvationists with the Army, he became in retirement the first director of the China Development Department, which since 1993 has initiated over 100 social service programs in twelve provinces of China, and wrote the stirring history of The Salvation Army in China, *Good Morning China*. He also authored several books that described the dynamic ministry of the San Francisco Corps. In 1997, in retirement, Yee was awarded the Army's highest honor, the Order of the Founder.

God's Flying Padre

During the Second World War, in 1941, Victor Pedersen joined the Royal Australian Air Force and became a qualified pilot. He later settled in Darwin, Australia's most northern city, its gateway to Southeast Asia, and one of the most isolated cities in the world.

While serving there in the Army's Red Shield ministry to servicemen, he had a vision for a spiritual ministry to the people in the outback of Australia. Pedersen made his dream a reality: he secured a small plane and pioneered the Flying Padre Service to outback Australia that links families living there to Army ministries. With his small open-cockpit, two-seater aircraft, for twenty-six years he "gave the Army wings." He brought hope and help to those in remote cattle stations in the vast northwest of Australia, and conducted weddings and funerals.

The arrival of his tiny aircraft at a station was a signal for everyone — stockmen, aboriginals, families — that a meeting would be held that night. Victor would accompany hymns with his concertina and then preach a gospel message. Sometimes he would show Moody Bible films, and often would distribute Bibles. He linked children in the Army's postal Sunday school operated from Melbourne and Sydney. The Sunday school he started with seven children in 1946 in Darwin ultimately became the Army's largest in Australia.

Known as the Army's "Flying Padre," his exploits and hair-raising experiences as a pilot became legendary among the Aussies. Once he crash-landed and was severely injured, but made a remarkable recovery. He aided the start of Army work in Bangladesh following cyclone re-

The Joystrings with Major Joy Webb at the keyboard

lief operations in 1970, and in his last appointment he served as the Army's prison chaplain for all of Australia, during which he inaugurated Bible studies for prisoners. Following retirement Brigadier Pedersen gave another five years of faithful service in the remote highlands of Papua New Guinea. A shining example of the Army's spirit of dedication, his outstanding service was recognized with admission to the Order of the Founder in 1999.

Innovative Music Evangelism

"Major Joy Webb demonstrated outstanding commitment to the creative and innovative use of music, poetry and drama in evangelism and worship, achieving unparalleled success in expressing the gospel in the popular idioms of the day while constantly reflecting the standards of the gospel in her personal life." So read the citation upon her admission to the Order of the Founder in 2004, by her U.K. territorial leader Commissioner Shaw Clifton.

In 1964, before Christian music made the U.K. charts, Joy Webb, a classically trained keyboard player and singer, was asked to get together a group of cadets with guitars to appear on a popular BBC program.

They called themselves the Joystrings. She later wrote in *Bridge of Songs* (London: Salvation Army, 2000): "From being amiably ignored by young people, we began to be able to draw and hold a crowd. So, from this time on it began to be clear that a change in the methods we had traditionally used in communicating our message was not only necessary but was, in fact, happening. It had yet to dawn on any of us that there was an enormous language barrier that had grown up between the Church and the ordinary man and woman. It took us a while to realize that we must both understand and overcome this."

With amplification and modern performance techniques, they played the highly popular music of the day such as that of the Beatles. Their new approach to evangelism became an instant national phenomenon, and they were besieged by bemused journalists intrigued at the idea of a religious group playing Christian rock music. Joy recalled, "We didn't really have any approach to evangelism and we most certainly did not have the music. But God had decided that my life was to go off at a right angle and that The Salvation Army was going to pioneer the first use the Church in Great Britain would make of the Sixties music culture."

That she did, and it snowballed. Within weeks she on the keyboard and her bandmates on guitar, tambourine, drums, and vocals were in the studio cutting their first record, using some of Joy's own compositions. Their music made the U.K. charts. International touring and albums followed. Joy Webb went on to write popular worship songs. She had moved The Salvation Army to the cutting edge of new music evangelism.

The appearance of the group on TV and at venues such as nightclubs scandalized some both within and outside the Army, and brought on a robust defense by General Coutts. He attributed their success to the realization that TV, radio, and records were now the way to reach people who had no contact with the church. "We are using TV as the street corner," he said.

These history makers, and the many others of their ilk, have left giant footprints in the Army's sands of time, and serve as models of what God can do when a life is fully yielded to him.

Twenty-Six

Heroes of the Faith

These were all commended for their faith.

Hebrews 11:39

Following in the train of the history makers are the heroes and heroines of the faith — those whose service was rendered in most difficult and dangerous places, all of whom paid a high cost, and some the ultimate cost of discipleship. The following, but a sampling of Salvationist heroes, call to mind Longfellow's memorable lines:

> Lives of great men all remind us
> We too can make our lives sublime,
> And departing, leave behind us,
> Footprints in the sands of time.

Hero with a Scalpel

Henry J. Andrews, a motherless child, was adopted by Emma Booth, daughter of the founder, and at age fifteen went with Emma and her husband Frederick Tucker to India. At age seventeen Harry, as he was called, became a Salvation Army officer, appointed accountant at divisional headquarters in Nagercoil. He worked by day in the office, but it was the people and their ailments that motivated him. Far into the night he pored over his small library of medical books. His leaders discerned his interest and allotted a tiny bathroom where he started an amateur dispensary that became the precursor of the Army's vast missionary medical work. At the time he had no medical training, but he was "a born doctor," and studied diligently all the medical works he could obtain.

Eventually his leaders arranged for him to take medical training in London. Following further medical study in Chicago, Harry at long last became Dr. Andrews, the first Army officer to earn a medical degree. Upon his return, through a donor's gift, a small hospital building was secured. In a short time the number of patients outgrew the hospital. Harry not only found land for a larger hospital but also designed the building and helped dig the foundation.

Henry began to treat patients in Nagercoil in 1893 and became known as "the father of Salvation Army medical ministry." His reputation as a healer grew rapidly, and patients walked miles to see him. Friends and relatives carried those too ill to walk. When deadly cholera raced through entire villages, he took his medicine to the people, treating the untouchables. Ultimately he helped found twenty-three Salvation Army hospitals and dispensaries in India.

In later life Lieutenant Colonel (Dr.) Andrews was requisitioned by the military for service during an uprising in northwest India. While attending the wounded, he was hit by a sniper's bullet, ending his life and compassionate ministry. For his bravery on the battlefield the British government awarded him one of its highest honors, the Victoria Cross; he is the only Salvation Army officer so honored.

Inspired by Andrews's vision and dedication, Army hospitals and dispensaries today continue their mission in India. A plaque over the door in the Catherine Booth Hospital, a 300-bed facility in Nagercoil, honors the birthplace of Salvation Army medical work.

In Jail Fifty-Seven Times for Jesus

One of the picturesque and indomitable pioneers of the Army was Joseph Garabed, a barrel-chested six-foot two-inch soldier in America known as "Joe the Turk." An Armenian, born in Turkey, he was converted in the Army in the heart of San Francisco's infamous Barbary Coast. He became a roving evangelist for the Army, gaining notoriety as an open-air preacher, and went to wherever the fight was the hottest. Clad in a fez and armed with a bugle and a yellow, red, and blue um-

Joe the Turk

brella, he paraded the streets of Los Angeles until the police were obliged to lock him in jail for disturbing the peace.

Wherever Salvationists were arrested for holding open-air meetings, Joe was there too, demanding a trial. "Arrested fifty-seven times for Jesus," he would, if convicted, keep on appealing until he won his case. He became an expert in court appeals in winning the right of free speech for Salvationists.

Fortified with decisions from superior courts in a dozen states, he could reel off the gist of them within seconds of entering a courtroom. With every victory came a decision to protect Salvationists who had been harassed. Early Salvationists in America owed their right to take the gospel to the streets to the one who went to jail many times to win their freedom for proclamation of the gospel.

Conquest of Devil's Island

Devil's Island had run its infamous torturous course of imprisonment since 1852. The Salvation Army received permission to work in French

Guiana's notorious penal colony, and in 1933 Ensign Charles Péan and five officers were sent to evaluate the possibility of the Army commencing work there. The governor of the island greeted Péan with the observation: "It's no use. This is a little hell that no man can conquer. Perhaps it's even too big a job for God." When twenty-seven-year-old Péan passed through the stone gateway, in his worst nightmares he could not have pictured the misery that greeted him — worm-infested huts, half-naked men, mosquito-haunted swamps.

Péan returned to help those confined there and to work for the abolishment of the colony. For twenty long years he labored on the island, enduring its draconian conditions. Often after gulping down the same foul-smelling messes as the convicts, he had to hasten away to vomit painfully. He once suffered sunstroke and collapsed in the street. An attack of malaria almost took his life.

Péan made an appalling discovery. Some 3,000 men faced a bleaker future even than the convicts. Under the infamous system, the law required that, following their release from the prison, convicts had to live in Guiana for a time equal to their forced labor time, or for sentences exceeding eight years, for the remainder of their lives; for most this equated to a lifelong quarantine. "When freedom is gained," ran a saying, "then your sentence begins."

Salvationists undertook to clothe, feed, and put the *liberes* to work. The rebirth of a man's self-respect became his reward. Hundreds of men were successfully repatriated. Péan wrote three books that brought pressure to bear on the government to close the settlement. His book *Devil's Island* was described in a review as "the most terrible account ever written by a Salvationist." In France and Algeria he pleaded passionately for abolition. Thousands flocked to the over 600 lectures he gave.

Some 70,000 convicts had endured life in that subhuman imprisonment. Péan reported that reform on the island was "far beyond the powers of the Penitentiary Administration and that the Penal Settlement should be abolished." In the meantime he worked with a twofold goal — moral and social. He helped establish clean homes and made available good and healthy food, a shelter, a workshop where men could exercise their former trades with a market for their labor, and also a marketing garden, an employment service, and "above all, an atmosphere of goodwill and hope."

Repatriation service for those free to return to France provided monetary aid for their passage, contact with family, and on arrival in France a welcome, clothing, and assistance in securing work. The country that had given such an inhospitable welcome to the Army's pioneers half a century earlier, now acclaimed this humanitarian approach to a social sore that had long been a reproach to this proud country.

Charles Péan had voluntarily lived on Devil's Island, considered the world's most infamous penal colony, to relieve the suffering of the men incarcerated there and to fight the French government for the colony's closing. In August 1945 Colonel Péan, then chief secretary in France, received a phone call from the Ministry of Colonies advising him that the government had decided to close the Guiana penal settlement. "Funds are available, and is The Salvation Army willing to take up the task of bringing them to France and make arrangements for their repatriation?" Péan did not require any time to answer the question — it was the crowning event of his long-sustained effort. Through the Army's advocacy the nation's conscience was stirred, and in 1946 Devil's Island was closed, with the final repatriation by the Army in 1953, the crowning event of a long-sustained effort.

Reader's Digest in March 1947 featured Péan's dramatic story in "The Man Who Conquered Devil's Island," by Clarence Hall. This infamous final remaining French penal settlement in French Guiana had been a living grave for 10,000 men.

It was indeed a job that seemed "too big." But Péan and his fellow workers, in their Franciscan dedication from 1933 to 1953, had a secret weapon — the power of God.

A Willing Captive

Herbert Lord, within six months of becoming a Salvation Army officer, along with Lieutenant Charles Sylvester, journeyed to Korea, arriving in Seoul by Russia's intercontinental railway in February 1910. There Lord would serve for over thirty years in varied appointments and in captivity, and would translate a number of books into Korean. In 1935 he pioneered the Army's work under difficult conditions in Malaya, where for his services in 1941 he was given the Officer of the Order of the British Empire award. The colonial secretary added a rider to the official citation, saying: "It is only since Colonel Lord and The Salvation Army came to Singapore that the social conscience of the community has been stirred." With the fall of Singapore in World War II, Lord suffered under Japanese internment.

Following release he returned to Korea in 1949 as territorial commander. In 1950, when North Korean troops crossed the thirty-eighth parallel, all missionary personnel were evacuated, with the occupying power suppressing all expressions of the Christian faith. Army buildings were seized, sold, leased, or vandalized. Rather than escape and leave his faithful flock, he remained, allowing himself to be captured by the North Korean army, again taken prisoner so as to be with his fellow Salvationists.

As a prisoner Lord became the leader and translator for those on the long notorious trek, known as "the Death March," to North Korea in blizzard conditions while wearing only light clothing. He and the column of marchers suffered severe privations in one of the most cruel and brutal experiences of the war. Many died or were murdered on the route, including nearly a hundred American soldiers and many civilians. Following three years of captivity, he was reunited with his wife and the Army, and was able to say: "To do one's duty, to do all things as unto God, conscientiously to seek God's will and to accept it happily, are lessons that a happy life for God has taught me."

He was regarded as a powerful thinker and preacher, and a dynamic personality, and was recognized as a hero both within and outside the Army. South Korean president Syngman Rhee in 1959 presented the retired commissioner with the country's highest honor for service to its people — the Korean Medal for Public Welfare.

Early in his ministry in Korea, Captain Herbert Lord visited a Mr. Chang, who was working in his rice paddy, and invited him and his family to the Army meetings. Chang, struck by the friendly demeanor of his visitor, responded, and with his family was converted to the Christian faith, he becoming a Salvation Army officer. In the mysterious ways of God, in 2007 retired Commissioner Peter Chang, living in the United States, wrote a book on The Salvation Army in Korea for its centenary in 2008. Peter, who himself had served as territorial commander in Korea, is the grandson of that early convert the young Captain Lord visited in the rice paddy. And fourth-generation Salvationists of the Chang family are presently serving in the United States. Herbert Lord's legacy lives on!

God's Servant in the Trenches

Major Eva den Hartog, trained as a nurse in the Netherlands, served in the most troubled spots of the world for over two decades. She tended the sick, fed the poor, comforted the dying, worked on medical teams in refugee camps, and nursed destitute Cambodians who had fled from starvation and genocide. She smelled the horrible stench of cholera, saw people dying of starvation, and witnessed dead bodies piled up, including those outside Calcutta in the refugee camps where they were being burned. She visited and did nursing in one camp into which 150,000 refugees, mostly women and children, were herded and dying in pitiful conditions. There was no water supply and scarcely any food. Sanitary conditions were indescribable. From 1974 to 1976 she took charge of the Army's work in Bangladesh, arranging for massive relief supplies; she was devoted to serving those most destitute with health needs, feeding, training, and clothing.

Billy Graham had this to say of the major's presentation, one of few to receive a standing ovation from 14,000 persons at Urbana '81, a national student missionary conference:

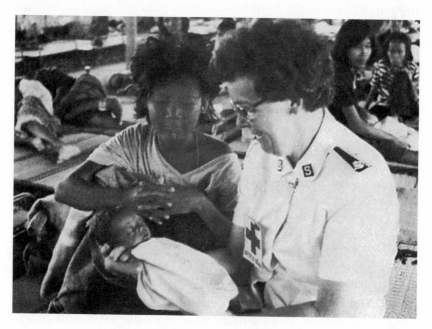

Major Eva den Hartog in refugee camp

The testimony tonight of Major den Hartog is still in my heart, because I've heard so much about this woman, seen so many pictures of
her in Zaire, Cambodia, Thailand, Bangladesh. I've heard my son tell
so many stories about her. Even where soldiers were afraid to go she
just went right on across the border to get to these refugees and take
care of the children, and lived in all the filth and all the dirt and all
the stench. She is one of the great people of our generation.

Such was the eloquent testimony of the world's leading evangelist
for a modern-day Salvationist heroine.

Modern-Day Martyrs

From the wars that ravaged nations in which the Army operated has
come a legion of stories of Salvationist sufferers and martyrs. In China,
Korea, and Eastern Europe under Communism, Christ's call to discipleship was costly. Many Salvationists paid the high cost of discipleship. The following serves as an example of those who, responding to
the call of Christ in the front lines of Army ministry, paid the ultimate
price.

Rhodesia, though haloed by natural beauty, has undergone unimaginable suffering of its people. In 1978 the Army world was shocked
and saddened to learn that a hail of terrorist bullets cut short the lives
of two young Salvationist teachers on the grounds of the Usher Institute, an Army secondary school for girls in Rhodesia, now Zimbabwe.
Lieutenant Diane Thompson, age twenty-seven, from England, and
Sharon Swindells, twenty-four, from Northern Ireland, as qualified
teachers had committed their lives to God in service at the school where
300 Rhodesian girls received full-time education.

At the time of this incident, Lieutenant Shaw Clifton (later to become general) and his wife Helen were corps officers at nearby
Bulawayo and had direct pastoral contact with the institute. The following is excerpted from his letter to this author.

We had personal experience of security problems due to the internal
conflict raging in Rhodesia at that time and the frequent episodes of
terrorist activity which selected missionary stations as soft targets.
The ultimate goal was to bring down the then white government. On

the night of June 7, 1978, we were leading a Bible study and prayer meeting in our quarters in Bulawayo. At about 8 P.M. the phone rang. It was Major Jean Caldwell, the principal. She said, "Shaw, it's happened." I knew exactly what she meant. I learned that two of our officers suffered gunshot wounds. I then asked about Lt. Diane Thompson and Sharon Swindells. Jean replied simply, "There is nothing anyone can do for either of them now." It was clear that Diane and Sharon were dead. The course of events that had taken place later became clear. A group of about 20 heavily-armed terrorists had taken up residence in the area, and at gunpoint rounded up all the teaching staff that could be found. Hearing the sound of an approaching vehicle, an order was given to open fire. This resulted in wounds to the teaching staff and in the immediate deaths of Diane and Sharon, both of whom were shot repeatedly in the back. They had been walking with their arms around each other and fell in this position. The worst nightmare had come true for all of us. The memories are etched forever, indelibly in my mind.

Clifton shares a capstone to the tragedy.

Sharon's father, when arriving at the airport, was asked, "Mr. Swindells, what do you think about the men who murdered your daughter?" Bill Swindells looked straight at his questioner and said in a steady voice, "I forgive the men who murdered Sharon." These words formed the headlines of the newspaper on the following day. I was in his presence regularly for many days after this and never once did I hear a single syllable of anything inconsistent with his airport interview statement. I realized that I was an eyewitness to the most powerful evidence of the Holy Spirit in this man's life and heart. This was grace at its most real.

It fell to Clifton to preach that Sunday morning; the Army hall at Bulawayo Citadel was packed to overflowing. He reported, "There were many seekers, among them Bob and Doris Thompson, parents of Diane, their only child. It was my great privilege to counsel them and lead them both into knowledge of Jesus Christ as their personal Savior."

As God so often does, in this crucible of suffering our heavenly Father brought blessing even out of brokenness.

Faithful unto Death

When in 1950 atheistic Communists invaded and took over Seoul, Korea, Major Noh Young Soo was sought out for questioning. He was ordered to march through the streets with his captors, after which he found himself facing extended gun barrels and an order to renounce publicly his Christian faith. Standing calmly but firmly, the major refused. Raising his Bible in one hand, and with The Salvation Army songbook in the other, he declared: "Whether I live or die matters not. Christ lives!"

As he knelt and prayed for his captors, rifle shots shattered the silence, and a modern martyr died for his faith. The merciless guards shouldered their rifles and marched away, leaving the body where it fell. But others cared, and the major's body was covered in a shallow grave — until, in 1958, his earthly remains were laid to rest in a more fitting place and his faithfulness recorded on a worthy memorial. History of the Army in Korea records that Major Noh was one of six Korean Salvationists "who died as martyrs for the Christian faith during the Korean war."

In *The Salvation Army Song Book* are words that challenge Salvationists today:

> I have read of men of faith who have bravely fought till death,
> Who now the crown of life are wearing;
> Then the thought comes back to me,
> Can I not a soldier be,
> Like to those martyrs bold and daring?

Faithful under Oppression in China

In 1990, a surprising and memorable moment came in London's Royal Albert Hall at the Army's international congress. General Eva Burrows called Salvationist hero Major Yin Hung-Shun to the lectern. "Major Yin," she said, "we remember how you helped The Salvation Army in China to remain strong after the missionary officers had to leave. We remember that during the time of the Cultural Revolution you were taken to the labor camp and there remained faithful to our Lord Jesus Christ. Your faithfulness to God and the Army, your endurance under persecution, and the inspiration that you have been to Salvationists would have

**Major Yin receives Order of Founder
from General Burrows.**

commended you to our Founder, William Booth. Therefore today it gives me great pleasure to admit you to the *Order of the Founder.*" Salvationists from around the world in London's Royal Albert Hall sprang to their feet with a prolonged ovation of esteem for this eighty-five-year-old stalwart hero.

What followed was one of the electric moments of Salvation Army history. Major Yin stepped forward, thanked the general "for this great honor" and the delegates for their welcome. He then asked the general if he could sing a chorus, and with her permission sang the chorus he had sung at the end of each day to keep his faith and Salvationism alive during his ten years in the labor camp, during which his wife died under incarceration. The general then invited the Salvationists from around the world to join the major in singing those words of consecration:

> All my days and all my hours, All my will and all my powers,
> All the passion of my soul, Not a fragment but the whole
> Shall be thine, dear Lord, Shall be thine, dear Lord.

A USA officer, Major Nancy Moretz, said to the author later that day on the street in London, "It was during the singing of that chorus that there took place the renewal of my covenant and love for the Army."

Such was the impact of that moment in Army history. The stirring saga of Major Yin is chronicled in the biography by General Arnold Brown, *The Mountain the Wind Blew Here.*

In the Crucible of Persecution

Brigadier Josef Korbel's autobiography, *In My Enemy's Camp,* is a powerful saga of heroic Salvationism. With his wife he served as corps officer in charge of the Army's work in Brno, a major city in Czechoslovakia. With the liquidation of the Army in his home country, in 1949 he was arrested in his home by Communist agents because of "his dangerous religious influence." Unwilling to renounce either his faith or The Salvation Army, he was imprisoned for more than ten years, during which he was often harshly punished.

In 1959, released from prison, he found severe limitations on his personal freedom and his family's activity. His youngest son, Viktor, had been shot and killed while attempting to attend a Good Friday service. The following year his oldest son was imprisoned on false charges.

In 1967 the Korbels fled their homeland and were reunited with The Salvation Army in Switzerland, and transferred in 1971 to the USA. When in 1990, after forty years of banishment, the Army reopened its work in Czechoslovakia, the brigadier returned to help reestablish it in his homeland. Later in Brno, he was present for the dedication of the 112-bed shelter named Josef Korbel House, a building returned to the Army by the government and completely renovated, a living memorial to the sacrificial devotion of its namesake.

As General Eva Burrows admitted him to the Order of the Founder at the Army's 1990 international congress, he stood with quiet dignity before the large assembly as an example of one who had proved the depth of his dedication in the crucible of persecution.

A Company of Unsung Heroes

Salvationist heroes and heroines are still quietly making their mark around the Army world, most often out of the spotlight and in dark corners of human need.

In a 2008 USA *New Frontier* article, "A Ministry of Presence," Major

Linda Manhardt, principal of the Army's training college in Tanzania, shared the following story.

> Among the first cadets to arrive were Peter and Pamela. I loved them from the start. They were energetic and eager to please and their eyes sparkled with humor and God's love. I know I was quite an oddity to the cadets — this single American officer with no husband and no children! In Africa, it is a strong cultural expectation for women to marry and have several children. I shared that although I had no children of my own, I could be their spiritual mother. Although I would lead them, I would also love them, and give them discipline and teaching, caring and nurturing. They started to call me "mamma" — a term of great respect.
>
> Not long after commissioning I heard that Peter and Pamela were going to have a baby. I was excited for them. Pamela had a beautiful baby boy, but a couple days after birth, in the hospital the baby unexplainably died.
>
> When I heard of the tragedy, I knew I had to go to them. They were stationed in a remote village in northern Tanzania, and I took a small plane to where they were.
>
> I found Pamela in the small quarters in a terrible state, with a blank look of despair. I had no words of wisdom, no profound insights, nothing to offer. So for three days, I simply sat with her, and we cried together. It was soon time for me to leave and I felt that I had been of little help.
>
> Pamela slowly came back to life. Later, she told me that she began to feel hope and cared about when I came to visit. She had needed a mamma, and when I came and simply grieved with her, she began to find comfort.
>
> It is miraculous the way God can take our simple, seemingly ineffective attempts at ministry and use them. We need to just keep on giving and loving. Through us, God can bring his healing. Sometimes the most effective ministry of all is this simple ministry of presence. I count it as one of my greatest joys to have been given the honor of being called "mamma" to a grieving heart.

A September 2007 newsletter from Majors Jim and Marcia Cocker, who in 2007 had gone from the United States as reinforcement officers to serve in Papua New Guinea, offers one such vignette.

Captain Michael Dengi, besides his duty as a corps officer, also travels on behalf of the government to teach and educate people in small villages about HIV/AIDS. He uses his earnings to pay for the supplies for his corps.

He had recently heard about an AIDS-infected woman in a village who was being inhumanly mistreated, and went to investigate. His trip involved a six day walk after an eight hour trip by car and canoe. Reaching this woman would be a test of both his faith and his physical stamina.

When Michael arrived in the village after dark, he discovered that the woman was tied up and literally living with the village pigs. She was forced to live there because it had been discovered that she had AIDS, and in the local culture of superstition no one would touch her. Angered at what he saw, but exhausted from his long journey and the hot equator sun which sapped his strength, he assured her he would return the following day after he had rested from his long journey.

In the early morning hours, Michael rang the village bell and gathered the town elders together, and then he walked them all out to the woman. She was filthy and covered in her own feces. Michael picked her up, untied her, took her clothes and burned them, gently bathed, and redressed her in clean clothes. Then he did something no one expected. He built a fire and prepared a cup of tea, all without saying a word. He gave the tea to the woman and asked her to drink. Following her tenuous, slow sip he took the cup from her and drained the tea from the very same cup.

He then turned to the crowd and told them that this woman could in no way infect any of them except through sexual contact. He took the woman's arm and slowly escorted her back into the village, where she took her rightful place not only in her home but also in the church.

Major Cocker writes, "Captain Michael is a simple man — in his words he is just a 'humble servant.' But that night as we sat in the dark on his porch and heard his story he became a giant of a man — one I will long remember even if I never have the opportunity to see him again, perhaps in eternity, where I know his Savior has a cup of tea waiting for him. In him I saw afresh the face of Salvation Army ministry. To be the hands and voice of Jesus I must do whatever it takes to fully restore lost people to the heavenly family. If that means walking for six days, is that too far? Captain Michael taught me the answer is 'no.'"

They are unsung, and unknown, but the Army still raises its heroes and heroines, doing God's work in trenches of the far-flung battlefields of human need, often exemplifying a Christlike ministry of "the basin and the towel."

TWENTY-SEVEN

Marching Forward

Fight the good fight of the faith.

1 Timothy 6:12

An army cannot long remain static or stationary. It is born to march forward. *The Salvation Army Song Book* presents a section of lyrics under the category of "Warfare."

Twenty-year-old Harry Read had been a soldier and hero as a British parachutist over France before dawn on historic D-Day — June 6, 1944. Following return from military service, he enlisted for a lifetime term as God's soldier. Captain Harry Read (later commissioner and nominee for general) wrote the following lyrics for a pageant at the United Kingdom's commissioning of cadets in 1962; the music is by Captain John Larsson (later general). Since then its martial strains have been a favorite among Army cadets, and its words describe The Salvation Army soldier who "marches as to war."

> God's soldier marches as to war,
> A soldier on an alien shore,
> A soldier true, a soldier who
> Will keep the highest aims in view.
> God's soldier goes where sin is found;
> Where evil reigns, his battleground;
> A cunning foe to overthrow
> And strike for truth a telling blow.

Assessment and Advance

"In order to meet the contemporary needs of humanity, The Salvation Army must remain flexible, constantly adapting its strategy while never changing its principles," stated John Gowans when elected general in 1999. He added, "Compassion is our stock in trade but there is nothing wrong with marrying compassion to the most sophisticated equipment and the most advanced training that we can afford. William Booth, the Army's Founder, was nothing if not a pragmatist, and sanctified pragmatism must remain the hallmark of the Army."

The emerging global culture of a postmodern world posed a new reality for the undertaking of the Army's mission. To respond creatively to this challenge, General Paul Rader established an International Commission on Officership, "to review all aspects of officership in the light of the contemporary situation and its challenges, with a view to introducing a greater measure of flexibility."

The twenty-three members of the commission, composing a widely diverse and balanced group, in due course presented twenty-eight recommendations to him shortly before his retirement. His successor, John Gowans, on entering office, launched the most comprehensive consultative process in the Army's history. All Army officers in the world were given opportunity to comment on the twenty-eight recommendations in the report dated February 2000. A consultation form, professionally designed and charted, was sent to every officer in the world, to provide a comprehensive analysis of the data gained, by zone, territory, age-group, gender, etc. Subjects included the covenant and conditions of officership, leadership models and development, cultural relevance, marriage regulations, women's ministry, the appointing process, officer ranks.

The recommendation was approved for moving away from authoritarian models of command and toward consultative models of leadership. A major breakthrough emerged with the relaxing of the sacrosanct and time-honored regulation that officers could marry only officers. It was approved, at territorial discretion, to allow in exceptional circumstances an officer to be married to a nonofficer, or to continue in officership when the spouse can no longer remain an officer. Furthermore, officers would no longer need permission from headquarters to marry, and age disparity restrictions on marriage were revoked.

A primary category for review was women's ministry, with the outcome that women officers be appointed to positions commensurate with their gifts and experience, and that gender balance be achieved in decision-making bodies. To allow more flexibility in officership, it was approved that "non-residential, all-age training will be permitted where a territory wishes it, to make officership a possibility for those who are called but because of circumstance are not able to take up the traditional two-year training college course." These, along with other considerations, ensured some foundational changes within the system and practice of the Army, although some moved forward at a slow pace. "It is likely," wrote General Larsson in retrospect, "that future historians will view this commission as having been one of the most influential in terms of the changes and thinking that brought it about."

As Salvation Army membership in Britain and Europe continued to suffer attrition, spiraling growth in developing countries produced a shift in the center of gravity for the Army. Numerically, two-thirds of the Army today is found in Africa and South Asia; Africa boasts 41 percent of the Army's senior soldiers and 66 percent of its junior soldiers. But two-thirds of the financial resources are in the Western world. African nations and Korea have become the Army's fastest-growing countries while its forces in the Western world have struggled for a stability of membership and mission results.

In 2004 General Larsson reported, "Growth is explosive in Africa. One corps officer was appointed to be in charge of 12 corps. By the time the officer left that appointment, he was in charge of 20 corps. The Lord is prospering the work in Africa." Church growth became a major agenda item, generating conferences, telemarketing, and new plantings. Cross-cultural ministries responded to the new demographics of ethnic populations. Adherents increased in prominence, offering a modified commitment to Salvation Army membership.

"Written Itself around the World"

The observation was made early in the movement's history that "The Salvation Army has written itself around the world." William Booth's *How to Reach the Masses with the Gospel* was the first publication of the Army founder in 1870. George Scott Railton, a young Methodist minister reading it, said, "It came like a trumpet call for action." It led him to join the Army, and in March of 1880 he and seven lassies led the Army's invasion of America. Catherine Booth's trenchant "Popular Christianity" influenced Samuel Brengle, a divinity student in Boston, to join the Army, and the salutary impact of this "Apostle of Holiness" upon the movement is incomputable.

One year after the Army was founded, its official publication, the *War Cry,* was launched, the first edition dated December 27, 1879. As the official publication of the Army, the *War Cry* appeared in each country where the Army was found, reporting on local events and printing articles of interest and spiritual nurture for its readers. In 1890 the United Kingdom edition already had a robust circulation of 300,000 copies, a colossus in the field of magazines, and a success story repeated in other countries. This record is especially impressive in that Army periodicals carry no advertising.

From its inception the Army has been blessed with a succession of skilled editors, competent historians and biographers, writers of teaching materials, and inspired devotional writers and poets. An amazing flow of Salvation Army books continued unabated into the early twentieth century. *The Warrior's Library* provided morning and evening readings from the writings of the general. Devotional books and biographies were at the top of Salvationist reading. A full three pages (361-364) of titles appear in Sandall's third volume of Army history (1955), with a plethora of additions since.

In 1884 the monthly periodical *All the World* was launched by International Headquarters; it continues to publish, now quarterly, and remains true to its original mission: "a record of the operations of the Army in all lands." In 1893 the *Officer* made its debut, and is still distributed to every English-speaking officer, conveying articles of international interest.

Preserving the Heritage

John D. Waldron, chief secretary and later commissioner, a foremost promoter of Army literature, in 1972 established in the USA East the Army's first Territorial Literary Council, resulting in an Army book published and distributed by a mainline publisher. The first Archives and Research Center both in the States and in Canada was his brainchild. Similar resources became replicated in other countries for the preservation of the Army's history and heritage, some with professional archivists and state-of-the-art technology. Waldron also founded the William and Catherine Booth College, in Canada, the Army's first degree-granting institution.

The Army's International Heritage Centre in London was initiated in 1988 by Lieutenant Colonel Cyril Barnes, noted Army author and historian. This vast compendium of historical data and artifacts provides valued research to the Army world, and was a source of data and photos for this volume, through its current staff member, Alex VonDer Becke.

In 1905 the Army's songbook was instituted for congregational use. Scores of new writers of songs and music also appear in the ongoing *Musical Salvationist* and *Band Journal.*

Since 1906 the Army has published an annual *Year Book* that reports on Army activity around the world during the preceding year. Featured are statistics, reports of work in each region of the Army world, a glossary of SA terms, a Who's Who of leaders, and details of international aid programs. It presents a veritable mine of information and is constantly updated; recent editions run to over 300 pages and include color photographs.

William Booth's bulky fountain pen never ran dry. He wrote numerous articles for the *War Cry,* in addition to the Army's *Orders and Regulations* and full-length books. Heading the list of Army books are those by and about the Booths.

Army books became popular with Hugh Redwood's *God in the Slums,* a small book describing the work of the Army in the slums of England, which sold a quarter-million copies within twelve months of publication.

In 1955 there appeared *The Soldier's Armoury,* a book of daily Bible reflections; it is published twice a year, and in recent years has been titled *Words of Life.* The book is distributed to tens of thousands around the world, all of whom read the same devotional thoughts each day; it is also sold in the bookstores of England.

The International Literature Programme, formerly known as the Missionary Literature and Translations Fund, established in 1979, with generous donations from territories, provides grants to supported territories toward the translation and production of literature and for the training of writers. Subsidized publications include literature for young people, soldiers, and officers, also Bibles, songbooks, devotional material, Army histories, and biographies.

Poets have graced the pages of Army publications and books. Commissioner Flora Larsson, fluent in six languages, wrote numerous articles for Army publications. One popular *War Cry* series, "Just a Moment, Lord," was published in book form in 1973, later in further editions and translations. Other prominent poets whose works grace the Army songbook and other publications include Herbert Booth, Ruth Tracy, Catherine Baird, John Gowans, and the Army's "Poet General," Albert Orsborn.

William Booth early realized the power of the printed word and set up his own printing shop in 1879; it was later expanded and named the Campfield Press. Situated beside a branch railway line with its own siding, the press published the weekly *War Cry* and other materials, which were expeditiously sent to Army centers. A "knee drill" (prayer meeting) preceded the day's work. The firm developed a reputation for fine printing, including leather binding. Among its customers was the United Kingdom Parliament, which had Campfield do its bound reports; upon ascension to the throne, Her Majesty Queen Elizabeth II was presented a leather-bound Bible by the press. From a peak of over 300 employees, changes and increased automation shrunk the workforce until its closure in 1991, with some employees having served for forty or fifty years.

For many years The Salvation Army elsewhere maintained its own printing facilities, in the United States, Canada, Britain, and the Netherlands, among others, facilitating the output of its literature. While today it takes advantage of the technology of modern printing presses outside the Army, its literature, including books, continues to roll off the presses and serves as a strong arm of the Army's outreach and mission.

A New Era

After 104 years of publication of the *War Cry* in the USA, in 1985 there was launched what was called the "new" *War Cry*, transitioning from a black-and-white tabloid to state-of-the-art full color, restyled to a magazine format, with coated paper stock, new text fonts, and new graphics design. Boilerplate pages were deleted, and the periodical offered a new genre of timely news, interviews, articles on issues of the day and family life, Bible study series, and an evangelistic page with the ABCs of salvation. At the same time, it went from a weekly to a biweekly, allowing more time for quality preparation and twice as long a shelf life. The new look and features pushed the magazine to a record circulation of over 500,000 per issue, and the quantum leap forward provided a new template for Army periodicals around the world.

In 1994 the national book plan in the USA was born, initiated by Colonel Henry Gariepy and carried forward by Lieutenant Colonel Marlene Chase, producing three books a year. Titled Crest Books, it printed 7,000 copies of each book for distribution to every officer and Salvation Army unit in the States, and sold them through its trade store outlets, with reprints as needed. The thirty-plus titles to date, all Salvation Army related, include biography, history, devotional topics, poetry, anthologies, and leadership books. Bylines include an international roster of Salvationists, from soldiers to generals. In recent years the plan has been modified for use in several other Army territories. The overall production adds significantly to the corpus of Salvation Army books, and helps preserve the heritage and history of the Army.

In 2008 General Shaw Clifton launched under IHQ auspices a program for reprinting Army classics and publishing new books. With sixteen titles to date, the program will network with Amazon.com.uk to make the books easily accessible worldwide.

The true life drama of The Salvation Army had given George Bernard Shaw impetus in 1905 to write the popular play *Major Barbara,* about a love affair of a Salvation Army officer engaged in slum work, first produced in London and with later incarnations overseas and as a film. A half-century later, in 1950, the Damon Runyon musical *Guys and Dolls* opened to rave reviews on Broadway. The Salvation Army had been discovered by playwrights and entered the major stages of the world.

Priority, put out by the USA East, is an example of the spate of recent publications that has emerged with state-of-the-art graphics, format, and content. Published quarterly and distributed nationally, its stated purpose is "to promote prayer, holiness, and evangelism through the life stories of God's people, intended for people both inside and outside The Salvation Army." *Caring,* a magazine of the USA West, treats the Army's social ministries with interest and insight. Eastern Australia has produced a flagship periodical, *Pipeline,* which sets a high standard of Army journalism.

Some Salvationist books, along with an increasing number of Army publications, both current and archival, are now available online. The technology of the day has ushered in a new era for the Army's literature and publications.

The Ubiquitous Kettle

The Army's ubiquitous Christmas kettles present at shopping malls and on street corners in major cities around the world have become a national institution, an integral part of the festive season. Often a Christmas *War Cry* or tract is given to donors, because in some countries more persons come in contact with the Army through this medium than any other.

On the occasion of the centenary of the kettle, a marker was placed in San Francisco that reads: "At this site, the old San Francisco Ferry Building, on December 16, 1891, the first Salvation Army Christmas kettle was inaugurated by Captain Joseph McFee in support of feeding

A Christmas tradition *(art by Karen Yee Lim)*

the hungry and clothing the poor. In the ensuing 100 years this has become an international tradition."

Little could the captain, in such an inauspicious beginning, have envisioned the tradition ultimately established and the good accomplished around the world by his simple act.

Americans contribute some $100 million to the Army's Christmas kettle campaign for providing Christmas cheer to the less fortunate. Kettle donations remain in local communities, supporting year-round services. In recent years the Wal-Mart Foundation and the Campbell Soup Company each contributed $1 million to the kettle campaign. The USA Christmas kettle tradition was too good to keep exclusive, and in recent years has been exported to other nations in which the Army serves.

Salvation Army Online

Modernization laid its heavy hand upon the Army. Computers and the explosion of new technology ushered the Army into the world of cyberspace, collapsing time zones and creating a new global network. Army media kept step with technology and the times as its publications sparkled with color and creative graphics. Multimedia and videos introduced a new age of communication. E-mail supplants the once official "snail mail" exchange. Blogs and Web sites from Salvationists around the world provide an extraordinary communication network for such an international organization.

Recognizing opportunities for a new cyber mission field, the Army's IHQ in London launched in 1995 its own World Wide Web page. Its first message from General Paul A. Rader extended a welcome and a challenge. He wrote to Internet users, "You may know the Army best as a humanitarian and social service agency with a global reach. We are that, but we are more. We are an evangelical part of the universal Christian Church, committed to sharing the Gospel of Jesus Christ." Other data on the Army's Web page included the Army's mission statement, news headlines and news items, and a reading from the Army's international daily devotional book, *Words of Life*. The move signaled the Army initiative to utilize the latest technology to communicate the gospel, with Web sites proliferating around the Army world. Territories in the developed world took advantage of the Internet to bring awareness of the Army's work to a new computer-savvy generation. Web sites also have been established by divisional offices, local corps, and individual Salvationists.

In June 1995, using a voice-activated video camera system from a London studio, General Rader communicated with Salvation Army leaders at Army headquarters in both Alexandria, Virginia, and Atlanta, Georgia. This thirty-minute intercontinental video conference held much potential for wider use in evangelism, education, and international communications.

Global Lotus Notes network became the lingua franca of the worldwide Army, allowing multilateral communication between Army centers around the world. It facilitated direct access and immediate response.

For the Army, the Internet came into its own as a bilateral communication tool as forums and chat rooms gave Salvationists and others a "virtual community" for airing their views. In 2007 it was reported that every month more than 84,000 people click on the Army's international Web site (www.salvationarmy.org). Following an explosion of Web sites by various headquarters and units, another third-of-a-million visits constitutes a virtual congregation almost as large as its flesh-and-blood one who click on its news and information pages.

The response of the North American public after 9/11 was a watershed in e-philanthropy. Subsequently the Internet serves as a fundraising tool for both disasters and ongoing support. This new resource of online fund-raising will continue to expand the Army's database of supporters and the building of "virtual" relationships with donors.

The Army continues to add to its Web-enabled publications, producing online editions of its publications or articles from them. The full text of its *Salvation Story — the Handbook of Doctrine* has been downloaded by over 2,000 users.

The Army founder, who once said, "Why should the Devil have all the best tunes?" were he alive today, would surely say, "Why should the Devil have all the best sites?"

Streamlining infiltrated Army buildings, fund-raising, programs, and uniforms. Though flexible in methodology, the Army remained firm in mission; though fluid in program, it remained fixed in purpose.

The Corps and Evangelism

The corps through the years has been the "core" of The Salvation Army. It has been the primary source of conversions and recruitment, as well as the venue and center for administration and services within a community. The officer in charge is known as the corps officer, and its ecclesiastical lay members as soldiers.

The Department of Women's Ministries hosts a variety of programs and meetings. Its mission is to bring women into a knowledge of Jesus Christ; encourage their full potential in influencing family, friends, and community; equip them for growth in personal understanding and in life skills; and address issues that affect them and their families. The Home League, an international component of women's ministry, was inaugurated in 1907 with the fourfold aim of worship, education, fellowship, and service. Every Army corps has a Home League geared to these four aims and also serving as a vital arm of support in the corps; they usually conduct weekly meetings.

Corps centers also sponsor Community Care Ministries, originally called the League of Mercy, which began in 1892 in Canada. Composed of people of all ages, it responds especially with visits and service to those institutionalized.

Some of the Army's venerable traditions gave way in the 1980s, including the near century-old bonnet for women and the high-collar tunic for men. Urban development rendered conditions inhospitable for the Army's traditional street-corner evangelism that had characterized both the beginning and over a century of the Army's evangelical thrust in what it called "open-air" meetings. The Army is ever exploring and exploiting new alternatives for evangelism, including TV, special meetings, online networking and blogs, and Web sites.

The Salvation Army in Academia

The Salvation Army may not normally be associated with academia, but no account of its work would be complete without reference to its involvement in the field of education. Worldwide it operates thousands of schools, from primary schools to high schools, colleges, and vocational training centers. The schools employ almost 16,000 teachers and host almost a half-million pupils. Among these institutions are 8 schools for the blind, 16 schools for the disabled, 27 boarding schools, and 27 colleges, universities, staff-training and distance-learning centers.

For many years some 10,000 students have been enrolled in the Army's schools in Hong Kong, the largest being the Ann Wyllie Memorial Primary School with 1,536 pupils. Education has long been a focus of the Army in India, where, for example, between 1983 and 1985, 35 adult education centers were started in the India Central Territory; they now serve 1,500 students.

In Africa, after nearly a century of educational activity, the *Historical Dictionary of The Salvation Army* reports that more than 2,900 schools are operated by the Army, ranging from primary schools to universities, as well as vocational centers, in sixteen nations. The Army in Ghana hosts 129 schools that enroll 24,000 students. The Howard Institute in Zimbabwe is an example of how the practical is interwoven with basic academic courses. Opened in 1923 with boarding accommodation, it eventually expanded to comprise a primary school of 1,200 students, a teacher-training school, a high school with 900 pupils, a weaving school, a manual skills unit, and a commercial studies course. Similar developments took place in other African nations, with Army schools achieving high standards of professionalism and prestige in Kenya, Nigeria, Zaire, and Zambia; even Liberia, in the wake of civil war, can boast 14 schools and 1,400 students.

"There is nothing else like this anywhere else in the Army world," observed General Wahlström of the Army's association with Asbury College at the dedication of the Army's 10,000-square-foot student center adjoining the campus amid the bluegrass hills of Kentucky. In the same year as the dedication, 1983, the Army's 126 students constituted 10 percent of the college enrollment. Salvationists have served as professors on the teaching staff and on the Board of Trustees, and Dr. Ronald Holz is professor of music literature and instrumental music and directs a Salvationist student band. Retired General Paul A. Rader was invited to serve as the college president (2000-2006). By 1997 over 234 Asbury graduates had served as Army officers, and several times that number as dedicated professional staff of the Army. Among them were eight commissioners and one general — Paul A. Rader. Honorary doctorates were conferred on Commissioner Israel L. Gaither and Generals Arnold Brown and Eva Burrows; Brown called the college the single most important educational influence upon the Army in the world.

Salvationists are often found as faculty in Christian colleges and universities. Roger Green, Ph.D., noted Army lecturer and biographer of William and Catherine Booth, is chairperson of biblical and theological studies at Gordon College. At Asbury College are Dr. Edward McKinley, professor of history and chairman of the Division of Business, History, and Society; Dr. David Rightmire, professor of Bible and theology, and author of scholarly books and articles; and Dr. Alan Moulton, who retired after thirty-five years of teaching at the college. Today Salvationist students are found in large numbers on the campuses of both Christian and secular schools of learning.

Salvationist Jonathan Raymond serves as president of Trinity Western University, the largest Christian university in Canada, having previously been president of the William and Catherine Booth College in Winnipeg. The latter was launched in 1982, established to strengthen the work of the Army and the church through the integration of rigorous scholarship, Christian faith, and active service to others. It offers university-level programs that combine faith-based study with hands-on experience for careers in social work, youth ministry, and urban mission.

**Commissioner William Francis,
Chancellor of Booth College**

In 2001 the college hosted the Army's first International Theology and Ethics Symposium, with delegates from seventeen countries, designed to "better equip the Army in its mission to 'save souls, grow saints and serve suffering humanity.'" Commissioner William Francis, an author and the Army's leader in Canada, with a master of divinity degree from Asbury Theological Seminary and an honorary doctorate from Houghton College, is chancellor. A milestone development was the opening in 2006 of a new college for officer training on the Booth College campus in Winnipeg, with the curriculum progressing toward a degree in biblical and theological studies. The new college replaces the long-standing former schools in Toronto and Newfoundland.

Canada's neighbor to the south entered into articulation agreements for its cadets with Houghton College and Nyack College in New York, Olivet Nazarene College in Illinois, Azusa Pacific College in California, and Asbury College in Kentucky. Each college provides credits toward degree programs. The USA West in 2000 established Crestmont College, designed to incorporate all training and education functions of the territory, offering specialized studies and a bachelor's degree for commissioned cadets.

War's Impact

Two world wars imposed major challenges to the international unity of the Army, the second one even more drastically than the first. For the first time in its history the Army had been forced into retreat. After the war ended in 1945, Communist governments both in Europe and in Asia banned the Army and forced it into a long night of separation from those countries in which it had formerly established both a beachhead and an accepted work.

World War II did not leave The Salvation Army unscathed. Members were imprisoned, some martyred, and the Army was outlawed in Communist-dominated countries as well as in those under Nazi control. Bombs often demolished Army properties, and training of cadets and recruitment came to an end. A number of countries were eclipsed from the Army's global network that transformed its "crown of glory" into a "crown of thorns."

The Army's suffering in Asia exceeded the severity of that in Europe. It was dissolved in Japan and its leaders imprisoned in the Philippines,

Malaysia, Indonesia, China, Korea, Singapore, and other countries under Japanese control. Countless Salvationists disappeared without a trace.

In Japan the Army was proscribed; in Indonesia it was formally dissolved by decree, though despite this liquidation a few Indonesian officers carried on incognito for a while. Five continents had instances where communication with international headquarters was severed.

The air warfare and bombing inflicted heavy damage and destruction on the Army's places of worship, hospitals, and homes in Europe and Asia. Some officers lost their lives, others endured, and some died in brutal internment.

The Army's firm refusal to divide the human race into "friends and foes" was illustrated by the edict that the word "enemy" could not be used in Army publications. The Army founder had early banned the word "foreigner" from the Army's lexicon, and during the Second World War General Carpenter had kept the word "enemy" out of his utterances and any paper passed by him for approval.

When hostilities ceased, the return of peace revealed that the war had not been able to break the unique and strong bond of the Army's world fellowship. The Salvation Army in those countries rose from the grave where its adversaries had deemed it forever dead and buried. The greatest demonstration of its unbroken worldwide unity came from August 10 to 23, 1950, with the International Youth Congress in London, which drew upwards of 1,200 delegates from five continents.

The Phenomenal Kroc Centers

Joan Kroc, philanthropist and widow of the founder of McDonald's, had a dream to help those labeled "at risk." "My greatest concern," she had said, "is for the future of our children and grandchildren, to provide opportunity for greater numbers of people around the world, especially disadvantaged women and children."

She became acquainted with The Salvation Army in San Diego, California, studied its history, and explored what it was doing to make a difference in her community and in the lives of the disadvantaged. She came to know and appreciate the century-long commitment of the Army in its holistic approach to those in need.

The Army's commitment was found to be trustworthy, leading her

Architect's rendering of Kroc Center for Dayton, Ohio

to endow the local corps with $82 million to build a twelve-acre multifunctional center, unlike any before in its history, to serve the needs of that community. She would occasionally drop in unannounced to see whether it was as she had envisioned, functioning as a "beacon on a hill" for the disadvantaged. The center, which stretches almost two city blocks, hosts a sanctuary-theater-library complex, a daycare center with a colorful playground, a full-size soccer field, a fitness center, three full-size basketball courts, a swimming pool, an ice-skating rink, classrooms, and a corps program, directed by Salvation Army officers. Each day some 2,400 people take advantage of its facilities and programs.

She must have liked what she saw, for she meticulously planned and executed what is the largest-ever gift to a private charity — her entire residual estate in excess of $1.5 billion — to be used in the construction and endowment of thirty-four more centers across the nation, each tailored to the needs of the community that surrounds it. A matching endowment for the ongoing operational costs will be raised by each community as its part of the program. As this book is being written, new centers are in various stages of development in major cities of the States, representing a milestone in the mission and ministry of The Salvation Army. In the future the Army's impact will be enhanced by these state-of-the-art community centers funded by America's largest one-time charity gift. For Joan Kroc, her gift was not just for a social service facility. She had a dream of community togetherness and enrichment no one had dared imagine, and became convinced that the Army could bring the highest return on her investment in human lives.

Some within the movement expressed concern that the cultural and recreational focus could dilute the Army's image as caretakers of the poor and its evangelistic mission. The substantial fund-raising required to generate operating dollars — from $30 to $60 million a year — could siphon money from other projects such as its trademark "corps centers" that aid individuals and disaster victims, and provide a spiritual outreach and home for its members. But Army leaders have stressed the commitment to always keep the primacy of its spiritual focus and core ideology as part of its holistic approach in these mega-centers of service.

A New Generation of Salvationists

The Salvation Army in 1976 entered the church growth movement — using modern means to bring persons into a relationship with Christ and into church membership. Led by Canada through links forged with Fuller Seminary in California, the headquarters of the movement, it soon spread to Australia and Britain. The ultimate stamp of approval was given by General Eva Burrows, who in 1989 convened an International Strategy for Growth Conference in London. The ninety-two delegates attending the meeting offered fifty-one recommendations that were shared and promoted around the Army world. The Army embraced five principles of church growth — the *presence* of Christ, *proclamation* where the people are, *persuasion* by use of heart language of words and music, *perfection* in mentoring converts, and *participation* that involves converts in the fellowship of believers. The new strategies, including telemarketing and church plantings, brought results of membership and corps growth in many of the territories where implemented.

Susie Swift, a teacher who graduated from Vassar College, in an 1890 edition of the Army's *All the World* magazine, gave her reason for joining the Army in London: "I do not find any other organization than the Army demanding of its members such uniform lives of gospel simplicity, purity and charity as are necessary to a permanent maintenance of spiritual life. I find these in The Salvation Army, therefore I cast in my lot with them." Many Salvationists, although distant from those of the first generation, share that sentiment and conviction for the decision they have made.

Today some in the ranks of the Army claim with pride to be fifth- and sixth-generation Salvationists. Each new session of cadets who train to become officers includes a significant number who bring a heritage of Army background, along with those newly introduced to the Army. These twenty-first-century Salvationists come into a more formalized style of worship and service quite different from the earlier days of the movement.

As a multinational movement, the status and trends of the Army are often quite different among its member nations. African and Korean Salvationists may exhibit a verve and spirit that in some settings may border on the charismatic. Bands and songster brigades may complement the corps' worship. In some parts of the Western world the standard church lectionary guides the sermon topics and worship content, and Sunday schools may use an interdenominational Bible study curriculum.

Today's congregation of worshipers in the Army no longer consists largely of "trophies of grace," although those saved from addiction or other defeats are still giving their "testimony" in many Army centers. But it is also not unusual to find those of upward mobility, a professor, a teacher, a doctor, or other professional, among those who call the Army their church home and place they render their Christian service. College and university students add to the mix. This cross-pollination of the intergenerational and the new, from varied social strata, brings a rich dimension of vital community and leadership resource.

But Army leaders and members around the world, as expressed through many of its commissions and communiqués, are not content with the status quo. They vigorously call for an Army moving forward with giant strides, to seek new and creative ways to fulfill its mandate for soul saving and the nurturing of spiritual life and action. Some of the dynamics cited in this volume give hope and impetus to the spiritual life of the Army, from the extraordinary 24/7 prayer of youth to the Spiritual Life Commission pronouncements of Army leaders.

Army's Template and Watchword

Today Booth's Army is one of the largest standing armies in the world. But it transcends that metaphor, for it is not "standing." It is forging ahead, marching forward to the cadences of "a Distant Drummer," to ever new battles and conquests for Christ. But an army also has to be ever on its guard, alert to subtle attacks on its mission, and ready to confront the challenges of a new day.

"Our primary purpose is, and always has been, to introduce men and women and girls and boys to Jesus Christ, the Savior of us all," stated General Shaw Clifton, in his foreword to the Army's 2008 *Year Book*. He added, "In every land where the Army flag flies, daily we seek to share the good news of Jesus Christ." Thus was summarized the core mission of the movement by its current international leader, and further amplified by the leadership and ministry of Commissioner Helen Clifton, world president of women's ministry, who shares with him the Army's covenant and mission.

The mission statement of the Army further amplifies the general's statement of purpose and continues to be the template and touchstone for all its endeavors: "The Salvation Army, an international movement, is an evangelical part of the universal Christian Church. Its message is based on the Bible. Its ministry is motivated by love for God. Its mission

Commissioner Helen Clifton and General Shaw Clifton,
international leaders of The Salvation Army

is to preach the gospel of Jesus Christ and meet human needs in his name without discrimination."

However, as earlier stated, there is ever the challenge to maintain the primacy of the spiritual, not to settle for the good rather than the best God has for the Army. Richard Niebuhr's words are as a glove thrown at the Army's feet: "Rarely does a second generation hold the convictions it has inherited with a fervor equal to that of its fathers, who have fashioned these convictions in the heat of conflict."

From the Army's founder, William Booth, comes a watchword for the challenges of the future. "The Army's future depends upon the Army. If she is energetic and faithful and steadfast, she will go branching out, this way and that way, going from great to greater things. If she is slothful and slackens her zeal, she will perish" — he nodded his head gravely. "Yes, I hope she will perish and be swept away, for dead things should not encumber the ground but should make place for the living."

In response to that challenge, Salvationists turn in their songbook to sing and affirm the words composed by the Army's late "Poet General," Albert Orsborn:

What a work the Lord has done
    By his saving grace;
Let us praise him, every one,
    In his holy place.
He has saved us gloriously,
    Led us onward faithfully,
Yet He promised we should see
    Even greater things.
. . . Give us faith, O Lord, we pray,
    Faith for greater things.

Doctrines of The Salvation Army

1. We believe that the Scriptures of the Old and New Testament were given by inspiration of God, and that they only constitute the Divine rule of Christian faith and practice.

2. We believe that there is only one God, who is infinitely perfect, the Creator, Preserver, and Governor of all things, and who is the only proper object of religious worship.

3. We believe that there are three persons in the Godhead — the Father, the Son, and the Holy Spirit, undivided in essence and co-equal in power and glory.

4. We believe that in the person of Jesus Christ the Divine and human natures are united, so that He is truly and properly God and truly and properly man.

5. We believe that our first parents were created in a state of innocence, but by their disobedience, they lost their purity and happiness, and that in consequence of their fall, all men have become sinners, totally depraved, and as such are justly exposed to the wrath of God.

6. We believe that the Lord Jesus Christ has by His suffering and death made an atonement for the whole world so that whosoever will may be saved.

7. We believe that repentance toward God, faith in our Lord Jesus Christ and regeneration by the Holy Spirit are necessary to salvation.

8. We believe that we are justified by grace through faith in our Lord Jesus Christ and that he that believeth hath the witness in himself.

9. We believe that continuance in a state of salvation depends upon continued obedient faith in Christ.

10. We believe that it is the privilege of all believers to be wholly sanctified, and that their whole spirit and soul and body may be preserved blameless unto the coming of our Lord Jesus Christ.

11. We believe in the immortality of the soul, the resurrection of the body, in the general judgment at the end of the world, in the eternal happiness of the righteous, and in the endless punishment of the wicked.

Articles of War: A Soldier's Covenant

Following an affirmation of the Army's eleven doctrines, the word "Therefore" introduces the following as part of the official document signed and received upon enrollment.

- I will be responsive to the Holy Spirit's work and obedient to his leading in my life, growing in grace through worship, prayer, service and the reading of the Bible.

- I will make the values of the Kingdom of God and not the values of the world the standard for my life.

- I will uphold Christian integrity in every area of my life, allowing nothing in thought, word or deed that is unworthy or unclean, untrue or profane, dishonest or immoral.

- I will maintain Christian ideals in all my relationships with others, my family and neighbors, my colleagues and fellow Salvationists, those to whom and for whom I am responsible, and the wider community.

- I will uphold the sanctity of marriage and of family life.

- I will be a faithful steward of my time and gifts, my money and possessions; my body, my mind and my spirit, knowing that I am accountable to God.

- I will abstain from alcoholic drink, tobacco, the non-medical use of addictive drugs, gambling, pornography, the occult, and all else that could enslave the body or spirit.

- I will be faithful to the purposes for which God raised up The Salvation Army, sharing the good news of Jesus Christ, endeavoring to win others to him, and in his name caring for the needy and the disadvantaged.

- I will be actively involved, as I am able, in the life and work, worship and witness of the corps, giving as large a proportion of my income as possible to support its ministries and the worldwide work of the Army.

- I will be true to the principles and practice of The Salvation Army, loyal to its leaders, and I will show the spirit of salvationism whether in times of popularity or persecution.

- I now call upon all present to witness that I enter into this covenant and sign these Articles of War of my own free will, convinced that the love of Christ, who died and now lives to save me, requires from me this devotion of my life to his service for the salvation of the whole world, and therefore do here declare my full determination, by God's help, to be a true soldier of The Salvation Army.

The Founder's Song

*By William Booth, in The Salvation Army Song Book,
and some other church hymnals.*

O boundless salvation! Deep ocean of love,
O fullness of mercy, Christ brought from above,
The whole world redeeming, so rich and so free,
Now flowing for all men, come, roll over me!

My sins they are many, their stains are so deep,
And bitter the tears of remorse that I weep;
But useless is weeping, thou great crimson sea,
Thy waters can cleanse me, come, roll over me!

O ocean of mercy, oft longing I've stood
On the brink of thy wonderful, life-giving flood!
Once more I have reached this soul-cleansing sea,
I will not go back till it rolls over me.

The tide is now flowing, I'm touching the wave,
I heard the loud call of the mighty to save.
My faith's growing bolder, delivered I'll be,
I plunge 'neath the waters, they roll over me.

And now hallelujah! The rest of my days
Shall gladly be spent in promoting his praise
Who opened his bosom to pour out this sea
Of boundless salvation for you and for me.

Countries and Territories

Dates given are those on which the Army work was officially opened.

Angola (1985)

Antigua (1903)

Argentina (1890)

Australia (1881)

Austria (1927)

Bahamas (1931)

Bangladesh (1970)

Barbados (1898)

Belgium (1889)

Belize (1915)

Bermuda (1896)

Bolivia (1920)

Botswana (1997)

Brazil (1922)

Burundi (2007)

Canada (1882)

Chile (1909)

China (1916)

Colombia (1985)

Congo (Brazzaville) (1937)

Congo (Kinshasa) (1934)

Costa Rica (1907, 1975)

Cuba (1918)

Czech Republic (1919, 1990)

Denmark (1887)

Dominican Republic (1995)

Ecuador (1985)

El Salvador (1989)

Estonia (1927, 1995)

Faeroe Islands (1924)

Fiji (1973)

Finland (1889)

France (1881)

French Guiana (1980)

Georgia (1993)

Germany (1886)

Ghana (1922)

Granada (1902)

Greece (2007)

Grenada (1902)

Guam (1992)

Guatemala (1976)

Guernsey (1879)

Guyana (1895)

Haiti (1950)

Honduras (2000)

Hong Kong (1930)

Hungary (1924, 1990)

Iceland (1895)

India (1882)

Indonesia (1894)

Ireland (1880)

Isle of Man (1883)
Italy (1887)
Jamaica (1887)
Japan (1895)
Jersey (1879)
Kenya (1921)
Korea (1908)
Kuwait (2008)
Latvia (1923, 1990)
Lesotho (1969)
Liberia (1988)
Lithuania (2005)
Macau (2000)
Malawi (1979)
Malaysia (1938)
Mali (2008)
Marshall Islands (1985)
Mexico (1937)
Micronesia (1993)
Moldova (1994)
Mongolia (2008)
Mozambique (1923)
Myanmar (1915)
Namibia (2008)
Nepal (2009)
Netherlands, The (1887)
New Zealand (1883)
Nigeria (1920)
Norway (1888)
Pakistan (1883)
Panama (1904)
Papua New Guinea (1956)
Paraguay (1910)
Peru (1910)

Philippines, The (1937)
Poland (2005)
Portugal (1971)
Puerto Rico (1962)
Romania (1999)
Russia (1913, 1991)
Rwanda (1995)
St. Helena (1884)
St. Kitts (1916)
St. Lucia (1902)
St. Maarten (1999)
St. Vincent (1903)
Singapore (1935)
South Africa (1883)
Spain (1971)
Sri Lanka (1883)
Suriname (1926)
Swaziland (1960)
Sweden (1882)
Switzerland (1882)
Taiwan (1965)
Tanzania (1933)
Tonga (1986)
Trinidad & Tobago (1901)
Uganda (1931)
Ukraine (1993)
United Kingdom (1865)
United States (1880)
Uruguay (1890)
Venezuela (1972)
Virgin Islands (1917)
Zambia (1922)
Zimbabwe (1891)

International Statistics

Countries and territories where TSA serves	118
Languages used in SA work	175
Corps, outposts, societies, new plants	15,175
Goodwill centers	1,155
Officers	25,974 (active 16,945; retired 9,029)
Auxiliary captains	143
Lieutenants (noncommissioned)	604
Envoys/sergeants full time	793
Cadets	998
Employees	107,902
Senior soldiers	1,082,166
Adherents	190,215
Junior soldiers	360,222
Corps cadets	36,374
Senior band musicians	25,653
Senior songsters	94,921
Other senior music members	45,753
Local officers	128,854
Women's ministries members	564,566
Community Care Ministries members	110,924
Over-60 club members	359,230
Men's fellowship members	74,072
Youth band members	10,652
Youth singing company members	79,665
Other youth music members	55,776
Sunday school members	612,533

Junior youth group members	236,067
Senior youth group members	79,912
Corps-based beneficiaries	2,845,288
Thrift stores	1,603

Social Program

Hostels for homeless and transients	647
Capacity	34,945
Emergency lodges	373
Capacity	21,047
Children's homes	209
Capacity	8,500
Homes for elderly	121
Homes for disabled	54
Capacity	2,583
Homes for the blind	1
Capacity	986
Remand and probation homes	36
Capacity	988
Homes for street children	31
Capacity	669
Mother and baby homes	40
Capacity	1,016
Training centers for families	27
Capacity	590
Care homes for vulnerable people	60
Capacity	808
Women's and men's refuge centers	68
Capacity	1,691
Other residential homes/hostels	113
Capacity	5,555

Day Care

Community centers	492
Early childhood centers	186
Capacity	26,195

Day centers for elderly	78
Capacity	22,744
Day centers for street children	10
Capacity	924
Day nurseries	174
Capacity	15,127
Drop-in centers for youth	183
Other day care centers	368
Capacity	48,137

Addiction Dependency

Nonresidential programs	57
Capacity	26,260
Residential programs	191
Capacity	15,245
Harbor Light programs	38
Capacity	70,361
Other services for addiction	1,695
Capacity	17,252

Services to the Armed Forces

Clubs and canteens	27
Mobile units for service personnel	18
Chaplains	18

Emergency Disaster Response

Disaster rehabilitation schemes	268
Participants	1,109,469
Refugee programs	
Host countries	3
Participants	138
Refugee rehabilitation programs	58
Participants	13,886
Other response programs	1,962
Participants	111,768

Appendix E

Services to the Community

Prisoners visited	409,014
Prisoners helped on discharge	151,405
Police courts — people helped	272,920
Missing persons — applications	10,143
Number traced	5,660
Night patrol anti-suicide — number helped	345,948
Community youth programs	2,780
Beneficiaries	189,837
Employment bureau applications	96,331
Referrals	185,630
Counseling — people helped	455,789
General relief — people helped	13,534,571
Emergency relief — people helped	1,632,409
Emergency mobile units	2,562
Feeding centers	1,066
Restaurants and cafés	121
Apartments for elderly	437
Capacity	6,700
Hostels for students, workers, etc.	86
Capacity	2,640
Land settlements (SA villages, farms, etc.)	21
Capacity	1,656
Social services summer camps	205
Participants	17,991
Other services to community	79
Beneficiaries	1,625,094

Health Program

General hospitals	11
Capacity	2,580
Maternity hospitals	24
Capacity	319
Other specialist hospitals	25
Capacity	1,956
Specialist clinics	68
Capacity	1,784

General clinics/health centers	133
Capacity	887
Mobile health clinics	63
Inpatients	281,110
Outpatients	981,568
Doctors/medics	3,459
Invalid/convalescent homes	29
Capacity	1,083
Health education programs	
HIV/AIDS, etc.	364
Beneficiaries	355,786
Day care programs	26

Education Program

Kindergarten/subprimary	732
Primary schools	934
Upper primary and middle schools	176
Colleges and universities	6
Vocational training schools/centers	253
Pupils	494,491
Teachers	15,831
Schools for blind (included above)	8
Schools for disabled (included above)	16
Boarding schools (included above)	27
Evening schools	2
Colleges, universities, staff training and development study and distance learning centers	27

Glossary

Salvation Army terms used generally and in this volume.

Adherent member of The Salvation Army church without a commitment to soldiership.

Advisory Board a group of influential citizens who, believing in the Army's spiritual and social service program, assist in its support.

Articles of War a covenant signed by a person upon becoming a soldier of The Salvation Army, in which he/she affirms acceptance of its eleven articles of faith, vows to live a holy life, and swears fidelity to the Army and its mission. (See appendix B.)

Auxiliary Captain a mature Salvationist who holds a warrant of appointment, with work similar to an officer, and, with time and further study, may receive a full commissioned rank of captain.

Blood and Fire one of the Army's mottoes; on the center of its flag; it refers to the atoning blood of Christ and the fire of the Holy Spirit.

Cadet a Salvationist in training for officership.

Chief of the Staff the officer second in command of the worldwide Army.

Command a region smaller than a territory, directed by an officer.

Community Care Ministries a group of Salvationists who visit prisons, hospitals, and homes of care, sharing the gospel, and in varied ways render practical aid.

Congress central gatherings attended by officers and soldiers of a territory, region, or division.

Corps a unit established as a church for spiritual ministry and community service. The nonordained lay leaders of a corps are designated local officers. It is not autonomous. Officers are appointed and supervised by divisional headquarters as approved by territorial headquarters.

Corps Cadet young Salvationist who takes a course of Bible study and practical training in his/her corps.

Corps Council a cross-section of corps members that serve in an advisory capacity.

Corps Sergeant-Major (CSM) the chief local officer who assists the corps officers with meetings and usually takes command in their absence.

Crest official emblem that symbolizes the movement's message. (See front part of book.)

Dedication of Infant the act of the parents who recognize children as a gift from God, and in a ceremony covenant to teach and train the child in the Christian way of life.

Division a number of corps and Salvation Army services grouped together under the direction of a divisional commander.

General the officer elected to the supreme command of the Army throughout the world.

High Council composed of the chief of the staff, all active commissioners, and officers in command of territories, convened for the sole purpose of electing the general.

Home League a fellowship of women that aids in development of Christian standards in personal and home life, and supports Army operations.

International Headquarters offices in London in which the business connected with the command of the worldwide Army is transacted.

International Management Council comprising the general, the chief of the staff, and international secretaries, the principal forum for discussing strategies, plans, and key issues.

International Secretary a commissioner who forms a link between the general, the chief of the staff, and territorial commanders with respect to the affairs of overseas commands, and facilitates administrative processes between prescribed territories and IHQ.

Junior Soldier a boy or girl who, having professed conversion and signed the junior soldier's promise, becomes a junior member of the church of The Salvation Army.

Local Officer a soldier appointed to a position of responsibility in the corps, without being separated from his employment or receiving remuneration.

Mercy Seat or Penitent Form a place where people can kneel to pray, seeking salvation or sanctification, or making a consecration to God's will.

Officer a Salvationist who has left secular concerns at God's call and has been trained, commissioned, and ordained to service and leadership.

Order of Distinguished Auxiliary Service international recognition to mark the Army's appreciation of distinguished service rendered by non-Salvationists who helped further its work.

Order of the Founder (OF) the Army's highest recognition, an order instituted in 1917 to honor such service as would, in spirit or achievement, have commended itself to the Army's founder.

Outpost a locality in which Army work is carried on, where a society or corps may develop.

Promotion to Glory the Army's term for the death of a Salvationist.

Salvation the work of grace by God in a repentant person whose trust is in Christ as Savior, who forgives sin and gives meaning and new direction to life.

Salvationist the denominational designation of those who are ecclesiastical members of The Salvation Army. It parallels the identification of persons such as "Baptist," "Methodist."

Society a small company of soldiers working together in a district.

Seeker a person who in a public meeting responds to the gospel by kneeling at the altar or who affirms commitment in some other way.

Self-Denial effort to raise funds for the Army's worldwide operations, now called World Services.

Soldier a converted person of at least fourteen years of age, enrolled as a church member of The Salvation Army after signing Articles of War.

Territory a country, part of a country, or several countries combined, in which Salvation Army work is organized under a territorial commander.

World Services an annual effort to raise funds for the Army's worldwide operations; also known as self-denial in some countries.

Endnotes

Chapter 1: In the Beginning

1. David Bennett, *The General: William Booth* (Longwood, Fla.: Xulon Press, 2003), p. 292.
2. Robert Sandall, *The History of The Salvation Army,* vol. 1 (Nelson, 1947), p. 18.

Chapter 2: Booth Finds His Destiny

1. Robert Sandall, *The History of The Salvation Army,* vol. 1 (Nelson, 1947), p. 37.
2. Andrew Mearns, "The Bitter Cry of Outcast London" (n.d.).
3. Harold Begbie, *The Life of General William Booth,* 2 vols. (New York: Macmillan, 1920), 1:329.

Chapter 4: An Army Is Formed

1. R. G. Moyles, *Come Join Our Army* (Alexandria, Va.: Crest Books, 2007), p. 110.
2. Henry Gariepy, *Mobilized for God: History of The Salvation Army,* vol. 8 (Grand Rapids: Eerdmans, 2000), p. 7.
3. Gariepy, *Mobilized for God,* p. 7.

Chapter 6: Early Persecution

1. *East London Evangelist,* December 1, 1868.
2. Bramwell Booth, *Echoes and Memories* (London: Hodder and Stoughton, 1925).
3. Lord Roy Hattersley, *Blood and Fire* (London: Little, Brown, 1999), p. 2.

Chapter 7: Women in Ministry

1. Diane Winston, *Red-Hot and Righteous* (Cambridge: Harvard University Press, 1999), p. 95.

2. Pamela J. Walker, *Pulling the Devil's Kingdom Down: The Salvation Army in Victorian Britain* (Berkeley: University of California Press, 2001), p. 243.

3. Eva Burrows, "The Dismantling of the Army's Glass Ceiling," *Caring Magazine* 11 (July 2005): 51.

Chapter 8: Attacking a Monstrous Evil

1. Bramwell Booth, *Echoes and Memories* (London: Hodder and Stoughton, 1925).

2. Roger J. Green, *Catherine Booth: Co-Founder of TSA* (Grand Rapids: Baker Books, 1997), p. 254.

Chapter 9: *In Darkest England*

1. Robert Sandall, *The History of The Salvation Army,* vol. 3 (Thomas Nelson, 1955), p. 65.

2. Harold Begbie, *The Life of General William Booth,* 2 vols. (New York: Macmillan, 1920), 1:424-25.

3. William Booth, *In Darkest England and the Way Out* (London: IHQ, 1890), pp. 85-87.

4. Sandall, *The History,* p. 87.

Chapter 10: The Army's Theology and Ecclesiology

1. Harold Begbie, *The Life of General William Booth,* 2 vols. (New York: Macmillan, 1920), 1:140.

2. Bramwell Booth, *Echoes and Memories* (London: Hodder and Stoughton, 1925), pp. 66, 67.

Chapter 11: The Sacramental Salvationist

1. R. David Rightmire, *Sacraments and The Salvation Army* (Metuchen, N.J.: Scarecrow Press, 1990).

2. Harold Begbie, *The Life of General William Booth,* 2 vols. (New York: Macmillan, 1920), 1:369-70.

3. Frederick Coutts, *The History of TSA,* vol. 7, *1946-1977* (London: Hodder and Stoughton, 1973), p. 315.

4. Needham, *Community in Mission: A Salvation Army Ecclesiology* (Atlanta: TSA, 1981), p. 8.

Chapter 13: "The General Lays Down His Sword"

1. Richard Collier, *The General Next to God* (New York: E. P. Dutton, 1965), pp. 247-48.

2. In *Fortnightly Review,* 1912.

Endnotes

Chapter 19: Serving the Armed Forces

1. Evangeline Booth and Grace Livingstone Hill, *The War Romance of The Salvation Army* (Philadelphia: Lippincott, 1919), p. 5.

2. Herbert A. Wisbey, Jr., "Religion in Action: A History of The Salvation Army in the United States" (Ph.D. diss., Columbia University, 1951), p. 326.

Chapter 23: Human Services

1. Bramwell Booth, *Echoes and Memories* (London: Hodder and Stoughton, 1925), pp. 13-14.

Chapter 24: At Front Lines of Tragedy

1. Evangeline Booth and Grace Livingstone Hill, *The War Romance of The Salvation Army* (Philadelphia: Lippincott, 1919), pp. 10-11.

Bibliography

BOOKS

Begbie, Harold. *The Life of General William Booth.* 2 vols. New York: Macmillan, 1920.

Booth, Bramwell. *Echoes and Memories.* London: Hodder and Stoughton, 1925.

———. *These Fifty Years.* London: Cassell, 1929.

Booth, Catherine. *Female Ministry.* London: Morgan & Chase, 1859.

Booth, Evangeline, and Grace Livingston Hill. *The War Romance of The Salvation Army.* Philadelphia: Lippincott, 1919.

Booth, William. *In Darkest England and the Way Out.* London: IHQ, 1890.

Booth-Tucker, Frederick. *The Life of Catherine Booth.* 2 vols. New York: Fleming Revell, 1890.

Brown, Arnold. *The Gate and the Light.* Toronto: Bookwright, 1984.

Clifton, Shaw. *Who Are These Salvationists?* Alexandria, Va.: Crest Books, 1999.

Collier, Richard. *The General Next to God.* New York: E. P. Dutton, 1965.

Coutts, Frederick L. *The History of TSA.* Vol. 6, *1914-1946.* London: Hodder and Stoughton, 1973.

———. *The History of TSA.* Vol. 7, *1946-1977.* London: Hodder and Stoughton, 1973.

Gariepy, Henry. *Challenge and Response.* TSA, 1994.

———. *General of God's Army: General Eva Burrows.* Wheaton, Ill.: Victor Books, 1993.

———. *Mobilized for God: History of The Salvation Army.* Vol. 8, *1977-1994.* Grand Rapids: Eerdmans, 2000.

Bibliography

Green, Roger J. *Catherine Booth: Co-Founder of TSA.* Grand Rapids: Baker Books, 1997.

————. *The Life and Ministry of William Booth.* Nashville: Abingdon Press, 2006.

Hattersley, Lord Roy. *Blood and Fire.* London: Little, Brown, 1999.

McKinley, Edward. *Marching to Glory: History of TSA in U.S., 1880-1980.* New York: Harper and Row, 1980.

Merritt, John G. *Historical Dictionary of TSA.* Metuchen, N.J.: Scarecrow Press, 2006.

Sandall, Robert. *The History of The Salvation Army.* Vol. 1, *1865-1878.* Nelson, 1947.

————. *The History of TSA.* Vol. 2, *1878-1886.* Nelson, 1950.

Satterlee, Allen. *Turning Points.* Alexandria, Va.: Crest Books, 2004.

Watson, Robert. *The Most Effective Organization in the U.S.* New York: Crown Business, 2001.

Wiggins, Arch R. *The History of TSA.* Vol. 4, *1886-1904.* Nelson, 1964.

————. *The History of TSA.* Vol. 5, *1904-1914.* Nelson, 1968.

Winston, Diane. *Red-Hot and Righteous.* Cambridge: Harvard University Press, 1999.

SECONDARY SOURCES

All the World (international periodical)

Archives and Research Center, U.S. National Headquarters, Alexandria, Va.

New Frontier (USA Western Territory periodical)

Priority (USA Eastern Territory periodical)

The Salvation Army Act 1980. International Headquarters

The Salvation Army International Heritage Centre, London

The Salvation Army Year Book (International Headquarters)

The Salvationist (United Kingdom periodical)

The War Cry (national periodical)

Index

The Author

Colonel Henry Gariepy served for the last fifteen years of his Salvation Army officership as national editor in chief and literary secretary for the USA. During that period he reported on events around the Army world, accompanied the generals on their USA tours, visited and published features on Army operations in England, Canada, and countries in Africa, Asia, and the Caribbean. In 1985 he launched what became known as "the new *War Cry,*" with major upgrading in format and content. In 1994 he coordinated the Army's first International Literary Conference with 160 delegates, and prior to retirement in 1995 initiated the Army's National Book Plan for the USA (Crest Books) and its *Word & Deed* theology journal.

He has authored twenty-eight books, including devotional writing, facets of Army history, and authorized biographies, including that of General Eva Burrows and Commissioners Israel Gaither and Andrew Miller. In 1994 he was commissioned by International Headquarters to write the official volume 8 of Army history. He has also authored segments of history including the Army's 100 years in Alaska and The Salvation Army in the USA, and is a major contributor to *The Historical Dictionary of The Salvation Army.*

His *100 Portraits of Christ* has gone through nine editions in several languages, and had 150,000 copies printed by Billy Graham for distribution to his mailing list. Others of his books also have gone into multiple editions and translations, including Chinese, Spanish, and Finnish. Besides more than 2,000 published articles, he is a contributing writer to more than forty books, and has an article in the *Reflecting God NIV Study Bible* (Zondervan, 2000). He is listed in *Who's Who in U.S. Writers* and in Wikipedia.

The Author

Gariepy earned bachelor's and master's degrees, and was honored by his alma mater in 1994 with its Alumni Lifetime Leadership Award. His "active retirement" includes teaching a weekly Bible class and Bible study seminars, being a literary consultant and instructor at writers conferences, and undertaking further books and writing projects.

As an adjunct instructor for fourteen years, he teaches Bible and Army history at its Schools for Officer Training, and also internationally with distant education.

In 1966 he attended the Army's International College for Officers in London and was elected president of his session. He has met and known personally thirteen of the sixteen elected generals, and most of the persons of recent times mentioned in this volume. In 2007 General Shaw Clifton conferred on him the Army's highest honor, the Order of the Founder.

His hobbies include reading, jogging (a three-time 26-mile marathoner), and outdoor sports. Henry and his wife Marjorie live in Lancaster, Pennsylvania, and take pleasure in their growing family and active ministry.